Rhetorics, Literacies, and Narratives of Sustainability

Edited by Peter N. Goggin

Routledge
Taylor & Francis Group
New York   London

First published 2009
by Routledge
711 Third Avenue, New York, NY 10017

Simultaneously published in the UK
by Routledge
2 Park Square, Milton Park, Abingdon, Oxfordshire OX14 4RN

First issued in paperback 2014

Routledge is an imprint of the Taylor & Francis Group, an informa business

© 2009 Taylor & Francis

Typeset in Sabon by IBT Global.

All rights reserved. No part of this book may be reprinted or reproduced or utilised in any form or by any electronic, mechanical, or other means, now known or hereafter invented, including photocopying and recording, or in any information storage or retrieval system, without permission in writing from the publishers.

Trademark Notice: Product or corporate names may be trademarks or registered trademarks, and are used only for identification and explanation without intent to infringe.

Library of Congress Cataloging in Publication Data

Rhetorics, literacies, and narratives of sustainability / edited by Peter Goggin.
  p. cm.—(Routledge studies in rhetoric and communication ; 1)
  Includes bibliographical references and index.
  1. Sustainable development. 2. Community development. 3. Human ecology.
  I. Goggin, Peter N.
  HC79.E5R4858 2009
  808'.06338—dc22
                                             2009006022

ISBN 978-0-415-80041-9 (hbk)
ISBN 978-1-138-80918-5 (pbk)
ISBN 978-0-203-87277-2 (ebk)

Rhetorics, Literacies, and Narratives of Sustainability

Routledge Studies in Rhetoric and Communication

1. Rhetorics, Literacies, and Narratives of Sustainability
Edited by Peter N. Goggin

For Maureen

Contents

List of Figures ix
Acknowledgments xi

    Introduction 1
    PETER GOGGIN

1 Rhetorical Techne, Local Knowledge, and Challenges in Contemporary Activism 13
    ELENORE LONG

2 Writing in the Third Space from the Sun: A Pentadic Analysis of Discussion Papers Written for the Seventh Session of the UN Forum on Forests (April 16–27, 2007) 39
    HANNAH SCIALDONE-KIMBERLEY AND DAVID METZGER

3 Creating a Rhetorical Space for Biodiversity: The Great Smoky Mountains Association 55
    ELIZABETH GIDDENS

4 The Vision or the View: Cape Wind and the Rhetoric of Sustainable Energy 78
    KIMBERLY MOEKLE

5 The Nine Mile Canyon Coalition: Rhetorical Landscapes, Responsible Public Land Use 97
    LYNDA MCNEIL

6	From Oral Tradition to Legal Documents: Words to Protect the Headwaters of the San Antonio River SALLY E. SAID	116
7	Acquiring Biospheric Literacy: Discursive Tools, Situated Learning, and the Rhetoric of Use ANNE FAITH MARECK	132
8	Alone on the Ark: Al Gore Reconstructed in *An Inconvenient Truth* JEFF BERGIN	150
9	Adventure Narratives and the Ethos of Survival DOUG CHRISTENSEN	164
10	Fixing Locke: Civil Liberties on a Finite Planet ERIC ZENCEY	180
11	Toward Sustainable Literacies: From Representational to Recreational Rhetorics DAVID M. GRANT	202

Contributors 217
Index 221

Figures

5.1 "The Hunters' Panel" in Cottonwood Canyon of Nine Mile Canyon, impacted by industrial traffic, dust, and chemical spray, in Fremont Style, ca. A.D. 500–700.   107

7.1 *Use* function triangle.   144

Acknowledgments

The idea for this book was inspired by the 2007 Western States Rhetoric and Literacy Conference, *Sustainability*. As the host for that year's conference, I was initially concerned that the focus would generate a low response. After all, although the subject was timely, it seemed there were few scholars in the field actually investing fully in this area of study. I needn't have worried—the conference was a success and proved that there was indeed a great deal of interest in rhetorics and literacies of sustainability, and many scholars are invested in this area who were excited to have a venue devoted specifically to their interests. The time was right for a collection to showcase some of that work and to contribute it to an emerging area of inquiry. I thank all the participants of the conference, especially Tarla Rai Peterson, who delivered the keynote, and Maureen Mathison, my codirector, who were instrumental in sparking this project.

My special thanks to the contributors to this collection. Editing *Rhetorics, Literacies, and Narratives of Sustainability* has been a rewarding experience, opening new ways of thinking about the complexities and discourses of sustainability, and illustrating the range of potential for research trajectories.

For providing the time and resources that have allowed me to develop this project, I thank the Arizona State University Department of English and the College of Liberal Arts and Sciences. I also thank Elenore Long for her collaborations with me on other sustainability projects and for her feedback on drafts of this book.

My thanks also to Routledge editor Erica Wetter for her enthusiasm and support for this book project and seeing it through the production process, and to the reviewers for their thoughtful and insightful comments.

My deepest thanks go to my spouse, Maureen Daly Goggin, who, as she does with every project I work on, provided intellectual contributions, editorial assistance, and unwavering support throughout the project. Finally, I thank my two border collie mutts, Soca and Kofi, for reminding me daily that it's not enough to just sit at the desk writing about sustaining the environment—you've got to get out there and experience it.

Introduction

Peter Goggin

> We enjoy the fruits of the plains and of the mountains, the rivers and the lakes are ours, we sow corn, we plant trees, we fertilize the soil by irrigation, we confine the rivers and straighten or divert their courses. In fine, by means of our hands we essay to create as it were a second world within the world of nature.
>
> —Cicero, *De Natura Deorum*

> Only rarely can one look at a landscape modified in some way by man and say with assurance that what one sees embodies and illustrates an attitude toward nature and man's place in it.
>
> —Clarence J. Glacken, *Traces on the Rhodian Shore*

Rhetorics, Literacies, and Narratives of Sustainability is a study of texts—literary texts, multimedia texts, legal texts, digital texts, political texts, popular texts, and so on—that write the future of biotic and social worlds. The epigraphs from Cicero and Glacken remind us that the concept of sustainability exists because of a growing acceptance that human activity has lasting impacts on the earth's ecosystems. That is, the quality of life for future generations depends on how we, as societies and civilizations, approach environmental and social development. Thus, sustainability is not a concept for preserving, conserving, or reserving the earth and nature solely for their own sakes, but also for their continuing benefit to human society. However, one key problem for enacting change toward a sustainable future is that on local and national levels, sustainability is defined and enacted in a multitude of ways, often to serve special interests and political expediency. Consequently charges of "sustainababble" insinuate that the concept of "sustainability" is too diffuse to be meaningful. Thus, while sustainability and sustainable development are certainly laudable ideals, it is also incumbent on people and societies to look critically and skeptically at who is doing the defining and to what ends.

For humanist scholars, who typically reside on the fringes, if at all, of actually implementing social and environmental change, compared with our colleagues in sciences, architecture, engineering, and commerce, this is perhaps where we can make our most immediate and direct contribution. As Charles Bazerman states:

> We have a responsibility to create the realities of the future through the plans, visions, and goals we inscribe. Our plans build and rebuild cities, build and rebuild communities and organizations, build and rebuild professions and institutions, build and rebuild schools and universities, build and rebuild the learning activities of each classroom. These objects of our future, responsibly grounded on our past experiences and current facts, need to go beyond the past and present to make a world more habitable and sustainable. The work of writing helps us live together better, more happily, in a world filled with all the richness we can support and sustain.

And that is where rhetoricians as teachers and scholars come in; the irony being that as we bring our analytical gaze to the who, why, how, and what of understanding, mapping, and perhaps even defining what people mean when they talk about sustainability, we are contributing to the very sustainababble that we are trying to make sense of. But I would contend that is what we do, and, to my mind, to gain an understanding of the multiple ideologies and discourses of sustainability is to generate the conditions for conversation within our own disciplinary frames. With notable exceptions, such as Owens, Dobrin and Weisser, Herndl, Peterson, and Killingsworth and Palmer among others, sustainability is a relatively untapped area of inquiry in rhetoric and in the humanities in general. However the desire, interest and need for study in this area is clearly in evidence.

Several universities in the US are increasingly encouraging research in sustainability beyond the more established disciplines of the sciences, business, and engineering. California State University at Chico, for example, has an endowed professorship of environmental literacy and encourages the integration of sustainability through all of its course offerings. Likewise, the University of Chicago's Division of the Humanities encourages programs in interdisciplinary studies and sustainability. Both Arizona State University (ASU) and Northern Arizona University have made wholesale commitments to a campus-wide emphasis on sustainability that is indicative of a growing movement across the nation's institutions of higher learning. ASU's School of Sustainability, together with the Global Institute of Sustainability, offers interdisciplinary undergraduate and graduate programs and research initiatives. The University of Kentucky Department of English offers its Summer Environmental Writing Program for graduate and undergraduate students. For recent scholarly conferences devoted to rhetoric, composition, and literacy studies, sustainability has become a key element, if not the primary subject for discussion. The 2008 Conference on College Composition and Communication, "Writing Realities, Changing Realities," emphasized sustainability, as did the 2008 Rhetoric Society of America Conference, "The Responsibilities of Rhetoric." The 2007 Western States Rhetoric and Literacy Conference had "Sustainability" as its theme, and the biannual Conference on Communication and Environment, with a strong emphasis on rhetorical analysis, has been operating continuously since 1991. In addition, venues that focus on or encourage interdisciplinary studies on sustainability and the environment such as the *International Journal of Sustainability in Higher Education*, the journal *Environmental Communication*, and a forthcoming special issue on sustainability in the *Community Literacy Journal*, illustrate an evolving space for rhetoric scholars to publish their work.

But there is a caveat here. All too often, it seems, as "new" areas of scholarly inquiry establish validity, there is a sort of land rush to publish on the cutting edge. This is hardly surprising in an academic and corporate climate that sponsors an almost insatiable demand for innovation (for example, see the Council on Competitiveness, a "group of corporate CEOs, university presidents and labor leaders committed to the future prosperity of all Americans and enhanced U.S. competitiveness in the global economy through the creation of high-value economic activity in the United States"), combined with "crises" of social and meteorological climates that demand immediate action. Yagelski invokes the notion of "crisis of sustainability," quoting environmental educator David Orr:

> The crisis of sustainability, the fit between humanity and its habitat, is manifest in varying ways and degrees everywhere on earth. It is not only a feature on the public agenda; for all practical purposes it is the agenda [. . .]. Sustainability is about the terms and conditions of human survival, and yet we still educate at all levels as if no such crisis existed (quoted in Yagelski)

Yagelski's proposed solution to this problem is that we reimagine "the literate self," but I would argue that we take care to do this in ways that are not driven solely by institutional drive for innovation (what Doug Brown refers to as the "Culture of Insatiable Freedom") but in ways that sponsor innovation and also sustain the humanistic ideal of critical reflection. Like the "slow food" movement, we should take time to savor the work we do and to build on an evolving, cumulative body of literature as a sustainable space.

Thus, the title of this collection, *Rhetorics, Literacies, and Narratives of Sustainability*, invokes at least three key elements of that space—not as distinct, separate entities, but as dynamic elements woven into each chapter in the forms of rhetorical theory and critique, case studies of rhetorical and literacy practice and *praxis*, and a journaling of events and the stories of people involved in them.

The rhetorical study of sustainability is well established in some areas, such as communication studies and law (it is telling that these disciplines have such specific, established fields of environmental communication and environmental law), but to a much lesser degree in English studies. Interestingly, many texts on the rhetoric of sustainability and environment are classified as science and social science texts by the Library of Congress, even if they are written solely by English scholars. Establishing sustainability as a valid subject of inquiry for humanists is no small task. As a member of an Institute of Humanities Research project at my own institution (Arizona State University), to establish the humanities' role in sustainability studies we have found it daunting not only to find a voice in discourse (and grant funding) already dominated by science and engineering, but to come to consensus among ourselves about what "the humanities" means, and how we define ourselves in terms of sustainability. To date we have established the following:

> Philosophers, rhetoricians, historians, theologians, and gender/sexuality scholars are examining the "human side" of sustainability: the politics and ethics behind sustainable and unsustainable practices; the varied impact of sustainable technologies on racial, ethnic, and gender groups; the social implications of a changing climate; the impact of human societies on the natural environment; and a host of additional, timely topics. (*Humanities & Sustainability*)

Within this overarching ideal, we have established rhetoric's contribution thusly:

> Rhetoric and Sustainability and its subfields provide a broad humanistic perspective on problems of ethics, epistemology, and discourse related to sustainability and ecology. . . . Rhetorical inquiry explores relationships and disconnects between discursive practices on sustainability in science, government, and business/industry. Further, rhetorical inquiry addresses professional objectivity that insulates enclaves of scientific specialization from the general public and the policies that inform social change and environmental impact. Ultimately, it promotes rhetorics of deliberation, and of social and scientific activism to ensure a sustainable future. ("Rhetoric and Sustainability")

Literacies of sustainability—the acquisition of textual (broadly interpreted) knowledges on sustainability—and narratives of sustainability further expand the possibilities for humanistic inquiry, particularly for such fields as literature, writing studies, English education, community literacy, and linguistics. For scholars and teachers who have long invested in environmental rhetoric and literacies of sustainability, and for those recently drawn to this area of interest, this is all very exciting. As one among the latter cadre (although, I suspect like many, my nonacademic activities and commitment to the ideals of sustainability, particularly the environmental, go back many years), I have experienced firsthand the enthusiasm of students I have worked with, both graduate and undergraduate, who are stoked at the prospects of devoting their future studies to sustainability. Many participants who attended and presented at the 2007 Western States

Rhetoric and Literacy Conference I hosted, on sustainability, remarked about how encouraging it was to have a conference venue devoted to a subject of such importance to them. The call for proposals for this very collection elicited a response in numbers of submitted abstracts and inquiries far beyond my expectations. Glen Love noted: "Given the fact that most of us in the profession of English would be offended at not being considered environmentally conscious and ecologically aware, how are we to account for our general failure to apply any sense of this awareness to our daily work?" (227). Similarly, Owens has argued:

> English studies is decades behind other disciplines in recognizing the importance of considering our research and teaching in light of local and global environmental exigencies. There is still a pervasive, if unacknowledged, belief that much of our work ought to focus on the triad of race/class/gender, whereas "environment" remains a category awkwardly associated with largely "white," middle-class values and geographies, and thus confined to the perimeters of our conversation. (3)

If this is so, then we have a lot of catching up to do. But I am optimistic, as the above examples and this collection suggest, that the interest and the commitment to ecological awareness *is* there, and increasingly applied in our daily work. I suspect this will continue to develop as environmental and ecological concerns become mainstream issues in the humanities as elsewhere.

Perhaps even more telling are the very positive reactions, assistance, and project input I have received from nonacademic activists and stakeholders invested in sustainability during my fieldwork on sustainability and environmental stewardship in small island communities. For these folks, their primary concerns are often immediate material outcomes and policy implementation, but they also want their stories told. To this purpose we should heed the words of Toni Morrison: "Narrative is radical, creating us at the very moment it is being created." In my work in Bermuda and the Isles of Scilly I was struck by the genuine enthusiasm by news editors, town council members, urban planners, wildlife management officials, land stewards, community activists, librarians, businesspeople, and all manner of local residents who wanted to talk about sustainability, voice opinions, provide me with mounds of documents, and offer suggestions and additional contacts. The fact that I was an English professor, and that my work was unlikely to appear outside of academic circles or influence immediate local consequences, seemed to matter little to these people. What they wanted was to tell their stories and to have them written into existence and validated no matter what. In part, this is what *Rhetorics, Literacies, and Narratives of Sustainability* accomplishes. It emphasizes that we not only theorize and critique the discourses of sustainability, but through case analyses we also contribute to telling the stories of actual events and the people who participate in those events. In doing so, we are also telling our own story. We are "being created" as this collection of original essays expands our body of scholarly literature on sustainability and explores some of the complex relationships between human endeavor and the natural world through a number of humanistic/rhetorical lenses.

As a subject of scholarly inquiry in the humanities, and in rhetoric and literacy studies in particular, a few scholars have made significant contributions in their work on environmental rhetoric and rhetorics of sustainability. They are cited frequently in this collection as important influences for this emerging area of inquiry and have established status as seminal reference texts. Among these are Killingsworth and Palmer's *Ecospeak*, Dobrin and Weisser's *Natural Discourse*, Muir and Veenendall's *Earthtalk*, Owens's *Composition and Sustainability*, and Tarla Rai Peterson's *Sharing the Earth*. Although still relatively scarce compared with available monographs on the subject, some edited collections on the rhetorics of the environment and sustainability are noteworthy, if now dated, precursors: Herndl and Brown's *Green Culture*, and Waddell's *Landmark Essays on Rhetoric and the Environment*. In the related field of communication studies, Senecah and DePoe's *Environmental Communication Yearbook* series (now a new journal, *Environmental Communication: A Journal of Nature and Culture*), and Meister and Japp's *Enviropop: Studies in Environmental Rhetoric and Popular Culture*, are further indicative of an emerging body of literature directly relevant to humanistic study on sustainability and related subjects.

Yet, as sustainability as a concept enjoys growing interest in the public sphere, and growing scholarly legitimization as an emerging area of inquiry across multiple academic fields and disciplines, what remains the question for many is just what do we mean when we talk about sustainability? For rhetoricians, and for this collection, the question itself is the answer.

In his oft-cited article "The Evolution of Sustainability," Charles Kidd identifies at least six related but different and often conflicting strains of thought, or "roots," on the relationships between economic, environmental, and social issues. They are the ecological/carrying capacity root, the resource/environment root, the biosphere root, the critique of technology root, the "no growth–slow growth" root, and the ecodevelopment root. Kidd contends that since the 1950s these multiple strains of thought have shaped the very emergence of sustainability as a widely accepted concept.

As a term related to promoting limits to growth, "sustainability" first appears in the early '70s in reports published by a group of scientists called the Club of Rome. These reports laid out a worldview for holding governments accountable for environmental problems and established a blueprint for enacting social change toward a sustainable future on a global scale. The report of the UN's Brundtland Commission in 1987, titled *Our Common Future*, popularized and authorized the notion of sustainable development as a political, industrial and social imperative. In 2002 UN representatives from around the world who had assembled in Johannesburg for the World Summit on Sustainable Development, issued the following statement:

> We assume a collective responsibility to advance and strengthen the interdependent and mutually reinforcing pillars of sustainable development—economic development, social development and environmental protection—at local, national, regional and global levels. (United Nations 1)

The resulting report lays out a detailed checklist for defining and implementing what constitutes good, socially responsible government, addressing conditions such as sanitation and health, poverty, education, communication technology, employment, and so on. All of these issues and systems are interdependent, leaning up against and overlapping each other with no one system, social ill, or solution standing in isolation from the rest. The summit's report and plan for action, ratified by the UN General Assembly, clearly emphasizes the magnitude and significance of sustainable development and serves to underscore global commitment toward a sustainable social future and provides a critical baseline for international institutions to work from. But it seems that "sustainability" as a conceptual term has been co-opted for just about any form of development marketing, and has become a catchall for justifying business as usual. *Building Magazine*, "the UK's oldest and best-read construction magazine," which specializes in articles and information on renewable and sustainable building practices and products, offered its readers a "sustainability buzzword generator" as a humorous "early Christmas present" in 2008 ("Play the Sustainability Buzzword Game"). The generator randomly selects terms from three columns that can be strung together (e.g., renewable responsibility tactics, holistic responsibility assurance, stakeholder long-term aspect, etc.) "to impress colleagues, industry contacts and clients with your sustainability know-how." Like the term "green," "sustainability" has become another buzzword that scholars must examine critically, if not cynically.

The rhetorical nature of definitions is that they are always constructed, and thus always contested. *Rhetorics, Literacies, and Narratives of Sustainability* does not presume to offer a solution or answer to the question "what do we mean when we talk about sustainability?" Rather, the essays in this collection offer a variety of perspectives that add to our understanding of what sustainability has meant in various contexts, and what it may mean, in various guises, as rhetoricians continue to delve into this area of inquiry. To this purpose I offer here four similar but contrasting definitions of sustainability from previous publications that inform the emerging study of rhetoric and sustainability and thus, to varying degrees, the chapters in this collection:

> If we could stop thinking of science as merely a data base for bolstering preformed arguments about environmentalist or developmentalist projects, and if we could consider the *form* of scientific discourse as a model of success, then new paths might open beyond the tangle of our

intractable problems.... An environmental discourse has begun to develop along these lines in ecological economics, in which the paradigm of *sustainability* has evolved as a challenge to the story of economic growth that proceeds in a never-ending upward spiral. Sustainability resists this economic version of the metanarrative of progress and thereby promotes maintenance and endurance of the ecological systems on which human life depends. (Killingsworth and Palmer 130)

Hastily defined, *sustainability* means meeting today's needs without jeopardizing the well-being of future generations.... Thinking sustainably requires that we envision ourselves less as autonomous individuals than as collaborators who are not only dependent upon but also literally connected to our local environments in complex ways. (Owens 1)

Whichever definition for *sustainable development* one chooses to adopt, there is general agreement that more mature ecological systems also are more sustainable (not necessarily stable) than less mature systems. This occurs because the most mature natural systems are tropical forests, which exhibit all the features of a mature system, as well as enormous biodiversity. In agricultural and urban systems, on the other hand, humans have altered the natural system to enhance productivity at the expense of system maintenance (or sustainability). The lesson from ecology, then, is that to create sustainable societies humans must focus more on a system's abilities to resist or recover from disturbances, stresses, and shocks than on its ability to produce goods. (Peterson 16)

How socially sustainable is the world if it provides a clean environment without addressing inequality, employment security, racism, and sexism, among others? ... Much of the coming debate around sustainability will not be whether or not it is "good" and is a socially worthy objective but will be about how it is defined. It will be a discourse issue. This is where progressive movements must play an active role. Its radical potential and ability to become the cultural paradigm for the next century will be determined by who shapes and influences its definition. (Brown 10)

Mindful of these diverse underlying definitions, *Rhetorics, Narratives, and Literacies of Sustainability* brings together essays on the following: conservation efforts in specific locales in the US; expressions for cultural survivance through various narrative forms such as documentary; social and political constructions of rhetorical place and space; community literacy; archival analysis of institutional politics, policies, and practices concerning the environment and economic growth and development; text analysis, and rhetorics of environmental remediation and sustainability.

Introduction 9

The contributors to this collection represent a range of specialization across a variety of scholarly research in such fields as classical rhetoric, social/cultural geography, comparative literature, literacy studies, digital rhetoric, communication, writing studies, rhetorical theory, linguistics, and discourse analysis.

A NOTE ON THE CHAPTERS

The essays in the first half of this collection (chapters 1 through 6) theorize and analyze how discourses of public engagement and rhetorical agency can help to build—and hinder—coalition building towards sustainability. They explore the situated contexts for conceptual constructions and enacted practices of sustainability in discrete geographical locals that become focal points for consideration of institutional and governmental rhetorics and regulations on environmental issues. These chapters provide detailed analyses of a wealth of texts generated during actual "living" events on environmental sustainability. As such, they offer insights, critiques, and lessons we can learn from the rhetorics, narratives, and literacies as they unfolded, and, in some cases, continue to evolve. Framing these chapters, the first essay, Elenore Long's "Rhetorical Techne, Local Knowledge, and Challenges in Contemporary Activism," begins with an observation: that both environmental rhetoric and community literacy call for more inclusive public discourse where the insights, values, and commitments of everyday people have a place at the table. Long argues that enacting such local public discourse also entails rethinking standard notions of invention, consensus, institutional sustainability, and conflict in public life. As her critical rhetorical analysis of three activist initiatives shows, community-based research stands to contribute significantly to such theory building even as its tools mobilize people locally to tackle tough problems in a risk-ridden world.

The two following chapters further illustrate the rhetorical complexities of enacting coalition toward progressive change in specific programs. The title of the second essay, Hannah Scialdone-Kimberley and David Metzger's "Writing in the Third Space From the Sun," evokes both Oldenburg's notion of community building in material social spaces ("third place") and Soja's postmodernist notion challenging the binaries of real and imagined spaces ("thirdspace"). Their Burkean textual analysis of the UN Forum on Forests illustrates how multiple stakeholders represent sustainability as they construct their identities as agents for forest management. The authors demonstrate the role of rhetoric in recognizing the discursive boundaries that occur in community building, and how to address them. Elizabeth Giddens's "Creating a Rhetorical Space for Biodiversity" addresses the complexities experienced by the Great Smoky Mountains Association in promoting environmental sustainability and biodiversity in a national park through its newsletters, brochures, and visitors' guides. Her essay raises questions about how institutions grapple with notions of public education and environmental literacy.

The next three chapters offer case analyses of actual events that have stirred up controversy on environmental sustainability. Kimberly Moekle's "The Vision or the View" looks at the case of the proposed Cape Wind project to establish a wind-turbine "farm" off Cape Cod. Illustrating that contemporary problems of "ecospeak" (Killingsworth and Palmer) persist, Moekle analyses how environmental discourse on the "public good" breaks down as stakeholders undermine the potential for complementary interests as they argue their cases from binary perspectives. In "The Nine Mile Canyon Coalition," Lynda McNeil looks at rhetoric in the public sphere through an analysis of discursive processes in adversarial rhetorics on industrial development in the Nine Mile Canyon in the Utah desert. Contrasting with Moekle's essay, McNeil describes how public scoping and deliberative democracy offer potential means to the emergence of coalition in the "reticulate public sphere." In an exploration of environmental sustainability that transcends historical time, the last case study, "From Oral Traditions to Legal Documents" examines efforts to protect the headwaters of the San Antonio River. Author Sally Said, a participant in the Headwaters Project, argues that the synchronic process of place-making works to erase chronologic time, effecting discursive practice that builds coalition, and ultimately enacting policy change.

The chapters in the second half of the collection provide discrete analyses of texts that address narratives of individuals, cultures, and social movements in terms of their relationships with the material and rhetorical places and spaces. In "Acquiring Biospheric Literacy," Anne Faith Mareck argues that difficulty convincing the public of the real and imminent environmental crises and the need for sustainability is due to the dominant social paradigm of unsustainability in the public sphere. Mareck presents a close analysis of the digital text of the Weather Channel Desktop to illustrate the ubiquitous rhetoric of use in everyday material discourse. She argues that this is why we must look to the ordinary if fast change toward a sustainable society is to occur. Next, in "Alone on the Ark," Jeff Bergin takes on another form of text, the documentary production of Al Gore's *An Inconvenient Truth*, which, he argues, uses visual literacy and rhetorical proofs to create the notion of truth and thus agency for (it is hoped) enacting social change. While Gore's film may have bordered on the extraordinary, Doug Christensen brings us back to Mareck's sense of the ordinary as the fulcrum for social change through his study of adventure narratives. In "Adventure Narratives and the Ethos of Survival," he argues that nature survival narratives promote the ethos of the individual rather than public sustainability, thus reifying an egocentric ontology that actually disconnects the hero (and us) from nature. Christensen invokes Thoreau to point to the potential for future survival narratives to promote sustainability by building symbiosis between nature hero and the environment.

As a challenge to the previous essays in the collection, Erik Zencey critiques the assumption of sustainability through rhetoric. In "Fixing Locke," Zencey examines the Western notion of civil liberties. He argues that the rhetoric in Lockean property law (eminent domain), manifest in the Fifth Amendment on property rights in the US Constitution, is inherently unsustainable, and to this day continues to encode a vision of nature as infinite resource. In a collection that focuses on the ways that texts write our understandings of sustainability, it is appropriate to conclude with David M. Grant's "Toward Sustainable Literacies," which provides an examination and critique of theories of ecocomposition. Grant analyzes the connection between writing theory and ecology, and argues that contemporary theory tends to emphasize the writer rather than writing, thus undermining potential for ecocomposition's role in enacting effective change toward real sustainability. He argues the need for a new literacy in and with the environment rather than about it.

Together these essays provide scholars of rhetoric with a window into the complex and often contradictory arena of discourse on sustainability, and illustrate some of the contemporary theory and research on sustainability in this important, emerging area of inquiry in the humanities.

WORKS CITED

Bazerman, Charles. *Conference on College Composition and Communication Call for Proposals.* NCTE, 2008.

Brown, Doug. *Insatiable is Not Sustainable.* Westport, CT: Praeger, 2002.

Cicero, Marcus Tullius. *De Natura Deorum. Academica.* Trans. from the Latin by H. Rackham. Loeb Classical Library. Cambridge, MA: Harvard UP, 1951.

Council on Competitiveness. *National Innovation Initiative Report: Thriving in a World of Challenge and Change* (December 2004). Jan. 24, 2005 http://www.publicforuminstitute.org/nde/sources/NII_Final_Report.pdf.

DePoe, Stephen P., ed. *The Environmental Communication Yearbook: Volume 3.* Mahwah, NJ: Erlbaum, 2006.

Dobrin, Sidney I., and Christian R. Weisser. *Natural Discourse: Toward Ecocomposition.* Albany: State U of New York P, 2002.

Glacken, Clarence J. *Traces on the Rhodian Shore: Nature and Culture in Western Thought from Ancient Times to the End of the Eighteenth Century.* Berkeley: U of California P, 1967.

Herndl, Carl G., and Stuart C. Brown, eds. *Green Culture: Environmental Rhetoric in Contemporary America.* Madison: U of Wisconsin P, 1996.

Humanities & Sustainability. Institute for Humanities Research, College of Liberal Arts and Science, Arizona State University. Jan. 25, 2009 http://ihr.asu.edu/ihr-sustainability.

Kidd, Charles V. "The Evolution of Sustainability." *Journal of Agricultural and Environmental Ethics* 5 (1992) 1–26.

Killingsworth, M. Jimmie, and Jacqueline S. Palmer. *Ecospeak: Rhetoric and Environmental Politics in America.* Carbondale and Edwardsville: Southern Illinois UP, 1992.

Meister, Mark, and Japp, Phyllis M., eds. *Enviropop: Studies in Environmental Rhetoric and Popular Culture.* Westport, CT: Praeger, 2002.

Morrison, Toni. "Nobel Lecture (1993)." *Nobelprize.org*. Jan. 25, 2009 http://nobelprize.org/nobel_prizes/literature/laureates/1993/morrison-lecture.html.

Muir, Star A., and Thomas L. Veenendall, eds. *Earthtalk: Communication Empowerment for Environmental Action*. Westport. CT: Praeger, 1966.

Oldenburg, Ray. *The Great Good Place: Cafés, Coffee Shops, Community Centers, Beauty Parlors, General Stores, Bars, Hangouts, and How They Get You Through the Day*. New York: Marlowe & Co.,1997.

Owens, Derek. *Composition and Sustainability: Teaching for a Threatened Generation*. Urbana, IL: NCTE, 2001.

Peterson, Tarla Rai. *Sharing the Earth: The Rhetoric of Sustainable Development*. Columbia: U of South Carolina UP, 1997.

"Play the Sustainability Buzzword Game." *Building Magazine: Sustainability Online*, Dec. 19, 2008. Jan. 20, 2009 http://www.building.co.uk/story.asp?sectioncode=747&storycode=3130368.

"Rhetoric and Sustainability" [MSWord file download]. In "Humanities & Sustainability—What do the Humanities Contribute?" Institute for Humanities Research, College of Liberal Arts and Science, Arizona State University, Jan. 25, 2009 http://ihr.asu.edu/ihr-sustainability.

Senecah, Susan L., ed. *The Environmental Communication Yearbook: Volume 1*. Mahwah, NJ: Erlbaum, 2004.

———. *The Environmental Communication Yearbook: Volume 2*. Mahwah, NJ: Erlbaum, 2005.

Soja, Edward W. *Thirdspace: Journeys to Los Angeles and Other Real-and-Imagined Places*. Cambridge, MA: Blackwell, 1996.

United Nations. *Report of the World Summit on Sustainable Development*. A/CONF.199/20 (2002). Feb. 20, 2009 http://daccessdds.un.org/doc/UNDOC/GEN/N02/636/93/PDF/N0263693.pdf?OpenElement.

Waddell, Craig, ed. *Landmark Essays on Rhetoric and the Environment*. Mahwah, NJ: Hermagoras, 1998.

Yagelski, Robert. "Computers, Literacy, and Being: Teaching with Technology for a Sustainable Future." *Kairos*, 6 (2) (2001). Sept. 29, 2004 http://english.ttu.edu/kairos/6.2/features/yagelski/INDEX.HTM.

1 Rhetorical Techne, Local Knowledge, and Challenges in Contemporary Activism[1]

Elenore Long

As different as the rhetoric of environmentalism and urban community action seem to be, they speak to the field's growing interest in activism and public engagement. They are also struggling with a shared couple of questions: how to elicit and validate local knowledge alongside discourses—whether discourses of policy, science or bureaucracy—that tend to dismiss it, and how to combine local knowledge with impact that is at once transformative and sustainable.[2]

Within the rhetoric of environmentalism, commitment to local knowledge is a corrective to top-down environmental initiatives that have earned big business, government, and industry reputations for being "insensitive," "disempowering," and "reductive" (Georg and Irwin 61). In keeping with the principles of widespread participation central to the United Nations World Commission on Environment and Development's *Brundtland Report*, attention to local knowledge signals respect for the "local expertise" and "local concerns" of "local people" (Georg and Irwin 61–63). Consider, for instance, the "ecological village" of Baarlarna, Sweden, initiated by a "local municipal housing society" (Georg and Irwin 66–68). Here, the local knowledge about daily life that residents contributed to the work of architects, biologists, and engineers resulted in innovations for the village's houses—from windows to furnaces to toilets—at once "imaginat[ive]," "resourceful," and adaptive (Georg and Irwin 63). Although local knowledge is affiliated with environmental practices that give "people a voice in their destiny" and honor the "right" for people to "empower themselves" (Ukaga and Maser 2), within sustainability studies, how local knowledge operates to make such a contribution has remained largely "in a black box" (Georg and Irwin 74).

Urban community action is the focus of community literacy. Here, local knowledge serves as a primary resource for intercultural inquiries into culturally loaded, locally situated social issues such as respect, responsibility, work, and welfare. Local knowledge signals the perspectival and partial nature of knowing (Dewey 132; Flower, Long, and Higgins 67; cf. Geertz). This situated fund of knowledge is a rich, experientially based resource for interpreting and problematizing familiar abstractions and stock solutions to problems that have not yet been fully understood. Below, Lorraine Higgins, Linda Flower, and I explain the use of local knowledge in this context:

> [D]ifferent stakeholders' situated knowledge can help groups construct and assess the unique situations and "complex social contexts" that lie behind problems (Flower, Long, and Higgins 6). When diverse stakeholders put their situated knowledge into play, the process helps all stakeholders at the table see their own situated knowledge in terms of the larger landscape (Young, *Intersecting* 67)—to recognize that the starting points from which others join the conversation are different from one's own (Langsdorf 316). Accessing the situated knowledge of others helps stakeholders critically assess and expand their own knowledge of a problem in ways that can have important consequences.

Once tapped, local knowledge can illuminate the unspoken motives, values, and assumptions that people use to interpret complex situations. Elicited and shared, local knowledge informs participants' realistic representations of complex social issues.

In each of these fields of study—the rhetoric of environmentalism and community action—the relationship of local knowledge to prevailing discourses has its own unique and dynamic complexities. Perhaps the most significant difference is that environmental rhetoric often requires residents to position, even subordinate, their situated understandings of an issue in relation to more formal scientific knowledge in order to contribute to public discussion—that is, participation requires that they "do their own science" (Simmons and Grabill 422). In contrast, community literacy's field of concern requires no such stipulation. In fact, it's often insights regarding gaps between the intent of medical, scientific, or bureaucratic discourses and how these discourses' polices and practices are experienced in the lives of ordinary people that local knowledge serves to illuminate within gate-keeping encounters (Cushman, *Struggle* 34) and intercultural dialogues (A. Young and Flower 79; Higgins and Chalich 2).[3]

This concern for local knowledge in public discourse is neither new nor unique to environmentalist rhetoric and community literacy. In 1989 Beverly Sauer published her analysis of a coal mine disaster in December of 1981. Prior to the accident, the wives of the miners knew something was amiss at the mine. How did they know? From doing their own science: observing, for instance, "the amount of rock dust in [their] wash cycles" (74). But they had no public forum to take their insights while their husbands were still alive, and their experiential knowledge lacked evidentiary status at the hearings following the disaster. Sauer interprets the disjuncture this way: "the conventions of public discourse privilege the rational (male) objective voice and silence human suffering, . . . the notion of expertise excludes women's experiential knowledge" (63). Over the last several decades, scholars in literacy studies (Cushman *Struggle;* Harris, Kamhi, Pollock), rhetoric (Fleming), technical communications (Sauer *Rhetoric*), and sustainability studies (Ukaga and Maser) have noted missed opportunities for knowledge building within public deliberation when residents' local knowledge is ignored or when the very design of technology undercuts citizens' efforts to draw on what they already know in order to conduct research that could contribute to the discussion at hand (Grabill *Writing;* Simmons and Grabill).

Activist rhetoric asks what can be done to improve the quality and consequences of public deliberation. What would it take to configure an alternative public discourse where everyday people and their local knowledge have a place at the table? Experience of having one's (or one's group's) knowledge shut out, ignored, or disregarded is not encountered according to our academic divisions, but rather in terms of the politics of daily life and institutional decisions that thwart the everyday struggle for resources, respect, and sometimes life itself—in whatever domain.

So, without eliding important differences between the rhetoric of environmentalism and community literacy and without space here to delineate further the role of local knowledge in each, my point is that concern for the questions of how to use local knowledge in discourses and how to combine local knowledge with impact that is at once transformative and sustainable involve even deeper conflicts over four substantial (and potentially divisive) issues:

- the role of rhetorical techne in public life
- the drive for consensus in public life
- the focus on sustainability in public life
- the function of conflict in the rhetorical invention of public life.

This chapter attempts to demonstrate the powerful role that rhetorical scholarship can play in articulating critical issues in activism in the field. A useful way to deal with these deep but also generative conflicts is to understand them from the perspective of both rhetorical scholarship and the emerging theory of local public rhetorics (Long 14–24).

TECHNE

The debate over the role of rhetorical techne or art in public life reveals both a dis–ease over intervention and a tendency to naturalize description as a more appropriate mode of academic involvement. Yet to do so, scholars such as Janet Atwill argue, comes at a cost: misunderstanding the first canon of rhetoric, invention. This suspicion of techne has already been used to urge theorists and educators to study and support students in the "more natural" process of discovery and immersion in both writing and community involvement. Below, I suggest that as a field we are at the cusp of articulating the implications that technai[4] have for writing in collaborative settings that require not simply awareness but public engagement (Flower, *Community* 86; Greene 441) and performative invention (Coogan "Sophists"; Simmons and Grabill 442).

The art of invention and intervention, techne is as old as rhetoric itself. In *Rhetoric Reclaimed*, Atwill draws on mythic characters from ancient texts to characterize techne: the forethought of Prometheus, for instance; the skill of Hephaestus, the cunning of Hermes, the indeterminacy of Athena (49–51). Through these characterizations, Atwill portrays techne as a special class of productive knowledge that is *"stable enough* to be taught and transferred but *flexible enough* to be adapted to particular situations and purposes" (48, emphasis added). Regardless of techne's prominence in ancient rhetoric and rekindled interest in invention within some academic circles, techne's place in contemporary local public life is hotly contested.

The debate over the use of techne in local public life is rooted in scholars' deep commitments to respond morally to the differences in time and resources that stack outreach in favor of university interests when scholars move from the library to the street. Regularly, for instance, scholars who describe service-learning or outreach initiatives beseech readers to join them in attending vigilantly to such questions as "who is serving whom?" (Goldblatt 292) and to consider "questions of time, space, credibility, knowledge, and success" (Mathieu 21)—or "Who speaks? Who pays?" (Mathieu 66).

Although the desire to respond morally to material and political inequities is central across community-literacy studies, a telling difference lies in the implications that scholars draw next. Some consider the very idea of intervention to be further evidence of university-driven interest and bias. For these scholars, intervention suggests intrusion—unwelcome and unwise interference. This is the connotation Goldblatt evokes when he credits his "non-interventionist" approach with earning him the "credibility" required "to participate in the organization-development process" (292). Likewise wary of academic arrogance, Paula Mathieu and Kirk Branch spurn academic involvement in community affairs that is protracted and systematic. The "clever uses of time" that Mathieu commends are those that erupt in the politically charged spirit of the moment and often influence public opinion in ways that not only defy easy prediction and measurement but are themselves "mysterious and unknowable" (48). Instead, Mathieu favors the tactical over the strategic (48)—a "trickster consciousness," explains Branch, that "use[s] hunger and cunning . . . to work in the service of covert, situationally grounded, and always constrained action" (189). Their greatest concern is that a systematic intervention will not respond to the nuances of the local situation and therefore will be intrusive and inappropriate.

Academics doubt the adequacy of their contributions for good reason. The issues that call together as a public the community and university are often tenacious and systemic. Here no one controls a sufficient or complete understanding of the rhetorical situation at hand (Higgins, Long, and Flower 12). For this context is laden with difference—differences of opinion and interest, cultural and socioeconomic background, and life experiences. Yet even as all this difference calls out for interpretation and understanding, it defies a single and comprehensive frame such as an A–B or condition–consequence problem statement that textbooks suggest for framing rhetorical situations in the workplace or academy (Booth, Colomb, and Williams 52; Huckin and Olson 97). Such complexity rightly curbs scholars' confidence to offer feasible and appropriate solutions to community problems. Such moral humility, for instance, guides Ralph Cintron to qualify his ideas for a "public forum" where members of gangs and mainstream culture could "document . . . the assumptions and beliefs of all parties so that they could be later deconstructed" (195). For as much as Cintron ventures forth, he is also quick to add an important qualification. "In the Angelstown of 1990 and 1991 such an approach would have been outrageous" (196). Conceding that his "solution . . . lacks the necessary subtlety," he also defends his musings on the grounds that "rhetorical invention must begin somewhere" (196).

In sum, within rhetoric and composition the very idea of techne, especially its connotation with intervention, remains a site of collective anxiety. Regarding this anxiety, Atwill asks her readers to consider the "'normalizing' traditions that work against interventions of any kind" (208). What is "[o]ne of the most powerful normalizing strategies" (Atwill 208)? Description. Atwill contends that in the field of rhetoric and composition, description has been naturalized to such an extent that its members are often more comfortable reading descriptive research than analyses of intervention and invention (207). I suggest that in community-literacy studies, this anxiety translates into a collective comfort level with scholars' descriptions of their own involvement pounding the streets to secure signatures on a petition, say, and with life-history research and critical ethnography—work that at its best is also highly sensitive and responsive to a complex array of community needs and interests. By extension, however, this anxiety has translated also into a general unease when intervention and invention go public—in accounts, for instance, of service-learning projects explicitly employing technai rather than encouraging students to move through a seemingly more natural process of discovery, articulation, and invention. This unease over techne manifested itself, for example, in a recent interchange in *College Composition and Communication* (*CCC*) charging David Coogan, in practicing materialist rhetoric in the community, with distorting rhetoric by prioritizing techniques over people. (Similar anxiety is expressed in Chris Warnick's recent review of Paula Mathieu's *Tactics of Hope*.) Granted, attempts at praxis typically merit refinement; Coogan is the first to recognize this fact ("Response" 813). For although intervention can be done well, it is never entirely sufficient to the situation. And yet only against the test of experience is techne's promise of *phronesis*—ethical action and good judgment for

18   Elenore Long

the public good—ever given meaning, let alone shared and refined. Atwill's arguments for reclaiming rhetoric suggest the unease reflected in the CCC interchange has more to do with how descriptive research and process pedagogies have been naturalized in the discipline at a cost to our abilities to imagine, test, and refine technai commensurate with the challenges of contemporary society than with Coogan's priorities.

Yet a kind of local public does exist that stands to benefit when activist scholars—or anyone else, for that matter—deliberately employ technai to scaffold public engagement. In "On Being Useful: Rhetoric and the Work of Engagement," Jeffrey Grabill describes the design of a community media center attentive to computer interface design that supports "effective citizens . . . becom[ing] effective researchers" (442), capable of both analyzing data and the very architecture of computer interface. It is such a site, he and his colleague Michele Simmons argue, that has permitted Concerned Environmental Citizens to "create [a] civic culture" to forestall a municipal decision to dredge a nearby harbor of hazardous waste (438)—a decision with possibly dire and heretofore underspecified environmental consequences. This kind of local public is most equipped to sustain the inclusive, deliberative discourse that ecocompositionists advocate for environmental discussions (cf. Dobrin and Weisser 97; Killingsworth and Palmer 168). Its discourse is capable, for instance, of formulating responses to the previously ignored needs of everyday people (e.g., Goldblatt), of bringing "business, policy, and neighborhood 'experts' together into a more sustained and interactive dialogue on timely . . . problems" (Flower, "Intercultural" 245), and of facilitating intercultural border crossing among disparate members of a public (Higgins and Brush 695).

Activist scholars involved in the partnerships that forge these local publics often consider intervention to be among the highest forms of rhetorical praxis. For them, it would be disingenuous and misguided to come to the table without offering possibly useful tools when ideas for them circulate within one's imaginative and professional repertoire. In the introduction to *City Comp: Identities, Spaces, Practices*, Flower commends rhetorical intervention as that special class of productive knowledge that allows everyday people to make informed judgments in the face of uncertainty—the very condition of human affairs (cf. Coogan "Sophists"; Simmons and Grabill 442). According to Flower, over the course of the "checkered history" of "town and gown" relationships ("Partners" 95), what has often foiled such initiatives has been not interventions per se but the logics motivating them: namely, the logic of cultural mission that puts patronizing distance between the university "doer" and the community "receiver"; the logic of technical expertise that assumes the discourse and tools of the university provide the only viable ways to frame solutions and structure relationships; and the logic of compassion fostering an "intensely individual consciousness" quite separate from "public action" (97–100). What's missing from each of these orientations is mutuality—moral and intellectual respect for others and vigilant attention to the question of who benefits from the collaboration and how. The logic for community outreach most rooted in mutuality is inquiry, specifically an approach that makes learning "a public act of shared knowledge making, . . . a problem-driven practice of mutual inquiry and literate action" (Flower and Heath 43). To promote mutuality, the logic of inquiry positions university partners as problem solvers deliberating not *about*, nor *for*, but *with* community members (Deans 20; Freire 74–90; Weisser 38). Within the logic of inquiry, technai permit scholar-activists to go beyond the limits of cultural criticism to participate with others in local acts of intercultural public engagement (Higgins and Brush 709–11). From such a perspective, technai do not exclusively wrap scholar-rhetors in the "purple robes of human agency" (Flower, "Transformation" 198), but they do call us to bring to the table the best that we have to offer.

And what a difference a techne can make. In "Service Learning and Social Change: The Case for Materialist Rhetoric," Coogan describes working with a community leader named Mrs. Brown, several community organizers, an educational consultant, and several dozen college students from 2002 and 2003, on a joint venture called Community Leadership in Bronzeville Public Schools. Coogan documents the groups' several false starts due to an insufficiently artful approach. Although it followed principles of good argumentation and effective document design, it missed what this rhetorical situation demanded. Coogan marks culturally loaded fragments of discourse with a special symbol: < >.

Coogan credits Michael McGee's material rhetoric—and its key method, ideographic analysis—with the rhetorical traction the group needed to mobilize local support of school reform. For the Community Leadership in Bronzeville Public Schools project, ideographic analysis identified the argument that community partners needed to win, one whose impact had the best chance of improving the lives of urban residents and for which it was reasonable to assume that college students—as legitimate participants in this local public—could make significant, if modest, contributions. Conducted behind the scenes, the analysis was protracted—over several semesters, in fact. The investment was worthwhile, however. For it revealed that the ideograph <local> wielded tremendous rhetorical power in the public arguments over school reform in Bronzeville. Yet when tethered to <control>, <local> harkened back to an earlier era of fractious local politics and dissipated contemporary public support. As long as public arguments alluded to this connection, Coogan and his partners could not mobilize significant local interest in school reform. Ideographic analysis led the group to revise its tack and recast their arguments to associate <local> not with <control> but with <responsibility>.

Method matters. More than an advertiser's clever shift of term, this new ideograph was generated from rhetorical research investigating the history of the controversy of public school reform in Chicago. In this configuration, <local> assumed an altogether different, more positive valance, "persuading parents [and other stakeholders] to take a more active role in [local] children's education" (Coogan, "Service" 688). Once focused on tethering

<local> and <responsibility> in public efforts to reform local schools, the Bronzeville partnership secured agreement and instigated action among diverse stakeholders by reframing the question to ask, "What would it take to increase parental involvement in fewer and more needier schools?"

On the one hand, this has been the point of technai all along: to let the writer do better work than he or she would otherwise, left to his or her own devices and default strategies or dependent instead on trial and error (Atwill and Lauer xi). What's new is the question Coogan explores: What might it take to reconfigure techne not as a tool of the lone orator preparing a public argument but as a community resource for framing joint inquiry and deliberation?

The question is significant. According to traditional rhetorical theory, deliberation begins at the point of stasis; however, in contemporary urban settings, "such argument seems premature; the problem space itself has not been defined" (Higgins, Long, and Flower 35). Consequently, materialist rhetoric allows deliberation to begin with the initial work of discovering with community partners the nature of the problems that bring them together and thus plausible responses to these issues. This analytical method seeks to cultivate consensus around the deepest commitments that a disparate body of stakeholders share.

Just as West's prophetic pragmatism urges cultural workers to apply the best of the Western intellectual tradition to contemporary issues even as they hold a searing eye to this legacy's arrogances and violations (30), scholars of classical rhetoric are adamant: techne is a valuable if overlooked component of this tradition. Both Atwill and Ekaterina Haskins seek to reclaim classical rhetoric for its applicability to contemporary democracy—Atwill by reclaiming "Aristotle's domain of productive knowledge" (11); Haskins by revisiting Isocrates's "model of rhetorical education and political performance" (133). Moreover, both argue that what's distinctive about rhetoric as a course of study is this focus on techne—the tools of discourse that take knowledge beyond the propositional and conceptual and into the realm of wise action. Yet whereas Atwill and Haskins commend the legacy of rhetoric for its attention to invention and intervention, both leave readers to design new technai that are up to the challenge of scaffolding the mutually respectful working relationships and intercultural knowledge building that contemporary public life demands (cf. Atwill 12–19; Haskins 130–36). Equipped with the tools of ideographic analysis, Coogan documents not only the collective intellectual demands involved in putting a techne to use, but also the benefits that can come from doing so.

THE DRIVE FOR CONSENSUS

Twenty years ago, scholarship made a case for dissensus in the composition classroom (Harris "Idea"; Trimbur). Even so, many theories informing compositionists' understandings of discourse communities tend to prioritize *agreement-expression* over *disagreement-deliberation*, leading educators to interpret conflict and dissension as bad because they threaten a cohort's unity and cohesion (Roberts-Miller 545). This misunderstanding comes at a high cost, writes Patricia Roberts-Miller: "To the extent that a theory (or pedagogy) assumes that a good community has minimal conflict it is almost certain to founder on the problems of inclusion and difference" (545). At issue now is how to make this debate actionable given the field's public turn.

From their own vantage points, both environmental rhetoric and community-literacy studies respond, in part, to the call of political philosophers to study the limits and possibilities of "actually existing democracy" (Fraser 109).[5] In *Ecospeak: Rhetoric and Environmental Politics in America*, Jimmie Killingsworth and Jacqueline Palmer, for instance, call for communicative rationality that respects the knowledge of the people (166–67). Especially pressing are efforts like Sidney Dobrin and Christian Weisser's *Natural Discourses* to focus on multiple rather than singular publics (97) in order to make room for previously excluded and silenced voices and communicative styles and to give serious consideration to issues of shared concern that have been previously bracketed as private.

On the one hand, efforts to rethink the public sphere call for scaffolding and documenting the alternative, multivocal deliberative discourses that Fraser calls for. Such discourse offers an alternative to the exclusionary rational-critical tenets of the traditional public sphere as well as scientific discourse.

On the other hand, however, the drive for consensus still prevails. In environmentalist rhetoric, for example, it's often assumed that the public worker's role is to help facilitate consensus among disparate parties (cf. Killingsworth and Palmer 168; Dobrin and Weisser 108). Amid the countervailing tendencies toward consensus and dissensus, it's easy for a public worker to feel like a string on a yo-yo caught in rock tumbler packed with cockleburs. A theory of local public rhetoric can help us recognize, distinguish, sequence, and abide legitimate impulses moving in both of these directions. Furthermore, such an orientation can help us bring appropriate technai to the distinct projects that follow, whether facilitating consensus or documenting and representing the knowledge present in sites' dissensus. But this choice requires us to understand—as a viable contribution to public life—the project of eliciting and documenting alternative interpretations of a shared concern and the consequences likely from following one course of action over proposed others.

According to Fraser, multiple alternative publics can overlap and inform one another—constituting new public configurations that allow people to listen and to learn from each other, who wouldn't otherwise. Fraser characterizes these publics as "multicultural"—requiring "communication across lines of cultural difference" through "multicultural literacy" (127).

Fraser's idea of multicultural publics is compelling. Yet research with community groups documents that invitations for cross talk are not enough. Residents often complain that talk simply dissipates after a public meeting (Flower and Deems 97), that the most boisterous in attendance often hog the floor (Mansbridge 60–62, 109), or those with professional knowledge often dominate discussion, whereby overshadowing those whose expertise may be grounded in a different set of experiences and in less authorized styles of discourse such as storytelling (Higgins and Brush 701–3). What would it take for intercultural groups to create together an alternative public discourse—one that would allow them not simply to rehearse familiar positions but to listen and to learn from one another?

A rhetorical model of community literacy strives to create a counterpublic discourse "in which marginalized voices bring significant expertise to solving a shared problem" (Higgins, Long, and Flower 31). This model challenges the normative exclusionary practices of public talk, and in doing so, it circulates distinctive texts that enact a new, inclusive practice for public discourse. Here vernacular discourses articulate with policy discourse, regional talk, academic analysis, personal testimonials, and narrative to create an alternative discourse for local public deliberation.

Flower's "Intercultural Knowledge Building" takes us behind the scenes to see what is required to create such an alternative discourse for public and personal inquiry and deliberation. Here the local public is the Community Think Tank that turns on its head the conventional think tank's selective invitation list, its prestige discourse (argument), and the singular voice that authorizes its publications (Abelson and Lindquist 39). The Community Think Tanks refers to a general practice demonstrated through a series of documented community problem-solving dialogues. For the point of its deliberation is the transformed understanding of individual participants made possible through the structured process of collaborative inquiry (Flower, "Intercultural" 245). To support these aims, the Community Think Tank depends upon a distinct set of design literacies, performance, and inquiry practices.

In "Intercultural Knowledge Building" Flower documents the rhetorical work of planning and preparing for a series of Community Think Tank roundtable sessions. She calls the process "designing an intercultural forum" (247). In keeping with that lexicon, I refer to the practices of researching and designing the materials to be used during these sessions as "design literacies" (Long 124–26). Design literacies include critical-incident interviews conducted with people who have firsthand knowledge of the problem at hand. These interviews identify features of the problem that are subsequently incorporated into paradigmatic problem scenarios, carefully contextualized written accounts of how people actually experience phenomena such as workforce development initiatives and urban health care. Design literacies then sequence a series of roundtable sessions: initial story-behind-the story sessions, asking participants to interpret these problem scenarios; decision-point sessions, shifting attention to actions and their consequences; and subsequent think tanks focusing on local action in individual community organizations or workplaces (Flower, "Intercultural" 255). Design literacies structure a rhetorical space where individuals can rethink how they understand a problem, and these same literacies coordinate this process for an entire group. When employed in text, design literacies also pull other readers into the process of negotiated meaning-making by dramatizing "critical features" of the problem at hand, "conditions under which [an option] might work out—or unravel, . . . possible outcomes and predictable problems" (272).

The Community Think Tank also capitalizes on the rhetorical force of performance to call into being a unique local public. Performance introduces and dramatizes issues for a Community Think Tank that—in the same public event—are focal points for public deliberative inquiry. For instance, at a think tank focused on welfare-to-work polices and practices, a union president, in the Bakhtinian sense of "ventriloquated," spoke for the experience of—and in the voice of—a bewildered new hire, and a human resource manager dramatically enacted the buddy system gone awry (Flower, "Intercultural" 262). Performances such as these harness the power of dramatization to focus participants' attention on a real problem.

A distinct set of inquiry practices further support participants' efforts to elicit one another's local knowledge of the issue at hand. The story-behind-the-story strategy supports narrative-based problem analysis by asking participants to narrate the "movies of the mind" they may call upon to interpret a complex situation. The strategy reveals a logic invaluable to deliberative inquiry: the hidden logic of often unspoken motives, values, and assumptions that people use to interpret complex situations—that is, local knowledge. Once articulated and shared, hidden logic permits other stakeholders to grasp the interpretative power of cultural knowledge other than their own (Flower, "Talking Across Difference" 40). Additionally, a strategy called rivaling helps think-tank participants to use difference to expand understanding, and the options-and-outcomes strategy helps them to explore options for wise action by seeing how a policy or practice might play out in the lives of those most affected by it. These strategies are tools of rhetorical invention, but in the context of intercultural deliberation they help participants figure out not just what to say but to invent with others the very discourse in which to say it. (For extended discussions, see Flower "Intercultural Knowledge Building" and Long 126–28.)

The Community Think Tank's alternative discourse neither promises nor documents consensus. In fact, this think tank is a response to other forms of community-based talk that often push toward consensus prematurely and at the risk of silencing some participants. This generative stance toward dissensus is represented throughout the think tank but perhaps nowhere more vividly than in the *Findings* it produces and circulates. The *Findings* is neither a policy piece nor a decision statement associated with the conventional think tank. Instead it is a heteroglossic text that employs an inventive "mix of narrative, argument, evidence, testimony, and practical plans" in order to document the new knowledge forged over the course of the think tank's roundtable discussions (Flower, "Intercultural" 255). Its purpose is to provide a culturally appropriate way to talk to diverse readers about the issue at hand while inviting readers to negotiate and integrate rival perspectives from the text for themselves. Grounded in Flower's social-cognitive theory of negotiated meaning making (*Construction*), *Findings* poses the question: How can you, the engaged reader, create options in your own sphere of influence that are responsive to the life experiences of others—social circumstances brought to life through your engagement with this text?

Although the Community Think Tank makes a case for public deliberation that spurs negotiated meaning-making at sites of dissensus, the fact remains that the desire to reach consensus drives much of environmental discourse and theories about it.[6] For instance, consensus is central to the alternative model of public environmental discourse that Killingsworth and Palmer call for. They write: "Where the lifeworlds of social subjects overlap . . . a space for action supported by 'intersubjective' consensus is created" (167). Although Fraser and others' efforts to rethink "the public sphere" have complicated the kind of intersubjective consensus that figures prominently in Jürgen Habermas's conception of the public sphere and that Killingsworth and Palmer rely upon (Benhabib 85–93; I. Young 52–57), consensus remains a likely and reasonable goal for at least some local forums at which people gather to speak for and about environments. What this process entailed, George and Irwin argue, need not remain in a black box. The Community Think Tank promises no such consensus. But Flower's study of intercultural knowledge building indicates not only the rhetorical work required to construct an alternative public discourse capable of eliciting and circulating participants' local knowledge, but also by extension the futility in complex, diverse contexts of pushing for consensus without first conducting intercultural inquiry and documenting the knowledge built in the process.

SUSTAINABILITY AND THE LIFE OF A LOCAL PUBLIC

Local publics are distinct and distinctly rhetorical entities. What does it mean, then, to sustain them?[7] The theory of local publics elaborated in *Community Literacy and the Rhetoric of Local Public* highlights two dimensions of a local public (its *local* dimension and its *public* dimension) that can seem to be at cross purposes. However, these features account for the unique rhetorical qualities of local public life. By way of Eli Goldblatt's "Alinsky's Reveille," here I'd like to suggest an implication: local public theory makes a case for measuring the viability of a local public in terms of the quality of the engagement and alternative discourse that it sustains, rather than longevity. From this perspective, local publics are sustained through technai that contribute specific kinds of rhetorical scaffolding at critical moments of a local public's rhetorical lifecycle.

Conceptually, the "public" part of "local publics" is discursive and abstract. The "public" in "local publics" refers to the social and discursive qualities of these spaces. Conceptually, the idea of a public moves in the direction of Habermas's and Michael Warner's more abstract theories of public discourse. In *The Structural Transformation of the Public Sphere*, Habermas identifies rational-critical deliberation as a model by which public talk supersedes force or coercion in efforts to determine matters of public concern, and he designates "the public sphere" as a discursive space separate from commerce or the state where people participate in democratic public life. Warner extends Habermas's work by identifying seven features that allow a public to exist, yet not as a material body, but rather through the circulation of discourse (67–114). For Warner the spatial connotations associated with the phrase "the public sphere" is the unfortunate consequence of a poor translation of Habermas's German to French and English (47). What's important, he says, is not a public's material manifestation, for the prominent image that equates "the public" with a deliberative body of decision makers is nothing but an "extraordinary fiction" (123). What can be accurately said about more formal publics is that they sustain the circulation of discourses—something that happens as a matter of course, and certainly without deliberate intervention—in a mainstream culture as media-saturated as our own.

In contrast, the *local* qualities of local public life are material and concrete. Conceptually, "local" in the phrase "local publics" refers to the situated and material dimensions of these spaces. They occur in space and time. As such, it would be tempting to think about a local public's sustainability in institutional terms: clarity of and consistency across its organizational mission, its services, its ability to attract funding, its measurable outcomes (Bryson). And yet research in community-literacy studies suggests that casting local publics more like formal institutions could cost local publics their inventiveness and responsiveness, features that make them so inviting and dynamic in the first place. The dynamism of local public life is evident, for instance, in each of the local publics featured in *Community Literacy and the Rhetoric of Local Publics*. So, too, is the pervasive threat of formal institutional discourse on local public life (Long 95). The equation is clearly demonstrated in a garden club's efforts to stop a city council from selling public land. Documented in David Barton and Mary Hamilton's *Local Literacies*, the garden club in a working-class neighborhood in Lancaster, England, maximized its ability to help everyday people to go public, not when it replicated top-down institutional practices—in fact, such practices alienated everyday people from participating in community life—but when the club invited members to bring whatever literate resources they had available to them (from a mimeograph machine to previous experience coordinating a letter-writing campaign) to the collective effort to stand their ground (227).

Consequently, if not for the materiality of local publics, we could perhaps rest confidently in the faith that local public life will likewise "just happen." But as Lancaster's garden club demonstrates, with a local public's situatedness comes its vulnerability to the "agendas, values, and practices of dominant domains that encroach upon local life" (Long 95).

Despite this uneasy relationship between local publics and institutions, work addressing sustainability in community-literacy studies has tended to define sustainability in institutional terms. Cushman, for instance, discusses the sustainability of the praxis of new media in terms of coordinated resources—material, disciplinary and institutional ("Praxis" 123). Likewise, when a foundation officer first hears a proposal for a new community-literacy initiative, she is likely to ask, "Is it sustainable?"—by which she is asking after plans for its sponsors to implement a funding mechanism once seed money dries up. Similarly, in reviewing service-learning opportunities for students, Joseph Harris equates the rhetorical value of these experiences with the solvency of the community organizations the students frequent—citing nonprofit agencies as one of the last and severely underfunded bastions of unregulated public space in the US. Don't get me wrong. The concern for institutional viability that provides community organizations and universities with resources to partner with one another is certainly legitimate. The point I want to make here, however, is that institutional factors alone do not account for the rhetorical work that Killingsworth, Palmer, Dobrin, and Weisser have called for—namely constructing an alternative, public environmental discourse where local knowledge has a legitimate place at the table.

Furthermore, local publics have a rhetoric lifecycle—a point that an institutional reading of sustainability can overlook. Greek concepts of time, *chronos* and *kairos*, help explain. In conventional terms, *chronos* refers to the quantitative dimension of time, that which unfolds, well, chronologically, on the continuum of time, minute by minute, day by day. In the community-university partnerships described above, *chronos* is the preparatory work involved in assessing the rhetorical situation and sequencing and structuring local public engagement. Ideological mapping served this purpose for the Community Leadership in Bronzeville initiative (669), design literacies for the Community Think Tank.

In contrast, *kairos* is the spatial and world-making quality of time that Lloyd Bitzer associates with the rhetorical situation. Within the scholarly debate over the objective and subjective dimensions of the rhetorical situation (Consigny; Vatz), it is generally agreed that the kairotic moment affords the discerning rhetor unique opportunities for world making (Miller 312). Coogan and Flower each credit performance with the world-making capacity that calls a distinct local public into being (*kairos*). In the end, Coogan writes, ideological mapping cultivates not "expert dissectors of texts" but "*agile performers* who cue their audience with a 'dense reconstruction' of the fragments" ("Service" 671, emphasis added). Similarly, Flower observes that of all the tools that Community Think Tanks employ—the crib sheets, the briefing books, the strategies—no tool has rivaled the power of dramatization to focus participants' attention on real problems.

In this *kairotic* moment, engagement can not last forever. To attempt to institutionalize such engagement would be to co-opt, deflate, and systematize the inventive rhetorical work that transpires when people pool their literate resources to respond to pervasive and complex issues that call them together as a public (Long 38; Peck 20; Tabouret-Keller 324). Yet under the right conditions, a local public may persist despite great odds, and thus merit our efforts to nurture it for as long as doing so honors the intent of the local public. This is the point I take from Goldblatt's "Alinsky's Reveille."

Open Doors, the community-organizing effort described in "Alinksy's Reveille," comes into being against stiff odds. In stark contrast to his university's manicured grounds, "[t]he terrain [of a neighborhood] is less defined and time isn't parceled out in fifteen-week intervals, but the needs are tremendous and the urgency persists like the stench of a hundred old oil-burning furnaces laboring in winter" (Goldblatt 286). Reasons and resources differentiate the partners' participation. In contrast to Goldblatt, Manuel Portillo—a community partner in Open Doors—"gains no tangible advantage in his organizing world for appearing in a learned publication; he still cannot get health benefits from the board of his small nonprofit organization until he brings in sufficient grant money in the next fiscal year" (289). So bringing key community leaders, such as Manuel and Johnny Irizarry, a director of an adult-education—along with Goldblatt's university colleague, Stephen Parks—together for a single meeting would have been significant. And yet it is not a single meeting but rather a sustained dialogue committed to consensus building and problem solving that Goldblatt has in mind, something that knowledge activism works to sustain.

The knowledge activism portrayed in Goldblatt's "Alinsky's Reveille" provides a techne (my term, not his) for scholars who want to help catalyze community-university partnerships that prioritize a community's needs over a university's interests. Knowledge activism is grounded in the work of the famous community organizer, Saul Alinsky, who cultivated in-your-face confrontational tactics to oppose the paternalistic attitudes and exploitative practices of big business and government that prioritize profit over everyday people's dignity and quality of life (Murphy and Cunningham 16–19). Knowledge activism takes Alinsky's approach to a "deeper level" by nurturing the process by which partners "talk through conflict and negotiate . . . tensions" in order to reach consensus regarding future joint action (289). A model practitioner, Goldblatt brought Alinsky's practical theory of action to bear on his own efforts in early 2002 to build connections across "the community-university divide" (289). Over an eighteen-month

28   *Elenore Long*

period, these partners constituted the Open Doors Collaborative that met to reconceptualize literacy education for adult non-native English speakers in North Philadelphia.

The knowledge activist draws on what he or she knows about the composing process to help university and community partners to reach consensus for joint action. The process connects leaders in the community, positions university interests and resources in terms of neighborhood needs, invests time and energy in the group's process without having to be in charge, and shepherds documents through the group's composing process. An alternative to standard university roles of principal investigator, expert, or committee chair, the knowledge activist seeks to preserve the integrity of the community-organizing effort.

Additionally, hospitality and a host of meeting literacies play central roles in knowledge activism.[8] An excuse to join community partners over hamburgers as the effort gets up and running, a community-organizing effort clears the space for partners in the embrace of friendship to ponder existential issues like "the effect that personal traumas have on one's vocational choices" (Goldblatt 285). Once gathered, participants' meeting literacies encourage them to persist in the face of conflict in order to reach more robust consensus. Underlying these literacies is the community-organizing effort's orientation to conflict. For Alinsky, conflict transforms problems into issues for action. Relying on talk and attentive listening, partners candidly express the needs of their own organizations and the neighborhoods they serve. (For extended discussion, see Goldblatt's "Alinsky's Reveille" and Long 110–13.)

Open Doors disbanded after eighteen months. According to institutional measures, Open Doors could be considered unsuccessful—a time-intensive investment with little observable return. And yet "Alinsky's Reveille" is not about sustaining an institution—an insight that has liberating implications for the disciplinary concern associating techne with institutional privilege. Instead, "Alinsky's Reveille" narrates an effort to sustain community partners' engagement on an issue of shared concern. As a local public, Open Doors lasted as long as was necessary to fulfill its rhetorical function: the inventive work of figuring out how to better serve adult ESL learners in North Philadelphia. Thus Goldblatt regards Open Doors "not as a failure but a long-term investment in helping neighborhood leaders identify problems related to literacy and work toward local solutions" (291). The final outcome of their meetings was a written purpose statement uniting the partners around a shared action plan which Goldblatt hopes will eventually improve the training of community educators in North Philadelphia, as well as the way that students at his university participate as writing tutors at neighboring community centers.

When we consider that the Open Doors partners were expert learners engaged in the activity of writing (Bazerman 428), it makes sense that they would disband when they had finished learning what it was that brought them together for local public-world making—in this case, a vision for a literacy initiative that would serve their diverse interests. Furthermore, by channeling so much of his energy toward writing, Goldblatt demonstrates the evidentiary function that writing can play in sustaining local public engagement. Throughout the community-organizing effort, Goldblatt persisted in listening to the partners' interests and represented them in the group's drafts that he crafted and circulated. Additionally, "Alinsky's Reveille" demonstrates how a rhetor in residence can help a group both to read a complex rhetorical situation and to manage often complicated power dynamics. This view of sustainability does not eliminate some stakeholders' concern for "deliverables" or resolve the difficulty of respecting process while producing effective results. Rather than invoking longevity as the gold standard, "Alinsky's Reveille" makes a case for measuring the viability of a local public in terms of the quality of the engagement and alternative discourse that it sustains.

In relation to Mathieu's concern for an implicit bias that slants techne toward institutional interests, this reading of Open Doors highlights that the meaning and significance of a given techne is ultimately inseparable from the context in which it emerges, the kinds of outcomes it generates, and the contributions it makes. That is, ethical valence is not predicated in techne itself but dependent on its use.

CONFLICT AND RHETORICAL INVENTION

Ambivalence toward techne and the drive toward consensus may keep us from better understanding conflict's central role in deliberation and the rhetorical invention of local public life. Conflict has a reputation for destabilizing a group's equilibrium (cf. Heller 67)—a reputation that conceals its generative potential. A rhetorical reading of community-based literacy initiatives shows the inevitability of conflict "when diversity sits down at the table" to deliberate over a shared problem (Flower, "Intercultural" 239) and, consequently, the need for technai that help intercultural partners (the multiculturally literate actors in Fraser's alternative publics) navigate this space. Under these circumstances, conflict can also prompt discovery and change.

Compare the community projects featured above. In each, conflict is the basis of the tacit or explicit account of rhetorical invention operating in the local public sphere—regardless of whether the group's intent was to reach consensus over an idea, or to use difference as a resource for inquiry and action.

In the Bronzeville project, conflict pervades ideographic fragments. Conflict gives ideographs their "primal force" as "blurry symbols of dissensus" (671). Conflict is also central to Goldblatt's knowledge activism. Here conflict refers to competing representations of neighborhoods' needs and interests. Partners "talk[ed] through conflict and negotiate[d] . . . tensions" in order to reach consensus regarding future joint action (Goldblatt, "Alinsky's Reveille" 289).

Likewise, conflict was "buil[t] into the very structure" of the Community Think Tank's design (Flower, "Intercultural" 250). First, the issues of race, class, and economics that it raises are controversial and conflicted ones. In addition, the Community Think Tank "enfranchises" alternative interpretations of the problem at hand, recognizing that whereas problem representations are "interconnected," they are not readily reconciled (248). Even the discourse expectations people bring to the experience are in conflict. It's not just the "conflict and tension" between competing discourses (Gee 8). In addition, these discourses carry histories of "mutual incomprehensibility" (Flower, "Intercultural" 250) and "suspicion of motives" (251). The think tank's response—asking everyone to suspend familiar discourses and stock responses to construct an alternative discourse for intercultural inquiry—pushes people from their comfort zones even as it dispels some competition among their default discourses. In that the Community Think Tank "reorganizes normal patterns of communication and authority," it also poses an unknown that's likely to make some people initially uncomfortable—yet another source of conflict.

The prevalence of conflict in community work is not surprising. What is instructive, however, is that across these three community projects, rhetorical invention occurs at sites of conflict; in other words, conflict is the basis of invention. Within Coogan's materialist rhetoric, invention is the process of discovery that first reveals how "public discourse has [previously] fared" in institutional circles ("Service" 690) and then produces more "probable means of persua[sion]" in light of this research (687). Here invention forges "the link between techniques of power and techniques of rhetoric" (690). It does so by tethering fragments of public discourse so to mobilize the consensus required to "pull down material resources" (688). In a material sense, rhetorical invention exposes disagreement over the capacity of an ideograph to contain a culture's commitments.

For knowledge activism, rhetorical invention is an indirect and protracted process of securing consensus, a by-product of three processes: forming relationships, building capacity, and communicating across institutional boundaries. In stark contrast to Habermas's version of the public sphere, where citizens bracketed their personal interests and differences in order to deliberate for the common good, for the community-organizing effort self-interests pose "a potent weapon in the development of co-operation and identification of the group welfare" (Goldblatt 282).[9]

More explicit still is the theory of rhetorical invention driving the Community Think Tank and the place of conflict within it. The think tank's heartbeat is the constructive process of negotiation through which rhetors transform conventional practices (such as a training program for new hires) into inventive and purposeful literate action. Here, "negotiation" and "conflict" are theoretical terms whose features have been named, identified, and made operational for the purpose of rhetorical analysis and theory building (cf. Flower, *Construction* 55). Negotiating conflict is the rhetorical work demanded of rhetors who deliberate over interpretations of a shared problem. According to negotiation theory, *conflicts* shape meaning-making in the form of "multiple 'voices' or forms of knowledge" (Flower, "Intercultural" 243). These voices include "the *live* voices" of those at the think tank roundtable and also "the *internal* voices of personal intention, knowledge and emotion, and the *internalized* dictates of convention, language, and ideology" (243). The conflicts that matter—those that have the potential to shape problem representations—are the ones that people actually attend to as "live options" (243). Of course, there's no guarantee that the restructured understandings will change the daily choices people make. But as an observation-based account of literate action, negotiation theory offers a plausible explanation of how socially situated individuals make difficult decisions in the face of multiple, internalized competing public voices.

Local knowledge transforms public understanding of a shared concern in such acts of negotiated meaning-making. According to Flower, participants restructure their understandings when they actively engage competing voices and forms of knowledge. Through such acts of negotiated meaning-making, people challenge the limiting effects of what Pierre Bourdieu has called "habitus"—the socially conditioned attitudes and behaviors that otherwise circumscribe so public a discourse (53). Negotiation lets people build more robust representations of the problem and consequently draw on these revised, enhanced understandings should similar situations arise for them in the future.

CONCLUSION

Whenever prevailing public discourse shuts out otherwise relevant knowledge, the consequences are real. People are degraded, their struggle for resources and respect made that much harder. Additionally, other members of the public miss out. Such acts of exclusion diminish a public's understanding of a complex issue and, very likely, its ability to imagine viable alternatives. Efforts to document the symbolic violence of exclusion are important; criticism that sheds such insight has significant value.

A rhetoric of activism takes another step to ask what can be done to improve the quality of public discourse. Community-based rhetorical scholarship has a powerful role to play in articulating and responding to this and other critical questions. Already this growing body of scholarship is testing the promise and limits of contemporary technai to help elicit and circulate local knowledge in public life.

The above rhetorical reading of local public life reveals <techne> and its frequent synonym <strategy> to be ideographs in their own right. For some scholars, they appear insidiously implicated in the interests of their institutional affiliations (cf. Mathieu 16, 20). Yet the rhetorics of local publics would suggest that the partnerships that elicit and circulate residents' local knowledge operate at the intersection of multiple institutional interests and concerns, neither entirely co-opted, controlled, nor—for that matter—free of any of them.

This rhetoric of activism adds observation-based methods to the approaches we customarily use to understand technai. These new methods have implications not only for understanding technai but for understanding activism itself. Surely characters from ancient Greek myths will help us articulate subtle features of techne's status as a non-normative knowledge (Atwill; Marcel and Vernant)—a goal as illusive as it is important. Likewise critical theory will help us predict (and revise) possible political implications that could follow when we employ technai, as Mathieu suggests when referring to Michel de Certeau's theory of institutional spaces to caution of strategies' "potentially colonizing logic that seeks to control the space of interaction" (17). And historical analysis will continue to provide insights, in the way that James Scott's analysis of Soviet collectivization, the Maoist Great Leap Forward, and the precisely planned city of Brasilia informs Branch's reading of techne and metís in *Eyes on the Ought to Be*.

Yet analysis of this historically rooted debate suggests another very contemporary implication. Not content to abandon the promise of techne to sites that are institutionally fixed and "proper" (de Certeau xx), community-based research puts to the test of observation whether in community-based contexts technai can "enable transgressive acts of the least powerful" (Simmons and Grabill 442) and support the "self-fashioning and institutional disobedience" characteristic of community literacy itself (Flower, *Community* 98). Constituting an emerging area of activist rhetoric, this work stands to inform both future environmentalism and urban community action.

NOTES

1. Linda Flower graciously read and responded to earlier conceptions of this chapter. I would like to credit and thank Jeff Grabill for offering the distinction between *chronos* and *kairos* as a useful framework for thinking about sustainability as it relates enigmatically to local public life. Graduate students in the winter 2008 class of AI 877: Community Literacies at Michigan State University drew my attention to the pervasive and enigmatic element of time in the rhetoric of local publics. Judy Holiday, Andrea Lewis, Sarah Dutton-Breen and Arlon Benson in ENG 556: Knowledge Activism have also contributed greatly to the ideas articulated here.
2. Work in rhetoric and sustainability occupies several subfields: environmental rhetoric, ecocomposition, cultural rhetorics and "green culture," and environmental discourse (Goggin). Here I focus on strains throughout environmentalism that draw from a host of methods and theories in order to interpret, refine, and respond to the call for the kind of communicative action that Jürgen Habermas distinguishes from the instrumental actions of industry, commerce, and the state in order for citizens to reason together about shared concerns regarding the environment and the fate of the planet.

Efforts to respond to this call are evident in work in sustainability studies ranging from Klaus Eder's *Social Construct of Nature: Theory, Culture* to Theo J. N. M. de Bruijn and Arnold Tukker's edited collection, *Partnership and Leadership: Building Alliances for a Sustainable Future*. Closer to home, efforts include Michele Simmons and Jeffrey Grabill's "Toward a Civic Rhetoric for Technologically and Scientifically Complex Places"; Simmons's *Participation and Power: Civic Discourse in Environmental Policy Decisions*; Sidney Dobrin and Christian Weisser's *Natural Discourse*; Nancy Coppola and Bill Karis's edited collection, *Technical Communication, Deliberative Rhetoric, and Environmental Discourse*; and Beverly Sauer's "Sense and Sensibility in Technical Documentation: How Feminist Interpretation Strategies Can Save Lives in the Nation's Mines" and *The Rhetoric of Risk: Technical Documentation in Hazardous Environments*. According to M. Jimmie Killingsworth and Jacqueline S. Palmer, such communicative action regarding the environment requires a shift from a culture that gives mere lip service to environmental concerns (ecospeak) to one "with environmentalism at its very center" (265); furthermore, this shift it entails constructing an alternative and sustained public discourse that is "valued-centered," "action oriented," and "open to contributions from diverse sources" (265).

3. Yet this concern for local knowledge is evident in the work of scholar-activists whose research spans both the rhetoric of environmentalism and community literacy. The intellectual trajectory of Jeff Grabill is a case in point. His early scholarship commended institutional participatory design practices attuned to the local knowledge—motivations, values, concerns, definitions of literacy—that attracted adults to community literacy programs in the first place. His subsequent work examines the relationship between computer technology and citizen action. His current theory of civil rhetoric reflects his and colleague Michele Simmons's action research with environmental groups including Midwest Citizen's Group and Concerned Environmental Citizens of Michigan, groups that challenge members to "make sense of public information from their own subject position" in order to participate "in deliberative discourse" (Simmons and Grabill 439–41).

4. I follow Janet Atwill's usage of "technai" (without italics) for the plural form of "techne" (e.g., *Rhetoric Reclaimed* 14).

5. For example, consider that in 1992, Killingsworth and Palmer drew on Habermas's notion of lifeworlds and communicative rationality to call for an alternative "public discourse that meets the public's demand for [environmental] change" (168). This alternative public environmental discourse would encourage citizens' active participation and would work hard to arrive at, not force, consensus among competing perspectives. Motivating the call was the untapped potential of everyday people's attitudes and insights that could put and keep environmental concerns on the national agenda. According to Killingsworth and Palmer, this alternative discourse would operate in distinct contrast to the instrumental rationality that has long governed mainstream environmental discourse. Instrumental rationality assumes "that people are confused about their own real needs, that impulses and emotions override rationality in public debate, and that good action depends upon expert guidance" (167). Furthermore, "the aim of instrumental documents is never to treat deviant discourses with respect but always merely to take note of them, to record them, and ultimately to treat them as 'noise' in the system, which needs to be ignored or expunged" (166).

A decade later, in *Natural Discourse*, Sidney Dobrin and Christian Weisser refine Killingsworth and Palmer's call for an alternative public discourse to address environmental concerns. Drawing on Nancy Fraser's critique of

Habermas's critical-rational deliberation, Dobrin and Weisser push against the concept of a singular public sphere where people deliberate over the common good. They note that this model discriminates against people unaccustomed to using the specialized codes and conventions that secure a certain class and gender (namely, propertied men) their places at the table. Habermas's concept of "the public sphere" also assumes that economic, cultural, and other differences are obstacles to be overcome rather than resources to inform understanding and to build new knowledge on issues of shared concern.

6. See, for instance, pages 90–113 of Ron Heifetz's *Leadership without Easy Answers*.
7. Phrasing the question this way prioritizes engagement over other things that are also worth sustaining—and treated in greater length elsewhere: for instance, a local public's ability to instigate organizational change (Faber 41–42), to inform public transformation (Flower, Higgins, and Long 32–34), to circulate alternative meanings of literacy (Comstock 46; Grabill 5), and to shepherd resources toward itself (Heller 67).
8. For more on meetings as rhetorically complex performances, see Grabill's "On Being Useful: Rhetoric and the Work of Engagement," in John Ackerman and David Coogan's edited collection, *The Public Work of Rhetoric: Citizen-Scholars and Civic Engagement*, University of South Carolina P, forthcoming.
9. Forming relationships means cultivating group trust so that conflict can spur creative solutions. Often what is in conflict is whether the plan on the table adequately responds to the needs of the various neighborhoods that the partners represent. Knowledge activism ensures that a literacy project's design is aligned with participants' own needs and interests. Quite simply, literacy projects attuned to participants' needs and goals are more likely to build the capacity of learners seeking their services (Grabill, *Community* 125). Knowledge activism also enacts "a new model" for neighborhood-based literacy projects, "one that comes from neighborhoods and draws on the university without being controlled by its demands" (284). The promise of communicating across borders is the power of institutional leverage: the ability to do more together than alone.

WORKS CITED

Abelson, Donald E., and Evert A. Lindquist. "Think Tanks in North America." *Think Tanks and Civil Liberties: Catalysts for Ideas and Action*. Eds. James G. McGann and R. Kent Weaver. New Brunswick, NJ: Transaction Publishers, 2000. 37–66.

Alinsky, Saul. *Reveille for Radicals*. New York: Vintage, 1946.

Atwill, Janet. *Rhetoric Reclaimed: Aristotle and the Liberal Arts Tradition*. Ithaca: Cornell UP, 1998.

Atwill, Janet and Janice Lauer, eds. *Perspectives on Rhetorical Invention*. Knoxville: U of Tennessee P, 2002.

Barton, David, and Mary Hamilton. *Local Literacies: Reading and Writing in One Community*. New York: Routledge, 1998.

Bazerman, Charles. "What is Not Institutionally Visible Does Not Count: The Problem of Making Activity Assessable, Accountable, and Plannable." *Writing Selves/Writing Societies: Research from Activity Perspectives*. Ed. Charles Bazerman and David Russell. Fort Collins: WAC Clearinghouse and Mind,

Culture, and Activity, 2002. 428–83, Dec. 21, 2008 http://wac.colostate.edu/books/selves_societies.

Benhabib, Seyla, "Models of Public Space. Hannah Arendt, the Liberal Tradition, and Jürgen Habermas." *Habermas and the Public Sphere*. Ed. Craig Calhoun. Cambridge: MIT P, 1993. 73–98.

Bitzer, Lloyd. "The Rhetorical Situation." *Philosophy and Rhetoric* 1 (1968): 1–14.

Booth, Wayne, Gregory Colomb, and Joseph Williams. *The Craft of Research*. Chicago: U of Illinois P, 1995.

Bourdieu, Pierre. *Outline of a Theory of Practice*. Trans. Richard Nice. Cambridge, UK: Cambridge UP, 1977.

Branch, Kirk. *Eyes on the Ought to Be: What We Teach When We Teach about Literacy*. Cresskill: Hampton P, 2007.

Bryson, John. *Strategic Planning for Public and Nonprofit Organizations: A Guide to Strengthening and Sustaining Organizational Achievement*. San Francisco: Jossey-Bass, 2004.

Cintron, Ralph. *Angels' Town: Chero Ways, Gang Life, and Rhetorics of the Everyday*. Boston: Beacon P, 1997.

Comstock, Michelle. "Writing Programs as Distributed Networks: A Materialist Approach to University-Community Digital Media Literacy." *Community Literacy Journal*. 1.1 (2006): 45–66.

Consigny, Scott. "Rhetoric and Its Situations." *Philosophy and Rhetoric* 7 (1974): 175–86.

Coppola, Nancy and Bill Karis, eds. *Technical Communication, Deliberative Rhetoric, and Environmental Discourse*. Stamford: Ablex, 2000.

Coogan, David. "Response to Heather Lettner-Rust." *College Composition and Communication* 59.4 (2008): 813–14.

———. "Service Learning and Social Change: The Case for Materialist Rhetoric." *College Composition and Communication* 57.4 (2006): 667–93.

———"Sophists for Social Change." *Rhetoric and Social Change: The Public Work of Scholars and Students*. Ed. John Ackerman and David Coogan, in prep.

Cushman, Ellen. *The Struggle and the Tools: Oral and Literate Strategies in an Inner City Community*. New York: SUNY P, 1998.

———. "Toward a Praxis of New Media." *Reflections: A Journal of Writing, Community Literacy and Service-Learning* 5 (2006): 111–32.

de Bruijn, Theo J. N. M., and Arnold Tukker, eds. *Partnership and Leadership: Building Alliances for a Sustainable Future*. Dordrecht, Netherlands: Kluwer Academic Publications, 2002.

de Certeau, Michel. *The Practice of Everyday Life*. Trans. Steven Rendell. Berkeley: U of California P, 1988.

Deans, Thomas. *Writing Partnerships: Service-Learning in Composition*. New York: NCTE, 2000.

Dewey, John. *Quest for Certainty*. Vol. 4 of *John Dewey: The Later Works, 1925–1953*. Ed. Jo Ann Boydston. Carbondale: Southern Illinois UP, 1988.

Dobrin, Sidney I. and Christian R. Weisser. *Natural Discourse: Toward Ecocomposition*. Albany: State U of New York P, 2002.

Faber, Brenton. *Community Action and Organizational Change: Image, Narrative, Identity*. Carbondale: Southern Illinois UP, 2002.

Fleming, David. *City of Rhetoric: Revitalizing the Public Sphere in Metropolitan America*. Albany: SUNY P, 2008.

Flower, Linda. *Community Literacy and the Rhetoric of Public Engagement*. Southern Illinois UP, 2008.

———. *The Construction of Negotiated Meaning: A Social Cognitive Theory of Writing*. Carbondale: Southern Illinois UP, 1994.

———. "Intercultural Knowledge Building: The Literate Action of a Community Think Tank." *Writing Selves, Writing Societies: Research from Activity Perspectives.* Ed. Charles Bazerman and David Russell. 239–70. Fort Collins: WAC Clearinghouse, 2002, Dec. 21, 2008 http://wac.colostate.edu/books/selves_societies.

———. "Intercultural Inquiry and the Transformation of Service." *College English* 65.2 (2002): 181–201.

———. "Introduction." *City Comp: Identities, Spaces, Practices.* Ed. Bruce McComiskey and Cynthia Ryan. Albany: SUNY P, 2003. 1–5.

———. "Partners in Inquiry: A Logic for Community Outreach." *Writing the Community: Concepts and Models for Service-Learning in Composition.* Ed. Linda Adler-Kassner, Robert Crooks, and Ann Watters. Washington, DC: American Association for Higher Education, 1997. 95–117.

———. "Talking Across Difference: Intercultural Rhetoric and the Search for Situated Knowledge." *College Composition and Communication* 55.1 (2003): 38–68.

Flower, Linda, and Julia Deems. "Conflict in Community Collaboration." *New Perspectives on Rhetorical Invention.* Ed. Janet M. Atwill and Janice M. Lauer. Knoxville: U Tennessee P, 2002. 96–130.

Flower, Linda, and Shirley Brice Heath. "Drawing on the Local: Collaboration and Community Expertise." *Language and Learning Across the Disciplines* 4.3 (2004): 43–65.

Flower, Linda, Elenore Long, and Lorraine Higgins. *Learning to Rival: A Literate Practice for Intercultural Inquiry.* Mahwah, NJ: Erlbaum, 2000.

Fraser, Nancy. "Rethinking the Public Sphere: A Contribution to the Critique of Actually Existing Democracy." *Habermas and the Public Sphere.* Ed. Craig Calhoun. Cambridge, MA: MIT P, 1993. 109–42.

Freire, Paulo. *Pedagogy of the Oppressed.* Trans. Myra Bergman Ramos. New York: Continuum, 1970.

Gee, James Paul. "Literacy, Discourse, and Linguistics: Introduction." *Journal of Education* 171.1 (1989): 5–17.

Geertz, Clifford. *Local Knowledge: Further Essays in Interpretive Anthropology.* New York: Basic Books, 1983.

Georg, Susse, and Alan Irwin. "Re-Interpreting Local-Global Partnerships." *Partnership and Leadership: Building Alliances for a Sustainable Future.* Ed. Theo J. N. M. de Bruijn and Arnold Tukker. 61–76. Dordrecht, Netherlands: Kluwer Academic Publications, 2002.

Goggin, Peter. "Rhetoric and Sustainability" [MSWord file download]. In "Humanities and Sustainability—What do the Humanities Contribute?" Institute for Humanities Research, College of Liberal Arts and Science, Arizona State University, 2009. http://iht.asu.edu/ihr_sustainability

Goldblatt, Eli. "Alinsky's Reveille: A Community-Organizing Model for Neighborhood-Based Literacy Projects." *College English* 67.3 (2005): 274–94.

Grabill, Jeffrey T. *Community Literacy Programs and the Politics of Change.* Albany: SUNY P, 2001.

———. "On Being Useful: Rhetoric and the Work of Engagement." *The Public Work of Rhetoric: Citizen-Scholars and Civic Engagement.* Ed. John Ackerman and David Coogan. University of South Carolina P, forthcoming.

———. *Writing Community Change: Designing Technologies for Citizen Action.* Cresskill: Hampton P, 2007.

Greene, Ronald Walter. "Rhetorical Pedagogy as a Postal System: Circulating Subjects through Michael Warner's 'Publics and Counterpublics.'" *Quarterly Journal of Speech* 88.1 (2002): 434–43.

Habermas, Jürgen. *The Structural Transformation of the Public Sphere: An Inquiry into a Category of Bourgeois Society*. Trans. Thomas Burger and Frederick Lawrence. Cambridge: MIT P, 1989.

Harris, Joseph. "The Idea of Community in the Study of Writing." *College Composition and Communication* 40.1, (1989): 11–22.

———. Review of *Writing Partnerships: Service-Learning in Composition*, by Thomas Deans. *Reflections: A Journal of Writing, Community Literacy* 2.1 (2001): 15–17.

Harris, Joyce L., Alan G. Kamhi, and Karen E. Pollock, eds. *Literacy in African American Communities*. Mahwah, NJ: Erlbaum, 2001.

Haskins, Ekaterina V. *Logos and Power in Isocrates and Aristotle*. Columbia: U of South Carolina P, 2004.

Heifetz. Ron. *Leadership without Easy Answers*. Boston: Harvard UP, 1998.

Heller, Caroline E. *Until We are Strong Together: Women Writers in the Tenderloin*. New York: Teachers College P, 1997.

Higgins, Lorraine, and Lisa D. Brush. "Personal Experience Narrative and Public Debate: Writing the Wrongs of Welfare." *College Composition and Communication* 57.4 (2006): 694–729.

Higgins, Lorraine and Theresa Chalich, eds. *Getting to Know You: A Dialogue for Community Health*. Pittsburgh, PA: Community Literacy Center and Rainbow Health Center, 1996.

Higgins, Lorraine, Elenore Long, and Linda Flower. "Community Literacy: A Rhetorical Model for Personal and Public Inquiry." *Community Literacy Journal* 1.1 (2006): 9–42.

Huckin, Thomas, and Leslie Olson. *Technical Writing and Professional Communication for Non-Native Speakers*. New York: McGraw-Hill, 1991.

Killingsworth, M. Jimmie, and Jacqueline S. Palmer. *Ecospeak: Rhetoric and Environmental Politics in America*. Carbondale: Southern Illinois UP, 1992.

Langsdorf, Lenore. "Argument as Inquiry in a Postmodern Context." *Argumentation* 11 (1997): 315–27.

Long, Elenore. *Community Literacy and the Rhetoric of Local Publics*. West Lafayette, IN: Parlor P, 2008.

Mansbridge, Jane. *Beyond Adversary Democracy*. Chicago: U of Chicago P, 1983.

Marcel, Detienne and Jean-Pierre Vernant. Eds. *The Cuisine of Sacrifice among the Greeks*. Trans. Paula Wissing. U of Chicago P, 1989.

Mathieu, Paula. *Tactics of Hope: The Public Turn in English Composition*. Portsmouth, NH: Boynton/Cook, 2005.

McGee, Michael. "The 'Ideograph': A Link between Rhetoric and Ideology." *Quarterly Journal of Speech* 6 (1980): 1–16.

Miller, Carolyn. "Kairos in the Rhetoric of Science." *A Rhetoric of Doing: Essays on Written Discourse in Honor of J. L. Kinneavy*. Ed. Stephen P. Witte, Neil Nakadate, and Roger D. Cherry. Carbondale: Southern Illinois UP, 1992. 310–27.

Murphy, Patricia, and James Cunningham. *Organizing for Community Controlled Development: Renewing Civil Society*. Thousand Oaks: Sage Publications, 2003.

Peck, Wayne. "Community Advocacy: Composing for Action." Diss. Carnegie Mellon U. 1991.

Peck, Wayne, Linda Flower, and Lorraine Higgins. "Community Literacy." *College Composition and Communication* 46.2 (1995): 199–222.

Roberts-Miller, Patricia. "Discursive Conflict in Communities and Classrooms." *College Composition and Communication* 54.4 (2003): 536–57.

Sauer, Beverly. *The Rhetoric of Risk: Technical Documentation in Hazardous Environments*. Mahwah, NJ: Erlbaum, 2003.

———. "Sense and Sensibility in Technical Documentation: How Feminist Interpretation Strategies Can Save Lives in the Nation's Mines." *Journal of Business and Technical Communication* 7.1 (1993): 63–83.

Scott, James C. *Seeing Like a State: How Certain Schemes to Improve the Human Condition Have Failed*. Yale UP, 1999.

Simmons, W. Michele. *Participation and Power: Civic Discourse in Environmental Policy Decisions*. State U of New York P, 2007.

Simmons, W. Michele, and Jeffrey T. Grabill. "Toward a Civic Rhetoric for Technologically and Scientifically Complex Places: Invention, Performance, and Participation." *College Composition and Communication* 58.3 (2007): 419–48.

Trimbur, John. "Consensus and Difference in Collaborative Learning." *College English* (1989) 51.6: 602–16.

Ukaga, Okechukwu and Chris Maser. *Evaluating Sustainable Development: Giving People a Voice in their Destiny*. Sterling, VA: Stylus P, 2004.

United Nations World Commission on Environment and Development. *Brundtland Report*. Oslo, Norway. 1987.

Vatz, Richard E. "The Myth of the Rhetorical Situation." *Philosophy and Rhetoric* 6 (1973): 154–61.

Warner, Michael. *Publics and Counterpublics*. New York: Zone Books, 2005.

Warnick, Christopher. Review of *Tactics of Hope: The Public Turn in English Composition* by Paula Mathieu. *Issues in Composition*. 34.1 (2006): 143–46.

Weisser, Christian R. *Moving Beyond Academic Discourse: Composition Studies and the Public Sphere*. Carbondale: Southern Illinois UP, 2002.

West, Cornel. *Keeping Faith: Philosophy and Race in America*. New York: Routledge, 1993.

Young, Amanda, and Linda Flower. "Patients as Partners: Patients as Problem-Solvers." *Health Communication* 14.1 (2001): 68–97.

Young, Iris Marion. *Intersecting Voices: Dilemmas of Gender, Political Philosophy, and Policy*. Princeton: Princeton UP, 1997.

2 Writing in the Third Space from the Sun

A Pentadic Analysis of Discussion Papers Written for the Seventh Session of the UN Forum on Forests (April 16–27, 2007)

Hannah Scialdone-Kimberley and David Metzger

> Far from being a burden, sustainable development is an exceptional opportunity—economically, to build markets and create jobs; socially, to bring people in from the margins; and politically to give every man and woman a voice, and a choice, in deciding their own future.
> —Kofi Annan, former UN Secretary General, lecture to the London School of Economics ("UN Secretary-General Kofi Annan Urges 'Coalition For Responsible Prosperity'")

This chapter focuses on the Multi-Stakeholder Dialogue Discussion Papers contributed to the United Nations Forum on Forests (UNFF) Seventh Session in New York on April 16–27, 2007. Our goals are to chart how these texts construct an expert position as a response to challenges associated with the development of multi-stakeholder dialogue and sustainability as coextensive values, and to identify how this expert position works within a "narrative of change" that emerges out of the stakeholders' and the UNFF's attempts to facilitate a multi-stakeholder dialogue on sustainability.

We restricted our attention to the UNFF given that the UNFF's Secretariat devoted considerable time and energy to the facilitation of multi-stakeholder dialogue. As reported in the Secretariat's published notes, participation in the multi-stakeholder dialogues did not initially meet the UNFF's expectations. For example, at the UNFF's second session in 2002, only two groups applied to participate, prepare position papers, and attend the conference: the "Scientific and Technology Communities Group" and the "Private Non-Industrial Forest Owners" group. The UNFF subsequently developed a financial assistance program and revised the application procedures by which interest groups and organizations might be officially identified as "stakeholders" (*Multi-Stakeholder Dialogue: Note by the Secretariat*, 2003, 2). Stakeholder participation increased for future

UNFF conferences: six groups attending in 2003, five in 2004, eight in 2005. However, in their position papers, these stakeholders began to express growing concerns regarding the role that they were invited to play in the UNFF's discussions. Chief among these concerns was the perception that guaranteeing a place in the dialogue did not guarantee stakeholders a place from which they could be heard (*Multi-Stakeholder Dialogue: Note by Secretariat*, 2005, 4). The UNFF Secretariat responded to these stakeholders' concerns by arranging to have stakeholders attend the UNFF meetings of the nation-state representatives. Eventually selected "stakeholders" were granted "expert" status, which afforded them the opportunity to speak at meetings of the nation-states (*Multi-Stakeholder Dialogue: Note by the Secretariat*, 2007, 1).

We also restricted our attention to the 2007 position papers, because the 2007 conference has been represented by the UNFF as the culmination of all its previous efforts—a benchmark year resulting in the development of a non-legally binding instrument on forests as well as the declaration of 2011 as the "International Year of the Forests." From the UNFF's perspective, the global community is setting itself on the path of change, and 2007 is a decisive moment in the history of forest sustainability.[1]

As we began to review the 2007 multi-stakeholder position papers, we used the language of Kenneth Burke's pentad (scene, agent, action, instrument, purpose) to chart the patterns of identification that emerged as each major stakeholder group located itself within the discussion of forests and sustainability (for example, the relationships between scene and purpose, and instrument and purpose). After we completed the pentadic analysis, we were in a position to identify quite specifically the discursive practices related to sustainability and the ways global and stakeholder identities were negotiated in dialogue with others.

Our methodological and theoretical perspective is taken from Kenneth Burke. Students of environmental rhetoric and eco-criticism may be acquainted with Burke through William Ruekert's 1978 essay, "Literature and Ecology."[2] Even so, a brief description of pentadic analysis will be helpful at the onset. Burke introduced pentadic analysis in his 1962 volume, *The Grammar of Motives*, and it has since become a useful tool for rhetorical analysis. The term "pentadic analysis" refers to Kenneth Burke's use of five discursive entities to identify how a particular text tells "it" like it is: scene (where something takes place), agent (who does something), action (what is done), agency (the tool by which an action is accomplished), and purpose (the reason some action is performed). Although this seems like a version of a journalist's heuristic (who, what, when, why, and how?), it's actually much more than that. Burke does not assume that what is identified as an action can only be identified as an action. What one text or rhetorical circumstance might identify as action may be identified as a scene in another. As a result, the identification of one pentadic element requires (if only by implication) the identification of other pentadic elements. At one level, this is quite commonsensical: the identification of an actor delimits and prioritizes the set of possible actions. For example, a person who is identified as a gardener may have mastered the appropriate cantillation for the Torah readings on Yom Kippur, but we would expect that she did so in her capacity as a cantor. After all, a cantor chants; a gardener gardens.

Now imagine that you have asked this cantor/gardener/academic colleague/friend a question: "What is sustainability?" It could happen! The friend, always helpful and responsive, points to a framed photograph on her office desk: she and her five-year old son are in their backyard vegetable garden in New Jersey. Surrounded by what appears to be a forest of tomato plants, your friend is on one knee, and she has her left arm around her son. If that is sustainability, what is it? Is the garden the scene? Are your friend and her son agents? Or is her son "the purpose"? Your friend (as agent) gardens (an action), in New Jersey (scene), because she wants her son (the purpose) to have a world (or at least a New Jersey) in which to live. Or is your friend teaching her son something, so the action is not so much the act of gardening as it is what she is trying to teach her son by way of gardening (now gardening is the agency and not the action)? What is the relationship of your friend to the person who took the picture? What was the photographer doing? Taking a picture, but why? To test a new digital camera, to capture a moment? And what was the son doing? Standing in the garden, working in the garden, using his work in the garden to be with his parents before running off to soccer practice? For the son, was the scene the garden or was the scene "not inside." The photograph captures a particular moment or event, but once that event has been captured/symbolized, it can be repurposed in a variety of ways. Notice too how the identification of one pentadic element may require the identification of another: if the action is gardening, then the agent would be a gardener; if the action is making the world safe for her son, then the agent would be a mother. If gardening is the tool, and the action is making sustainability local, then the agent is a (g)local citizen. Burke has a name for this relationship among pentadic elements; he calls it a ratio. Note, as well, how many identities your friend has accumulated over the course of our imaginary analysis. If we limit her identity to the position of the agent, she's a mother, gardener, wife, friend, and teacher, and our attitude toward her might even be a reflection of how often she acts like a teacher when we identify her as a friend.

It is not surprising that a particular person might deploy or be understood in terms of a number of identificatory positions over the course of a day. Now imagine a situation where the explanatory anchor used in our example (our friend's "picture of sustainability") could not be taken for granted. As we enter in conversation with others about this picture ("Did you see the picture on her desk? It—"), the pentadic elements would still represent a particular way of understanding that picture, but they would also encompass it. Indeed, if we should ever have the opportunity to see the picture ourselves, it might be difficult to see the picture except as it has already been seen for us. This point, in and of itself, is not surprising if we understand it as a description of the ontological status of constructed/discursive entities.[3] However, Burke is not simply saying that one person's agent (for example, "teacher") is another person's instrument (teaching allows me to have a captive audience), or that one person's agent ("parent") is much like the same person's other agent ("teacher" or "friend"). Burke proposes that the pentad is a means to chart the ongoing movement of identifications from one discursive site (identified with a pentadic element) to another (also identified with a pentadic element). What is more, this movement takes place within an ongoing conversation that is not limited to the speech of an individual speaker or her representatives. We are left then with a picture of identification as the movement of a group of pentads and pentadic elements, each stretching and twisting to offer their terministic resources for the identification of other pentads and pentadic elements. The distinctiveness of an individual or individual group's discourse is thereby understood as a map of the differences in the idiosyncratic passage of a term of identification from the position of scene, for example, to the position of agent, to instrument, to purpose, and so on.

Granted, all of this discussion about the pentad may sound like a description of a map of Rhode Island, which is all well and good if one has heard of Rhode Island. But if one hasn't, it is difficult to see how the pentad is a tool for understanding how discourse serves as a vehicle for identity construction. Let us now turn to the UNFF position papers themselves to exploit the descriptive and predictive power of Burke's insight into how discourse works. More specifically, we will start with the question, "how might Burke's pentad help us to describe the discursive work required in the UNFF's multi-stakeholder dialogue?"

By 2007, seven different major groups were participating in the UNFF's multi-stakeholder dialogues. The corpus of 2007 position papers includes statements prepared by seven major groups: Business and Industry, Children and Youth, Farmers and Small Forest Landowners, Non-governmental Organizations, Indigenous People, Scientific and Technological Communities, Workers and Trade Unions, and Women.[4] Each of these majors groups is made up of representatives from a variety of organizations endorsed by either the UN's Economic and Social Council (ECOSOC) or the UN's Commission on Sustainable Development (CSD) (UNFF Frequently Asked Questions). For instance, the Business and Industry major group aligns itself with "associations around the world, International Council of Forest and Paper Associations, [which is a] trade association from 39 countries representing industries from 75% of world's paper production and more than 50% of world's wood production." And the Children and Youth major group aligns itself with the International Forestry Students' Association and the Global Youth Network (3).

As one would expect, each of the major groups carefully identifies its unique contribution to the common discussion on forest sustainability.

However, the means by which these unique contributions are asserted are remarkably similar. As major groups participating in a multi-stakeholder dialogue, they identify themselves as agents whose unique contribution to the discussion is identified as "knowledge." As participants in a multi-stakeholder dialogue on forest sustainability, their knowledge is essential for the implementation of sustainable forest management, and this knowledge makes it impossible for another group to speak on their behalf. The Business and Industry major group notes that, given the number of organizations it represents, it is itself "a forum for joint action" (3). The Children and Youth major group notes that they can "provide a source of innovative thinking, new ideas, [and] fresh perspective" in the role in sustainable forest management, which may help inform forest policy from their perspective via educational programs (7). The Farmers and Small Forest Landowners can present a "wealth of practical knowledge and know-how" about forest management and suggest that all of the major groups be treated as equivalent associates in "formulation and implementation of non-binding instrument" (1, 5). The Non-governmental Organizations and Indigenous People major groups argue that they are able to bring "forest-related traditional knowledge" to the discussion on forests and note that they should be a part of monitoring, assessing, and reporting on the performance of proposals and involvement in the process of forest sustainability (4). The Scientific and Technological Communities major group offers "scientific knowledge generation and development and adaptation of forest technologies" as well as "forestry education and . . . training" (5). The Women major group brings a "gender aspect" to the discussion, which is essential given the "critical importance of women's contributions to the implementation of the proposal for actions" (3). Lastly, the Workers and Trade Unions major group offers to bring "knowledge of social aspects of sustainable forest management" to the discussion and notes that the Building and Wood Workers' International Union (BWI) has helped to give a "wake-up call for unions to integrate forestry issues into workplace concerns."

Using the language of Burke's pentad, it appears that the major groups identify themselves as agents whose defining characteristic might—in another context—be understood as an agency or tool: namely, knowledge. In addition, "knowledge" might also be understood to be an attribute of the scene inasmuch as a "lack of education" is an attribute of a scene that impedes the actions/efforts of particular agents. The association of the position of "stakeholder" with the position of "one who has discrete knowledge" (a particular kind of expert) might then be understood as a complex relationship (Burke would call it a ratio) between scene and agent, set in motion by the identification of the attributes of each (whether scene or agent) as instruments for action/change.

As noted earlier, the 2007 *Multi-Stakeholder Dialogue: Note by Secretariat* marks a significant change in the participation of major groups at the UN Forum on Forests. Rather than the major groups presenting their prepared discussion papers either to each other or to the general assembly of nation-state representatives, the major groups were asked by the UNFF Secretariat to engage in "more meaningful opportunities" in the Forum, such as consulting with the Secretariat on "focal points" and suggesting that member states offer support to major groups in the form of financial resources and time in order to increase "networking" and "capacity-building" opportunities for the major groups to build "a group perspective based on common concerns" (2).[5]

It is possible that the UNFF's call for stakeholders' involvement and knowledge regarding forest sustainability associates "expertise" as a tool by which to change/perfect the scene of the multi-stakeholder dialogue by increasing the interaction of major group meetings with nation-state members. Likewise the UNFF Secretariat's redefinition of some major groups as "experts" could be viewed as an attempt to change/perfect the major groups as agents and to find a place for them in the UN's administrative structure. Indeed, the Secretariat notes that the major groups have already significantly added to the discussion of forest sustainability as authorities on "traditional forest-related knowledge" and "gender aspects of sustainable forest management" (3). And the Secretariat further recommends that the major groups work alongside other "experts," such as "representatives of civil society organizations" (3). This being said, the UNFF's identification of the major groups as "experts" enables these groups to participate on committees that are restricted to representatives of nation-states and content-area experts (1). This new identity, then, provides the major groups with the opportunity for greater participation in future UNFF conferences.

Burke also shows us that a new set of rhetorical challenges may also accompany this new identity. Their new identity as "experts" may support the identity of "nation-state representatives" as "rational citizens" who are always in need of more information in order to make correct decisions. And the role of expert has already been scripted: experts are agencies (instruments) by which some other rational agent might be perfected into action. And these newly identified experts will no doubt experience the frustration expressed in the Scientific and Technological Communities major group's 2007 call for better integration of information and policy making (8). After all, being an expert means that a person has something to say; but it isn't a guarantee that someone is going to listen. However, the identification of major groups as experts could also provide the opportunity for extending and localizing the notion of the rational agent in a way that does not simply contrast the interests of rational global agents and rational local agents. In other words, what is the nature of an expert contribution? Does an expert contribute to the scene of the discourse and thereby enable the actions of those who are in a position to act? Or does an expert herself serve as an agent capable of action if only she were given the appropriate tools or opportunities?

The rhetorical exigency prompting this dual identity may be related to the dual nature of sustainability itself. As Tarla Rai Peterson has observed in her landmark book *Sharing the Earth: the Rhetoric of Sustainable Development*, the concept of sustainability is itself grounded on a powerful ambiguity inasmuch as "sustainability" means "sustainable development." In her discussion of sustainable development, Peterson notes that the "rhetorical strength" of sustainable development "lies in its philosophical ambiguity and range." Further, Peterson explains that sustainable development is an "oxymoron," a "term [that] both draws attention to the obstacles intrinsic to resisting exploitation (which brings temporary losses but future losses) and encourages the invention of alternative forms of resistance" (36). On the one hand, the earth is the scene within which a particular agent requires resources; agent, scene, and resource are distinct from this standpoint. The basic discursive move that supports the notion of "development" is to treat "resources" as parts of the scene that, upon the emergence of the agent, are transformed into the tools by which the agent accomplishes the task of living. On the other hand, as Burke noted years ago, when the term "earth/ecology" becomes simply a container of "resources" at a particular agent's disposal, the "scene" is no longer the proper habitation or container for the resourceful agent:

> Among the sciences, there is one little fellow named Ecology, and in time we shall pay him more attention. He teaches us that the total economy of this planet cannot be guided by an efficient rationale of exploitation alone, but that the exploiting part must itself eventually suffer if it too greatly disturbs the balance of the whole (as big beasts would starve, if they succeeded in catching all the little beasts that are their prey—their very lack of efficiency in the exploitation of their ability as hunters thus acting as efficiency on a higher level, where considerations of balance count for more than considerations of one-tracked purposiveness). (Kenneth Burke, *Attitudes toward History* 150)

This sentence from *Attitudes toward History* is almost a commonplace in eco-critical writing. We quote it here to foreground the predictive value of the discursive relations (the pentadic ratios) that it implies. In one version of the story, the predator finds that more and more of the scene might be understood to be its prey; here the identity of the agent is foregrounded as the scene continues to be instrumentalized (scripted as "resources"). In the other version of the story, the predator finds that less and less of the scene might be instrumentalized (scripted as "resources"); here the scene is foregrounded as the agent fails to instrumentalize it (as "resources"). Burke is asserting two basic terministic formulae: 1) "agent = scene—instrument" with the corollary "scene = agent + instrument"; 2) "scene = agent—instrument" with the corollary "agent = scene + instrument." However, these are not arithmetic formulas; rather they are brief expressions of how each of the pentadic elements might be understood as a reservoir of terms from which the "identity" of the other pentadic elements might be drawn.

For Burke, "sustainability" is always already "sustainable development," inasmuch as the promise of any discussion of sustainability would be to strike a balance between the two orientations toward the world expressed in the formulas above. In one orientation, the identity of the agent emerges as the scene continues to be identified as an instrument; in the other, the identity of the scene emerges as the agent continues to be identified as an instrument.

How does this help us to understand the emergence of the "epistemological agent" or "expert" as an identity position in the UNFF stakeholder papers? First, Burke identifies the principal pentadic elements in the discourse of sustainability: agent, scene, instrument. Second, Burke suggests that two competing orientations toward the world emerge out of the relationship among those pentadic elements. For those familiar with Burke's work, this will not come as much of a surprise, inasmuch as the dominance of these two ratios are developed in *A Grammar* as a conflict between two major orientations to the world: materialism and idealism. The following analysis extends Burke's discussion to suggest that these two ratios also figure prominently in the discourse of/for change.

There are those (in *A Grammar of Motives* Burke calls them materialists) who argue that change is only possible when the scene for change is perfected (131). For example, the materialist assumes that real change regarding the environment requires the eradication of the scenic prompts for environmentally harmful practices: poverty, violence against the marginalized, war, etc. This program also requires that the materialist posit an agent capable of making such a change in the world. Because the task is to change the world as scene, this agent must become the determining forces that the materialist identifies as the scene of war, poverty, and violence. The Business and Industry major group recommends that the UNFF create "basic principles and minimum requirements," which require "national commitments" for sustainable forest management (4). The Non-governmental Organizations and Indigenous People major groups argue that if actions to stop forest destruction are to be achieved, those actions must include respect, support, and implementation of indigenous rights (6). Further, they note that the non-legally binding instrument is too ambiguous and is "based on the commercial aspects of the forests," which ignores its "cultural and spiritual" aspects (7). The Women major group argues that gender inequality and poverty are major concerns for women within the realm of forest sustainability (4). The Workers and Trade Unions major group suggests that workers are able to work in conditions of freedom, equity, security and human dignity" in order to increase the link between sustainable development and decent work (3). They also urge that the non-legally binding instrument "remain . . . flexible yet prescriptive" and that the multi-year program of work consider "poverty alleviation . . . the Millennium Development Goals, gender dimensions . . . land tenure issues, and human rights of indigenous peoples" with regard to the role of forests (4). Each of these examples could work to impede change in forest management in that each major group focuses on the problems that must be solved before it will be possible to achieve forest sustainability. Potentially this position could lead to postponing commitment to the actions of sustainability while the scene for sustainability is being constructed. Here the resources for change are also impediments for change.

Burke situates the position of the idealist in contrast to that of the materialist. There are those, he tells us, who argue that change is only possible when the agent for change is perfected (172). These "idealists" assume that real change regarding the environment requires that an agent's inherent rational and ethical capacities be engaged to motivate a needful change. Because the task is to change the world by affecting it one agent at a time, each agent must be outfitted with the necessary tools or understanding with which she or he will perform the actions associated with sustainability. The Children and Youth major group suggests that "education" and "capacity-building" for children and youth should be included in the UNFF's non-legally binding instrument as a way to ensure forest sustainability (5). The Farmers and Small Forest Landowners major group advocates for major groups to be included in the creation and implementation of the UNFF's non-legally binding instrument and the multi-year program of work, which should include "capacity-building, education, and training at local and regional levels" for children and youth (6). The Scientific and Technological Communities group recommends that future international agreements such as the non-legally binding agreement need to "enhance the interface between science and policy" as well as expand research capacity-building and funding in order for scientific knowledge and technologies to participate in forest sustainability (11). The Women's major group recommends that (along with implementation of the non-legally binding instrument) in order to achieve gender equity in reference to forest management, women be afforded "capacity-building" for leadership, "gender-mainstreaming skills and expertise within all forest-related institutions," "resources," funding and "partnerships between Governments and civil society and with regional and global organizations, specialized in gender mainstreaming, to assure the implementation of gender-sensitive sustainable forest management initiatives" (8–9). The Workers and Trade Unions major group suggests that resources for "capacity-building of civil society and trade unions" be distributed (3). These examples impede change in that it seems impossible to make a rational argument regarding a time frame that severely limits the goals of sustainability. Here education, funding, and capacity building might never be enough for sustainability to happen. Likewise the goal of sustainability may become lost when these tools are used for purposes that have not been reconceptualized in terms of sustainability.

The dominance of these two orientations/ratios (materialist and idealist/ scene and agent) may also help us to identify another obstacle to change.

Whether one conceives of the solution as the perfection of a scene or the perfection of an agent, it is necessary to identify who might be responsible for these ameliorations. And, as one attempts to concretize these perfections, responsibility can be shifted to another entity who is understood to be both outside and wholly implicated with the problem at hand. There is a danger that the United Nations might become just such an entity. Although each major group has different interests at stake, they all see the United Nations as a group that is responsible to act on the discussion on sustainability. From this context, the multi-stakeholder dialogue reinscribes an independent/dependent binary between stakeholders (the South) and the United Nations (the North). Here it may be possible that the North-South binary reemerges within this attempt to create the scene of sustainability—a scene within which the "North" is always in the position to give up something and the "South" is the position to give up on something. In *Sharing the Earth*, Peterson discusses the North-South binary originally portrayed in the Brandt Commission report, "[which] describe[d] the world as a division between north and south . . . and portray[ed] its programs as claims of justice owed from North to South (19). She noted that the authors of the *Brundtland Report* worked to supplant the key word "justice," used in the Brandt Commission report, with the key word "sustainability," which "enables political leaders of developed countries to advocate international policies on the basis of national interests, rather than domestically unpopular claims alleged to be owed to noncitizens, plac[ing] citizens of developing countries in a position of equality to those in developed nations" (19).

To see how the development of expert agents responds to the rhetorical exigencies that we have associated with the dominance of materialism/idealism and the North-South binaries, we will focus our attention on the 2007 position paper submitted by the Women major group.

As with all the major groups, the Women major group is made up of "focal points," or points of contact and representation. The Woman major group selected Women Organizing for Change in Agriculture and Natural Resource Management (WOCAN) as one of its UNFF major group focal points (UNFF Major Group Focal Points). The WOCAN Web site describes WOCAN as "a women-led global network of professional women and men engaged in agriculture and natural resource management who are committed to organizational change for gender equality and environmentally sustainable development" (WOCAN Home Page).

WOCAN, as a representative of the Woman major group, has been instrumental in enacting a "productive ambiguity" using the resources of materialism and idealism to reconstruct "expertise" so that it is compatible with both the perfection of the agent and the perfection of the scene. Within the United Nations, "expert" can mean one who is invited to provide information to nation-state representatives. And it is precisely this use of the term that is invoked when the Woman major group recommends in their 2007 position paper that they contribute their "expertise" to a committee of experts in order to "promote and facilitate the implementation of the non-legally binding instrument" (7). An ambiguity emerges, however, when the Woman major group identifies women foresters themselves as experts. In a speech developed by the Women major group and presented to the Commission for Sustainable Development at the United Nations May, 2008, Jeanette Gurung (WOCAN's director) notes the following:

> As said by our group before, the MG Women seeks recognition of the primary roles of women as farmers and environmental managers. Rather than being regarded as a vulnerable group, women—through their extensive knowledge, experience and substantial roles related to land use—are experts in agriculture and natural resource management. They are key agents—not vulnerable victims—in the way forward and as such, should be placed forefront and centre of a transformation of institutions (including those of the UN system) that generate policies, technologies, knowledge and programs so as to orient structures and processes to address women's needs as food producers and environmental managers through gender mainstreaming (Speech by Major Group Women)

The term "expert" includes both women farmers and forest managers—reconceptualizing them in terms of action, or what Burke refers to as the "scenic overtones in action" (*A Grammar of Motives* 14). On the one hand, as experts in the field, women draw their identity both from the scenes and from the agents of forestry. On the other, as members of the Women major group, their expertise emerges as an instrument by which nation-state representatives might be informed.

The Woman major group uses this ambiguity to respond to the materialism/idealism binary by making arguments for change in both the scene and agent. In its 2007 position paper, the Women major group devotes considerable attention to a partnership between WOCAN and the Ministry of Forest and Soil Conservation of Nepal, engaged in "bridg[ing] the gender gap by training and mentoring rural and professional women as group promoters and gender focal persons from livestock and forestry departments" (8). As reported by the Women major group, this partnership was successful, inasmuch as it led to a policy shift in the Ministry of Forest and Soil Conservation of Nepal, which developed a "national strategy for gender mainstreaming action plans until 2015" (8). As an agent, a nation-state can partner with a nongovernmental agency (NGO) in order to accomplish a particular task exhibiting an "exemplary performance in project implementation through . . . effective collaboration" (7). As a scene, a nation is the particular site for such a partnership. In their collaboration with nation-states, NGOs might also participate in the dual identity of the "nation" as scene and agent.

In creating a formal connection with the Ministry of Forest and Soil Conservation of Nepal, the Women major group uses its "expertise" to situate gender mainstreaming in the context/realm of sustainable forest management. In their position paper, the Women major group offers the following recommendations: "to strengthen linkages with the Ministry in Nepal by establishing a formal relationship for at least the next three years, to assess the effectiveness of an NGO/Government partnership strategy; identify gaps in the Ministry's efforts in gender mainstreaming in programmes and organizational aspects; and make recommendations" (8). Here the scene of the United Nations is a source for action, especially because the Women major group identifies other nation-states (South Africa and the Philippines) as potential partners for building the same kind of linkage with the Women major group.

There is more at work in this list of nation-states than the assertion that "we did it before and we can do it again." What we see here is a complete transformation of the scene. But we will need a little more Burke in order to see it. In *A Grammar of Motives*, Burke discusses the usefulness of ambiguities: "[I]nstead of considering it our task to 'dispose of' any 'ambiguity,' we rather consider it our task to study and clarify the *resources* of ambiguity," for it is in the areas of ambiguity that transformations take place" (xix). Burke further explains how such ambiguity might be achieved:

> Terms like "adjustment" and "adaptation" are ambiguously suited to cover both action and sheer motion, so that it is usually difficult to decide in just which sense a thinker is using them when he applies them to social motives. This ambiguity may put them in good favor with those who would deal with the human realm in a calculus patterned after the vocabularies of the physical sciences, and yet would not wholly abandon vestiges of "animism." Profession, vocation, policy, strategy, tactics are all concepts of action, as are any words for specific vocations. Our words "position," "occupation," and "office" indicate the scenic overtones of action (14)

In the above quotation, Burke refers to the difference between motion and action. For example, imagine a young girl in motion. Now visualize her skipping down the sidewalk. We now have two views—the young girl skipping and the young girl in motion. The young girl skipping is an action inasmuch as it is related to an attitude with respect to the motion as well as a motive for the action. If the young girl is "letting off steam," then it is doubtful that she skipped across the room; it is more likely that she stomped.

This distinction between motion and action helps us to see that in the discourse of the United Nations, the scene is often associated with what Burke calls motion, the movement of a reality unmediated by human motive. The scene of idealism is understood in these terms as a collection of victims as well as deficiencies, problems, and obstacles to change. The Women major group's particular construction of "expertise" opens up the scene as a resource for action by identifying the experts within that scene. That is, the scene itself is made up of agents capable of action. To demonstrate that "women" are not simply victims is to say that they are not simply potential agents trapped in or by a particular scene. We say "demonstrate" in this case to suggest that the acknowledgement of this "fact" requires more than a simple assertion, because the call for justice and equity is often prompted by the acknowledgement of victims. It requires that the scene itself be understood as a locus of action: a nation-state within which women are already experts. "Gender equity" is not then only an issue of injustice (the perfection of the scene) comparable to other injustices; "gender equity" involves the recognition and capacity building of women as experts.

We see here how "action" is filtered into the discourse of the United Nations as implementation. Following Nepal's example may not be attractive to another nation-state. However, using the example of Nepal as a source of information in order to implement a sustainability project is more so, because the agent of implementation is the individual nation-state under whose aegis the implementation would take place. In the instance of the WOCAN-Nepal partnership, each agent is equipped with the tools and understanding by which both groups may carry out the actions associated with sustainability of the forests. In this manner, the Women major group exploits idealism (the perfection of the scene) and materialism (the perfection of the agent) to develop a sustainable rhetoric for change.

Likewise, in this instance, the North-South binary is also addressed in that the Woman major group has constructed a synecdoche: where a part (Nepal) of the whole of nation-states (the United Nations) represents the actions for which the whole might be responsible. Notice how the identification of responsibility does not mean that no action is to be taken should the whole (as perfected agent) not respond.[6] The part is already responding and should continue to do so. But the quality of the part's action has been transformed, because to act as Nepal has done more fully perfects the actions of the whole (understood as the individual actions of each nation-state). "Perfection" is thereby scripted in terms of a hybridized scene/agent rather than as a dependent agent ("the South") who relies on another agent's ("the North's") generosity or sense of justice. In this instance, the Women major group has successfully made arguments for change in both the scene and agent, arguments that do not focus on the scene and the agent as mutually exclusive identificatory positions.

Insofar as rhetorical theory might be understood as both descriptive and predictive of discursive practices, this analysis runs the risk of inventing new words to render common sense or practical rhetorical judgment. That being said, our use of Burke's pentad has identified not only the development of a new identificatory position but it has contextualized that development in terms of the affordances of a generalized rhetoric of/for change. In short, Kofi Annan's statement regarding the opportunities of sustainability—which prefaced our discussion—is more than simply a hope; it is a positive and realizable goal when its discursive burdens are also acknowledged and addressed.

NOTES

1. "Following intense negotiations, the Seventh Session of the Forum adopted the landmark Non-Legally Binding Instrument on All Types of Forests" ("About UNFF").
2. Seigel's "One Little Fellow Named Ecology: Ecological Rhetoric in Kenneth Burke's Attitudes Toward History" contests the view that Burke is the "father of ecocritism" by carefully reconstructing the public conversation about ecological issues in 1930's America.
3. For a more detailed discussion of Burke's responsiveness to an ongoing constructivist project, see Chapter 1 of Robert Wess's *Kenneth Burke: Rhetoric, Subjectivity, Postmodernism*.
4. Produced at the 1992 "Rio Conference," Agenda 21 is commonly acknowledged as the first substantive call for multi-stakeholder dialogue regarding sustainable development. Agenda 21 differs from earlier calls for policy implementation by identifying multi-stakeholder dialogue as a key feature for any future implementation strategy for sustainable development: "Critical to the effective implementation of the objectives, policies and mechanisms agreed to by Governments in all program areas of Agenda 21 will be the commitment and genuine involvement of all social groups" (Agenda 21: Chapter 23: Strengthening the Role of Major Groups). The 2007 UNFF Secretariat's "note" on multi-stakeholder dialogue also suggests that Agenda 21 identifies who these stakeholders might be. And, between 2000 and 2007, the UNFF welcomed nine major groups to participate in its multi-stakeholder forums following recommendations made in Chapter 23 of Agenda 21: Women, Children and Youth, Indigenous People, Non-governmental Organizations, Local Authorities, Workers and Trade Unions, Business and Industry, Scientific and Technological Communities, and Farmers and Small Forest Landowners.
5. The UNFF has granted various organizations to represent each major group (such as the Global Youth Action Network, which represents the Children and Youth Major Group) to retain "consultative status" with the UNFF. This focal point system consists of focal points from each major group and works to "coordinate planning and discussion on UNFF issues within and between major group networks" (UNFF Major Group Focal Points).
6. In *A Grammar of Motives*, Burke notes, "The 'noblest synecdoche,' the perfect paradigm or prototype for all lesser usages, is found in metaphysical doctrines proclaiming the identity of 'microcosm' and 'macrocosm.' In such doctrines, where the individual is treated as a replica of the universe, and vice versa, we have the ideal synecdoche, because microcosm is related to macrocosm as part to whole and either the whole can represent the part or the part can represent the whole. (For 'represent' here we could substitute 'be identified with')" (508).

WORKS CITED

"About UNFF." *United Nations Forum on Forests*. May 30, 2008 http://www.un.org/esa/forests/about.html.

"Agenda 21: Chapter 23: Strengthening the Role of Major Groups." *United Nations Division for Sustainable Development*. Dec. 15, 2004. May 30, 2008 http://www.un.org/esa/sustdev/documents/agenda21/english/agenda21toc.htm.

Burke, Kenneth. *A Grammar of Motives*. Berkley: U of California P, 1969.

———. *Attitudes toward History*. Berkley: U of California P, 1984.
"Frequently Asked Questions." *United Nations Forum on Forests*. Feb. 1, 2008 http://www.un.org/esa/forests/faq.html#p2.
Multi-Stakeholder Dialogue: Discussion Paper Contributed by Business and Industry Major Group. United Nations. United Nations Economic and Social Council, Forum on Forests, 2005. 1–5. Feb. 1, 2008 http://www.un.org/esa/forests/documents-unff.html#5.
Multi-Stakeholder Dialogue: Discussion Paper Contributed by the Non-Governmental Organizations and Indigenous Peoples Major Group. United Nations. United Nations Economic and Social Council, Forum on Forests, 2007. 1–7. Feb. 1, 2008 http://www.un.org/esa/forests/documents-unff.html#7.
Multi-Stakeholder Dialogue: Discussion Paper Contributed by the Scientific and Technological Community Major Group. United Nations. United Nations Economic and Social Council, Forum on Forests, 2007. 1–7. Feb. 1, 2008 http://www.un.org/esa/forests/documents-unff.html#7.
Multi-Stakeholder Dialogue: Discussion Paper Contributed by the Small Forest Landowners Major Group. United Nations. United Nations Economic and Social Council, Forum on Forests, 2007. 1–6. Feb. 1, 2008 <http://www.un.org/esa/forests/documents-unff.html#7.
Multi-Stakeholder Dialogue: Discussion Paper Contributed by the Women Major Group. United Nations. United Nations Economic and Social Council, Forum on Forests, 2007. 1–9. Feb. 1, 2008 http://www.un.org/esa/forests/documents-unff.html#7.
Multi-Stakeholder Dialogue: Discussion Paper Contributed by the Workers and Trade Unions Major Group. United Nations. United Nations Economic and Social Council, Forum on Forests, 2007. 1–4. Feb. 1, 2008 http://www.un.org/esa/forests/documents-unff.html#7.
Multi-Stakeholder Dialogue: Discussion Paper Contributed by Youth/Children Major Group. United Nations. United Nations Economic and Social Council, Forum on Forests, 2007. 1–7. Feb. 1, 2008 http://www.un.org/esa/forests/documents-unff.html#7.
Multi-Stakeholder Dialogue: Note by Secretariat. United Nations. United Nations Economic and Social Council, Forum on Forests, 2007. 1–4. May 23, 2008 http://www.un.org/esa/forests/documents-unff.html#7.
Multi-Stakeholder Dialogue: Note by Secretariat. United Nations. United Nations Economic and Social Council, Forum on Forests, 2005. 1–5. June 5, 2008 http://www.un.org/esa/forests/participation-msd-papers.html#unn5.
Multi-Stakeholder Dialogue: Note by the Secretariat. United Nations. United Nations Economic and Social Council, Forum on Forests, 2004. 1–2. June 5, 2008 http://www.un.org/esa/forests/participation-msd-papers.html#unff4.
Multi-Stakeholder Dialogue: Note by the Secretariat. United Nations. United Nations Economic and Social Council, Forum on Forests, 2003. 1–3. June 5, 2008 http://www.un.org/esa/forests/documents-unff.html#3.
Peterson, Tarla R. *Sharing the Earth: the Rhetoric of Sustainable Development*. Columbia: U of South Carolina P, 1997.
Ruekert, William. "Literature and Ecology: An Experiment in Eco-criticism." In *The Ecocriticism Reader: Landmarks in Literary Ecology*. Eds. C. Glotfelty and H. Fromm. Athens: U of Georgia P, 1996, 105–123.
"Rio Declaration on Environment and Development." *United Nations Environment Programme: Environment for Development*. 1992. Apr. 23, 2008 http://www.unep.org/Documents.Multilingual/Default.asp?DocumentID=78&ArticleID=1163.
Seigel, Marika. "One Little Fellow Named Ecology: Ecological Rhetoric in Kenneth Burke's Attitudes Toward History." *Rhetoric Review* 23.4: 388–403.

"UNFF Major Group Focal Points." *United Nations Forum on Forests.* May 1, 2008 http://www.un.org/esa/forests/contacts-major_groups.html.

"UN Secretary-General Kofi Annan Urges 'Coalition for Responsible Prosperity.'" *United Nations Information Service Vienna.* 26 Feb. 2002. United Nations. Apr. 28, 2008 http://www.unis.unvienna.org/unis/pressrels/2002/envdev624.html.

"United Nations Forum on Forests (UNFF) Documents." *United Nations Forum on Forests.* 2000–2008. November 12, 2008 http://www.un.org/esa/forests/documents-unff.html#7.

Wess, Robert. *Kenneth Burke: Rhetoric, Subjectivity, Postmodernism.* Cambridge: Cambridge UP, 1996.

WOCAN. November 2008. Women Organizing for Change in Agriculture and Natural Resource Development. November 12, 2008 http://wocan.org/index.html.

3 Creating a Rhetorical Space for Biodiversity
The Great Smoky Mountains Association

Elizabeth Giddens

"A wondrous diversity of life" serves as a slogan for the Great Smoky Mountains National Park (GSMNP). It appears—illustrated by a lush display of native plants and animals—on Web pages, T-shirts, posters, and coffee mugs, especially those promoting a research project to identify all the species in the park. The phrase is adapted from Edward O. Wilson's remark in the closing chapter of *The Diversity of Life* that "[t]here can be no purpose more enspiriting than to begin the age of restoration, reweaving the wondrous diversity of life that still surrounds us" (351). In keeping with Wilson's view of the need to maintain biodiversity, the slogan highlights the park as a preserve of biodiversity, which it unquestionably is. As a park Web page explains:

> No other area of equal size in a temperate climate can match the park's amazing diversity of plants, animals, and invertebrates. Over 10,000 species have been documented in the park: Scientists believe an additional 90,000 species may live here." (National Park Service, "Nature & Science")

In particular, the park is renowned to scientists and naturalists for its one hundred species of native trees, "more than in any other North American National Park" (National Park Service, "Nature & Science") and for being the salamander capital of the world. At least thirty species of salamanders live in the park, including twenty-four lungless species that breathe through their skin; some of these live nowhere else (National Park Service, "Amphibians").

But a visitor survey shows that this famed biodiversity is unlikely to be the first image that a park visitor thinks of before or during a trip to the Smokies (Littlejohn iii). Visitors are more likely to think of scenic views of tree-covered mountain ridges blanketed in mist, of black bears ambling along slopes, of mountainsides blazing in fall colors, of glorious springtime wildflower blooms, and of the self-reliant homesteaders who once lived and farmed the mountains and coves before they were forced out when the land became a park in 1934. Consequently the park faces a challenge in linking its public image dominated by the hallmarks of the Appalachian mountains to its identity as a diverse and important natural area.

The mission of the National Park Service (NPS) requires that park management give equal attention to both the natural and cultural resources of the park and the "enjoyment" of these resources by the public (National Park Service, "Caring for the American Legacy"). So the rhetorical situation of those who write for and about the park in an official capacity is complex; because park visitors are likely to be most interested in topics other than the area's biodiversity and because park management is charged both with meeting the needs of visitors and protecting the unique resources of the park, publications must be carefully crafted.

The Great Smoky Mountains Association (GSMA) is the congressionally authorized nonprofit cooperating organization for the GSMNP. In existence for over fifty years, the association supports the park by "promoting greater public understanding and appreciation through education, interpretation, and research" (GSMA, "About Us"). Although it does many things for the park, the association is best known for running the bookstores in the visitor centers, sponsoring demonstrations throughout the park, and publishing the park's quarterly newspaper and interpretive brochures. The proceeds from association publications, sales of other items, and membership dues are contributed to the park as aid, which has been significant for maintaining vital park services during the last twenty years. According to Barbara Muhlbeier, a board member of the association, one year during the 1990s the association and the Friends of the Smokies, another organization supporting the park, together contributed about 25 percent of the park's budget because of federal cutbacks. Since its creation in 1953, the association has contributed over $18 million to the park; in 2006–2008, annual budgeted aid to the park has averaged $1.7 million and has increased every year (see *Bear Paw* newsletters for 2006, 2007, and 2008). The association serves as an important supporter of the park financially and educationally.

In addition to a full range of T-shirts, coffee mugs, toys, and park-logo items, association stores sell many books and booklets that it develops and publishes in cooperation with Park Service professionals. These include a set of field guides about hiking trails, wildflowers, birds, ferns, and trees; an auto touring guide; children's storybooks and junior ranger guides; books about Native American culture in the park; as well as booklets about the Appalachian farmers and their way of life in the nineteenth and early twentieth centuries, the logging industry that cut timber throughout the Smokies from 1900 to 1938, and the Civilian Conservation Corps that built much of the park's infrastructure from 1933 to 1942. Although Steve Kemp, interpretive products and services director for GSMA, views the association as primarily a retailer rather than a publisher, much of his time and that of his publications staff of four is devoted to the ongoing production of new publications and the revision of existing ones, all vetted by park management for accuracy and message appropriateness. In short, the association exists "exclusively" to serve the park, as Muhlbeier explains, and publications are a significant part of this support.

Through its many and diverse publications, the association functions as the voice of the park to visitors. To succeed in this role, GSMA has developed a rhetorical strategy that indirectly and pragmatically promotes biodiversity as it meets visitors' pressing needs and initial interests. The strategy is pragmatic because it takes into account the multiple rhetorical constraints that inform its situation: the park's mission; a high standard of factual accuracy in content; the business concern of the association to meet a payroll, monitor inventory, and donate aid to the park; and the needs and psychology of park visitors and the local community. Although association publications are in harmony with green values such as protection of habitats and species, and limits to human knowledge and the ability to control nature (Jamieson 480–81), they espouse them quietly. As they balance these constraints and values, GSMA publications provide park visitors information and facilitate positive park experiences, noting the park's biodiversity along the way. Similarly, the association avoids falling into environmental communication traps that will limit its effectiveness with constituencies: expensive publications or a mix of publications that would not be profitable (Kemp, personal interview; Muhlbeier), a preachy or overly dogmatic tone (Killingsworth and Palmer 15, Plevin 137, and Moser 71), dullness (Jacobson 186), and overt challenges to a materialist culture in a society focused more on jobs and security than on nature (Corbett 2, Biodiversity Project 74). In contrast to the instrumental rhetorical model between government and the public that Killingsworth and Palmer describe in Chapter 5 of *Ecospeak: Rhetoric and Environmental Politics in America*, which analyzes the lack of sincere dialogue and understanding between parties in environmental impact statements, the GSMA successfully enacts a Habermasian rhetoric of communicative action between the Park Service and GSMNP visitors. This rhetoric is marked by mutual respect and need as well as a desire on the part of GSMA writers to inform readers about the park's stunning biodiversity and contemporary threats to it. Though GSMA publications are transactional in that they advise, suggest, and occasionally warn readers, their sensitivity to their readers' current interests and immediate needs reveals them to be sincerely dialogic.

AN AMBIGUOUS CONTEXT

Before examining GSMA's approach to its communications, the fundamentals of the park's context and history need to be explored. GSMNP is now and has traditionally been the most visited park in the National Park Service, due in part to its accessible southeastern location. According to a NPS press release, in 2007 9.37 million visits were made to GSMNP. These numbers are more than double those for Grand Canyon National Park, 4.4 million visits, the second-ranked park ("National Park Service Attendance"). In addition, the Smokies have a significant economic effect on the gateway communities to the park in Tennessee and North Carolina: In 2005, GSMNP was highest among all national parks in economic benefits through local jobs, personal income, and "non-local visitor and park payroll spending" ("Study: National Parks Huge Economic Return"). But a check to the park's popularity and the economic benefits it brings to the region is lingering bitterness from the time of its founding. Unlike many western parks, GSMNP was established on land that was owned by large logging companies and by homesteaders; it has a rich and relatively recent human history. (Of course, before Europeans settled in the area, parkland made up a part of the Cherokee territory, so Native American history is also a feature of the park's cultural heritage.) Indeed, though local resentment has faded, when the park was created, families were required to leave their homes, logging operations were bought out, businesses were closed, and a way of life in the park was lost. Few individuals now survive who once lived in the park, so community resentment about resettlement is minimal. But for many years this history colored the relationship between the park and local communities. In the past, Tennessee and North Carolina state leaders have not always supported the park through legislative efforts to enhance funding via special appropriations; the park was sometimes seen as "an intrusion by the federal government," according to Kemp, and in the years following the park's establishment, regional legislators did not work to secure federal funding for special park projects, a sharp contrast to the support of legislators in the districts and states surrounding the Grand Canyon and Yellowstone, which has led to a perennial underfunding of the Smokies. In the last decade, local communities and state and federal representatives have warmed to the park—indeed most now see the park as the great natural and economic asset it is—but park and association employees are aware that they need to continue to be sensitive to the displacement of families at the time of the park's founding.

Furthermore, because parkland was established where communities had flourished, it cannot be said that GSMNP is a pristine wilderness, given the logging, farming, and commerce of the pre-park era. Cabins, mills, railroad beds, and fields remain—and some are preserved—as a record of this period. Of course, many areas of the park are remote and wild; a few are untouched by logging and farming. This history cuts both ways. Unlike the history of Yellowstone Park concessions and management told by Barringer in *Selling Yellowstone: Capitalism and the Construction of Nature*, in which the loss of prepackaged, idealized experiences caused visitors to resent changes to park concessions and tours as well as those responsible, the Smokies have not been traditionally viewed as unspoiled wilderness, so a conflict between conserving nature and building tourism was not cast in sharp relief when ecological management practices became the norm in the 1960s. Rather, the park's establishment in the midst of populated communities led to a slower recognition of the Smokies' ecological value generally and especially to those in towns and communities surrounding the park's boundaries. Encouraging an understanding of how the Smokies are unique ecologically—while continuing to acknowledge and respect their important cultural heritage—has been the management challenge.

A broader contextual issue for GSMA publications is a national trend *away* from nature-based recreation and park visits; park and association staff wonder what it may mean to the park in terms of funding and preservation. Since 1999 the number of park visits nationwide has been in decline ("National Park System Attendance Rises"). In a 2008 statistical study of national and international park use, Pergams and Zaradic found that "all major lines of evidence point to an ongoing and fundamental shift away from nature-based recreation" (2295). These findings, Pergams and Zaradic concluded, lead to concern about general public support for conservation efforts:

> We think it probable that any major decline in the value placed on natural areas and experiences will greatly reduce the value people place on biodiversity conservation. Accordingly, it becomes less likely that attempts to raise public awareness of the current biodiversity crisis will succeed. In the long term, conserving biodiversity may depend on our appreciation of nature's intrinsic value. (2295)

Peter Kareiva of the Nature Conservancy and Environmental Studies Institute concurs with this view and worries that people seem to be more "disconnected from nature" and that consequently they may be "less likely to value nature" (2757). He notes that "[p]eople care about what they know, and people need to know something about nature to solve environmental problems" (2757). Kemp interprets the trend in social and political terms: "National Parks are protected by law, but those laws only exist because people want them to. Parks can get decommissioned in the wink of an eye." So the challenge for GSMA and its writers is to connect, or reconnect, park visitors to nature in ways that, over the long term, will lead to such support. An oft-quoted comment by Senegalese conservationist Baba Dioum on the links between affection and political will echoes this point: "In the end, we will conserve only what we love, we will love only what we understand, we will understand only what we are taught" (quoted in Wilson 320). Biodiversity is, of course, a key component of the concept and practice of sustainability in society's interactions with the nonhuman world. This notion must also be taught in order for society to protect habitats and species; it is critical that more people grasp the relationship between preservation of biodiversity and the establishment of social practices that can sustain a high quality of life in both short and long terms.

A PROFILE OF PARK VISITORS

Given this context, the audience for GSMA publications becomes a critical question, and though the association store sells its literature and merchandise online and ships purchases anywhere, it considers its core audience to be park visitors who pick up free publications during a trip or buy others before, during, or after their visit. Anticipating Ingham's recommendation that park interpreters "start with forging actual connections with the audience" through audience analysis in order to "reveal where discussions of the issues . . . might be elaborated" ("Rhetoric of Disengagment," 145), GSMNP has attended to the question of who the park's visitors actually are. The most recent survey of visitors to the park was conducted in the summer and fall of 1996, with the purpose of providing a profile of visitors and their visits to the park, the services they used, and their views of the quality and necessity of those services. It found that family groups comprised about 73 percent of visitors while very few (less than 2 percent total) entered the park as part of guided tours and school groups (Littlejohn iii). Many visitors were repeat visitors (65 percent in summer and 79 percent in fall), and more than half viewed the park as their primary destination (Littlejohn iii). In both seasons, "viewing scenery, viewing wildlife/wildflowers, photography, and visiting historic sites" were the most popular activities even though two-thirds spend less than one day in the park (Littlejohn iii).

These data show why Kemp envisions his audience largely as tourists who need basic information:

> One thing I always notice about people who visit the park is that they're almost always looking at a map. . . . They don't know where they are. They don't know what's here. They don't know where they want to go. So they're first consumed with basic knowledge about the park. . . . The majority of the people are not college educated, liberal, green folks. You do get a good cross-section of people who come to national parks, especially in the east here where it's a pretty economical trip, so you've got an opportunity to connect with people who aren't singing in the choir.

This observation also fits another key finding of Littlejohn's report: The most used information services were the park brochure/map, visitor center information desk, and park newspaper, though visitors did think other publications available in the visitor center were both "important" and "very good" in quality (46–58). Notably, about one-third of visitors used road-guide booklets (46–47, 57).

The goals of GSMA publications are obvious. They are to help visitors to know the park, to have affection for it, and to support it. Promoting the park's biodiversity and its value as a natural resource are two of the first key aspects for actually "knowing the park." However, Chess and Johnson remind us of the "tenuous" and "fragile" link between information and behavior (223); many people do not act on environmental information that they possess. Consequently it becomes equally desirable for the association to help instill in visitors a love for the park that perhaps over the long term will result in their willingness to support the park. Kemp explains the interrelationships between these goals for the park as a process of building a personal relationship between the park and its visitors:

> A person's relationship with a national park is the same as a person's relationship with another person. You've never seen them, you never met them, you've never heard of them, you don't care that much about them.... Who cares about them? But you know when you meet somebody, learn their name, see what they look like, talk to them, you immediately begin to care about them to some extent. The more you get to know them, the more you care about them. So I see our role as just that—facilitating, spending some time in a mostly non-dogmatic way.

As Reardon explains, "the greatest enemy of persuasion is assumption,... [y]ou must know what *does* matter to [your audience], not what *should* matter to them" (10). An examination of key GSMA publications demonstrates how the organization addresses its audience—the somewhat hurried, potentially confused, partially informed, recreationally minded park visitor. People come to the park to see the mountains and what's in them, to take a break from their routines, and to enjoy themselves. These motivations must be respected if GSMA is to produce publications that help visitors value the park's "wondrous diversity."

RHETORICAL STRATEGIES FOR BIODIVERSITY RECEPTIVENESS AND AWARENESS IN THE SMOKIES

Plevin suggests that if an organization seeks Habermasian communicative action (or understanding of its and even other groups' concerns) over the long term, as opposed to instrumental action, in which control and success are priorities, then approaching a rhetorical situation such as that of the park and association by "[f]ocusing on 'communication free from domination' and grounded in 'mutual trust'" is likely to be preferable to strategies that make individuals feel guilty of their environment-related behaviors and choices or, equally limiting, discouraged by dire circumstances of biodiversity or the difficulty of sustainability (238–39). The association's approach—coping rationally with contextual complexity by recognizing what can be achieved through its publications and what messages and goals may need to be set aside—embodies communicative action. An activist might think that in accepting such constraints association writers and park staff are selling out or foregoing opportunities to reach, teach, or inform a larger group of people. But a communicative action approach offers the attractive safeguard of ensuring that it will not alienate its audience from the park, park service staff, or the association.

A critical review of GSMA publications reveals four strategies that follow from the choice of a communicative action approach:

- to provide visitors with tools to help them enjoy their visit to the park
- to interpret the park for visitors, rather than to teach directly
- to balance negativity about the problems the park faces with positive messages
- to encourage visitors to make connections between the park's natural and cultural history by identifying with families who lived in the park and with contemporary visitors, experts, and park staff.

The remainder of this chapter will describe how these strategies are enacted in individual publications and how they work collectively to convey messages of the relevance and importance of biodiversity to society.

PROVIDING TOOLS TO ENSURE A GOOD VISIT

The most pervasive rhetorical strategy of GSMA publications is to provide park visitors with information during a park visit that will help them organize, navigate, and enjoy their time in the park. The psychology of this strategy is clear: If visitors have a good time in the park, if they see interesting places, learn a bit about what they see, and, importantly, are able to avoid traveling frustrations (such as wrong turns and time-consuming traffic jams) and dangers (such as weather hazards, accidents, and harm from insect and snake bite or even bear attack), then their associations with the park will be positive. Consequently they may become more intrigued by the park and may pursue that interest by returning another time, getting off the roads and onto the park's walkways and trails, learning more about the value of the park's natural resources to the region, and perhaps supporting or even volunteering for the benefit of the park.

The free park newspaper *Smokies Guide* and many free (or donation) brochures for the park, its nature trails, and other attractions are the primary vehicles for this strategy. The newspaper is available at visitor centers, and roadside and trailside brochures are distributed at kiosks near entryways to their designated focus.[1]

Although the basic park brochure, containing the standard NPS park map, is the most distributed publication, *Smokies Guide* functions as the best introduction to the park and is also distributed in large numbers; Kemp estimates that probably 350,000 copies are distributed each year. This quarterly newspaper, typically a 16-page, half-size, simple-fold paper, always includes a map on its back cover, phone numbers for information and emergencies, a list of driving distances between key park locations, and announcements about road closings, fishing regulations, pets in the park, campgrounds, and special events—everything a visitor needs to navigate the park. In addition to this boilerplate, the paper features short descriptions about seasonal park destinations and activities and tips for avoiding crowds; it also summarizes key park news and promotes park educational events and organizations. Beyond these basics, the paper includes brief news summaries about park research on broad-ranging issues such as Native Americans, animals, plants, and air and water quality. These articles focus on the biodiversity of the park and will be discussed shortly.

Another key tool for park visitors is the *Smokies Road Guide* by Jerry DeLaughter. This five-by-ten-inch, 150-page, color-illustrated guide to all the roads of the park helps the large number of visitors who tour the park by automobile make the most of an experience that, by definition, keeps visitors removed from much that the park has to offer. Coping creatively with the limitations of a driving tour, the *Smokies Road Guide* provides concise descriptions mile by mile. For example, the first tour in the book is about Newfound Gap Road, the main road that bisects the park and links the northern Tennessee and southern North Carolina parts of the park. This tour presents 22 points of interest, organized by mile marker. Some of these alert the driver to upcoming attractions like visitor centers, picnic grounds, overlooks, and trailheads, but others advertise and explain exhibits on park habitats such as cove hardwood forests (15); streams (16–18); rivers (29–30); geologic formations such as the Anakeesta Ridge, formed by a slide in 1975 and the shearing off a mountainside that revealed bare, acidic rock (20); and the northern hardwood forest found above 6,000 feet elevation, composed of tree species common to New England and left behind after the last ice age (21–22). Kemp explains the logic of the popular guide:

> It gets you into the car, very easy, and it's going to tell you about some of the things you're going to see instead of just driving by on a rainy day and not seeing very much. Even if [visitors] don't read [the descriptions] that much in the car, they wait until they get back into the motel room and look through them and say, ah, yeah, we saw that; ah, yeah, we were there.

The modest but pithy guide in and of itself makes a qualitative difference in a family trip across Newfound Gap, one of the most traveled roads of the park, and one that is often backed up with traffic. Instead of idling in line for fifteen minutes to move a half mile, visitors using the *Road Guide* can read about what they're seeing and perhaps be persuaded to stop, get off the road and out of the car, and take a longer look while the traffic clears.

The association's set of field guides (on trees, wildflowers, ferns, birds, reptiles and amphibians, hiking trails, waterfalls, and short walks) are similarly transactional; each pocket-size book is organized in a way that opens the subject to a novice user. For example, the wildflower guide is organized by flower color, rather than by flower family, an approach common in guides intended for botanists and students. The tree guide is organized by leaf shape, and the fern book, which must use some specialized descriptive terms, nonetheless offers photos chosen to "emphasize important macroscopic characters" in an effort to make the somewhat confusing differences between species clear enough for amateur identification (19). The trail guide organizes trails alphabetically by name but keys each trail to a map, which is included with the purchase of the book, so hikers can plan routes involving more than one trail and see how trails intersect. In addition each trail's narrative begins with a call-out section stating its length, highlights, cautions, use by horses and hikers, and trailhead location. But perhaps the best feature of the guide is its trail profiles that show hikers the elevation change of the trail by half-mile on a simple line graph, allowing hikers to see whether a hike is likely to be very steep or only moderately so. All of these guides are intended for active use as tools to make a park visit more enjoyable and meaningful, and less prone to delays or accidents.

Though rhetoricians may often think of Habermas's prescription for understanding an audience's concerns on the level of how worldview affects one's position on a deliberative issue, in the context of creating a rapport in which park visitors are open to hearing about biodiversity at all, respecting the logistical and physical needs of the audience as well as their own desires for their trip to the park is an essential first principle. In most cases the audience's immediate concerns are significantly more mundane than a consideration of park ecosystems. Before the topic of biodiversity can be raised, basic physiological, safety, social, and self-esteem needs must be met; then higher levels of need and satisfaction can be entertained (Maslow). The most accessible association publications need to supply basic information that will make a material difference in the success of a park visit. Because the newspaper and various guides show a GSMA recognition of this reality, biodiversity messages included in these and other publications may become relevant to park visitors.

INTERPRETING BIODIVERSITY

Of course, the newspaper and guides do more than facilitate trip planning; they interpret the park, making visitors aware of the park's resources and attractions, and connecting these resources in entertaining, hands-on ways to broader concepts such as the park's cultural heritage and natural history. Interpretation is a well-established field for park rangers, with professional training courses and standards, but the discipline's relevance to association writers may be understood quickly by Jacobson's distinction between interpretation and education:

> [Interpretation] attempts to communicate meaning and relationships in a thematic and informal presentation, rather than by reciting facts.

> Interpretation also differs from formal teaching in that it generally targets a voluntary audience, people who are interested in self-improvement, entertainment, or simply passing time. Besides translating technical information, interpretation entertains and interests the target audience. (186)

Obvious interpretive elements of association publications are their liberal use of illustrations, photographs, and simple tables, as well as attractive and sometimes even whimsical design elements. The publications rarely present pages of copy for visitors to wade through; the routine practice is to combine language and visuals, presenting topics in concise but illuminated formats. As Jacobson explains, "Like exhibits, qualities of attractiveness, brevity, clarity, and dynamism are crucial to hooking your audience [in publications about conservation topics]. Then you need good content to keep their attention" (205).

For example, most *Smokies Guide* issues offer two to four pages of short, interpretive articles about the natural history of the park. The Winter 2007–08 issue included a one-page piece about where neotropical migrant songbirds that nest in the park during the summer go during the winter months, one page about homesteaders' choices of wood for cabin building and typical construction strategies, and a third page about winter tree identification (11–13). All three pages are heavily illustrated with drawings and photographs. The article "Snow Birds" includes detailed drawings of five neotropical migrants and small maps of their migration routes; "Tree I.D. in Winter" displays nine round photos of distinctive bark patterns, tree silhouettes, and details of bud shapes. The article about cabin construction, "Into the Woods," devotes half of its space to illustrations, a line drawing of a traditional cabin and small drawings showing tools, tree-felling approaches, and joinery types for cabin corners. Taken together, these articles offer visitors a primer about the diversity of the park's bird and tree species, as well as how this diversity is important internationally (through bird migration to Central and South America) and regionally (through forest health and diversity), and culturally through human uses of woods from trees like shagbark hickory (to flavor and cure meat), dogwood (in looms, horse collars and gears in grist mills), black locust (fence posts), and American chestnut and tulip tree (for cabin logs) (12–13). A reader can scan these pages in a few minutes and take away the important points even though the copy is limited to about two sentences per bird or tree species.

Many other association publications have a primary interpretive purpose, notably publications intended for children, including several storybooks and the series of junior ranger booklets. The storybooks, *The Great Smoky Mountain Salamander Ball* and *The Troublesome Cub* (Horstman), and the collection of offbeat natural history articles that comprise *The Smokies Yukky Book: Weird, Creepy, and Completely Gross Stuff that Really, Really Happens Here* (Gove), intended for independent readers, age ten and older, all introduce—through humor, rhyme, and charm—the central concepts of biodiversity: the unique habitats of the Smokies, the great range of animal life that lives there, why these animals are important, and the best ways for humans to respond to them.

The junior ranger series extends the interpretive reach of GSMA publications. The series began as one booklet for children ages 5–12, but in 2007, the association published four separate booklets, one each for children 5–6, 7–8, 9–10, and 11–12. These activity books are intended for children to fill out during a visit to the park so that they can earn a badge from the Park Service when the completed booklet is shown to a ranger at a visitor center. Each sixteen-page, full-color booklet contains twelve activities, such as word games, guided scavenger hunts, and picture puzzles that ask children to look carefully at exhibits, plants, and animals in the park and then record their observations. The booklets have been very successful, says Kemp:

> By having more activities [in age-specific books], some of the feedback that I've gotten from people is that families are having to extend their stay in the park so the kids can get the badge. You can't do it all in three hours. We doubled participation. . . . [Rangers] make a big deal of it when kids get their badges in the visitor centers; they make an announcement over the public address.

Consequently, a child who completes a booklet—and her family too, perhaps—will have acquired some new awareness of the Smokies and have been rewarded for the trouble. This strategy helps NPS rangers, and association staff as well, fulfill their oft-cited role as "ambassadors, or cheerleaders, or hosts," according to Kemp. In addition, it helps visitors make personal connections to the park through the family memories that they gain, a source of emotional links that, according to Farrior, help pave the way for biodiversity messages that will have a lasting effect (2). Moreover, the interpretive approach makes the abstraction of biodiversity, which the Biodiversity Project report *Engaging the Public on Biodiversity* describes as a "challenging concept to convey to the public in simple terms" (11), much more tangible to both children and adults. Focus group research has found that the word "biodiversity" "communicates different types of life, but it does not imply other key concepts surrounding biodiversity like interconnectedness and ecological relationships" (Biodiversity Project 74). Publications such as the junior ranger booklets and the natural history articles in *Smokies Guide* tell tales that teach these concepts, even if environmental or scientific terms are rarely used.

BALANCING NEGATIVE AND POSITIVE MESSAGES

Given that the primary audience for association publications is the typical park visitor, and recognizing visitors' likely desire for a pleasant, relaxing trip, association writers need to be cautious in their approach to conveying bad or troubling news about environmental threats to the park. The park faces a number of serious threats to its unique ecosystems: air pollution that causes acid rain and affects the health of plants, animals, and even people in the park; loss or decline of signature animal species, such as the river otter, elk, and red wolf that have traditionally lived in the park; exotic plants that are crowding out native species; exotic insects without local predators to control them that have devastated important tree species such as the Fraser fir and eastern hemlock. It is critical that the NPS and the association provide information about these topics to visitors in order to explain the apparent effects of the problems and to educate park supporters about what is being done and how they can help. But it is equally important that visitors are not overwhelmed by bad news through fear appeals or made to feel blamed for problems whose causes are complex. Moser has found that the negative emotional impact of climate-related news in and of itself may cause communication efforts to fail (65). Fear appeals, in general, have been found to be limited in their usefulness to cause long-term behavioral change; also, different audiences respond to fear appeals very differently, some with "defensive avoidance," some with increased but unproductive anxiety, and some with marked resistance (Ferguson 166). Further, rhetorical scholars Killingsworth and Palmer and Plevin persuasively argue that whereas guilt appeals may be effective for engaged and concerned audience groups, they usually turn off those who are not already environmentally oriented; similarly, Moser summarizes more than twenty empirical studies done in the past thirty years that concur with the theorists:

> The implications are twofold: one, guilt appeals are unreliable as motivators of environmentally benign behavior; and two, people will maintain their sense of self and identity before changing an environmentally damaging behavior, unless the new behavior is consistent with who they want to be in the world. (71)

Kemp knows the dangers of too much negativity from watching park visitors; he recounts his view, based on professional practice and observation, of how negative messages affect park visitors:

> I think a lot of mistakes people in the education business, especially in parks, make is that the first thing they want to tell people is what's wrong: "Do you know that acid rain is killing everything?" That's one of the first messages. "Do you know that the air is so polluted today that you can't go up to Clingman's Dome and go for a hike?" And you know that these poor people just coming in from Cincinnati have just heard about the Smokies. They've never seen it. They think that there are mountains or something, but they don't know what it looks like and what you do here, and all the sudden people come out and

start shrieking Chicken Little. Go look in Sugarlands [Visitor Center], and probably the first thing you will see is the air quality exhibit, and though that is an important message, educationally, I think it's different. Think of stair steps. You've got to get people oriented, get them comfortable, get them acclimated to a place and facilitate a way for them to connect with the place.

This strategy accounts for how association publications, in light of visitors' likely receptivity, balance the facts about the real threats to biodiversity and ecological sustainability in the park with other information of more immediate use and with less apocalyptic overtones.

The *Smokies Road Guide* exemplifies this approach. As previously discussed, the guide helps automobile tourists enjoy the park, so the mention of environmental issues is limited to slots where this type of visitor is likely to see something directly relevant to biodiversity and sustainability. The Newfound Gap Road tour, for example does not mention any ecological threats to the park until the fifteenth stop, Webb Overlook at mile 17.7, which describes declines in the raptor populations in the park from human development and sport shooting. The guide notes that "thanks to a concerted effort by the National Park Service, the Peregrine Fund, and many others, Peregrine Falcons are again nesting and rearing young atop jagged Smoky Mountain cliffs. Golden Eagles, Bald Eagles, and Osprey are also being returned to other areas of the Southern Appalachians" (27). The next stop features an exhibit on logging and describes the effects of the logging industry on the Smokies following a similar pattern; the devastation caused by logging is stated plainly—the *Guide* says that about three-fourths of the park was heavily logged—but the section closes with a paragraph noting that some virgin forests stands have been preserved and that "given time and human care, the land will heal itself," as evidenced by the forest view available at this point in the tour (28). Current threats to the park, such as the two exotic adelgids, or aphid-like insects, attacking the Fraser fir and eastern hemlock, are discussed briefly later in the book, at points when these species (or the remnants of them) dominate the scene (36–38, 87) in subsequent chapters. The air pollution and acid rain issue is described in a stop titled "Haze," along the Cherokee Orchard Road and Roaring Fork Motor Nature Trail (85), and the text focuses on the degrading views of the mountains in the last fifty years, which is what a reader is likely to see at this point, rather than on the multiple, damaging effects of the pollution to park habitats and species. The bad news about the park is available to visitors, with audience- and situation-appropriate explanations. If visitors inquire, more detailed discussions of problems are readily available.[2]

Americans are a nation of optimists, a South African friend of mine once observed to me, and I agree. Consequently, an open but controlled approach to publicizing problems can keep the park from becoming a house of horrors to visitors. The Biodiversity Project found that two tacks on biodiversity typically reach audiences: "One is the stewardship value, expressed by some as responsibility to family and future generations and to others as responsibility to care for God's creation. On the flip-side, [is] self-interest—'what's in it for me?'" (8). If threats to the park are approached through the avenues of what visitors experience and, secondarily, how they can help—avenues that fit these two successful themes—then writers do not need to resort to relatively ineffective fear and guilt appeals.

LINKING CULTURAL AND NATURAL HISTORY

The previous three strategies are used by GSMA to reach visitors and meet their needs, and though they enable visitors to learn bits about the park's natural history painlessly, these strategies are not proactive in their voicing of the significance of the park's biodiversity. They have focused on creating a rapport between the park (via GSMA's ventriloquy) and its visitors. The fourth strategy is different in character in that it asserts biodiversity more directly. But it does so by appealing to visitors' interest in people, rather than nature, and specifically in the people who have lived and worked inside what are now the park's boundaries. This approach cultivates visitors' personal connections to the park by asking them, for example, to imagine what farming in the mountains might have been like and identifying with the resourcefulness and hardiness of homesteaders. By reading contemporary stories, visitors learn about the personalities and careers of teachers, park rangers, naturalists, and other professionals who work in the park as well as other visitors who enjoy the park. The strategy draws on common interests in American history, nostalgia, and the pioneering spirit of facing the physical challenges, and the pastimes and pleasures of living in small communities and remote areas. A second kind of answer to the "what's in it for me?" question that the Biodiversity Project claims helps people understand the importance of natural resources is to link them to cultural heritage. Jacobson states that "one sure way to hold an audience's interest is to relate the interpretive material to their lives and experience" (189); more broadly, in *Environmental Interpretation*, S. H. Ham advises, "Link science to human history" (quoted in Jacobson 190). Kemp confirms the success of this strategy:

> People really connect with a lot of the historic stories of the park. They like the idea of simpler times, people who had to do more things themselves, people who were more self-reliant, people who had more control over their day-to-day existence, who were maybe skilled in a wider variety of activities, who lived or died because of their own actions. They like to look back—I hate to say it's sentimental, but some of it is. They like to look back on those times as so different from our own and pretty exciting.

70 *Elizabeth Giddens*

This strategy also involves the stewardship appeal, as many visitors will infer a responsibility to help maintain the places where ancestors lived or where a slice of American culture flourished.

The Walker Sisters of Little Greenbrier, by Rose Houk, serves as a good example of this strategy. This sixty-page book tells the story of six sisters who, for their entire lives, lived together in a cabin and ran the farm their parents established. This period spanned the years between 1870, when the oldest, Margaret, was born, and 1966, when the last surviving sister, Louisa, died. This household of single women resisted multiple buy-out offers from the federal government and finally negotiated a sale that included a lifetime lease on the land even after it became part of the park. The book recounts the outlines of their lives, their family history, individual personalities, beliefs and education, way of life, and skills to maintain themselves comfortably in a log cabin without electricity or indoor plumbing. The prose is illustrated with photographs of the women going about their chores and of their home, tools, furniture, cookware, firearms, clothes, quilts, hats, medicines, and writings. Although the cabin was complete and fully furnished by the time their father died in 1921, for more than forty years afterward the women kept a garden and livestock, fed and clothed themselves, and maintained the cabin and its numerous outbuildings. Before the deal with the park, they also hunted, fished, gathered herbs, cut wood, and grazed livestock. Their self-sufficiency compels a reader to reflect on the values that guided their lives, but it also speaks of how fully integrated their lives were with the land and resources around them. This point is especially salient in Houk's description of their gardening:

> The Walker sisters were organic gardeners and guardians of biodiversity long before these ideas became trendy. A gate behind the house opened onto a huge vegetable garden, fenced with hemlock stakes and surrounded by prolific orchards. (19)

The sisters claimed that their "land produces everything we need except sugar, soda, coffee, and salt" (24). As DeLaughter says of the life portrayed at the Mountain Farm Museum in Oconaluftee, "We call it a 'simple' life, but it had its own complexities and rewards. . . . Most mountain folk were smart and resourceful people, imaginative and self-reliant. They had to be. We can learn much from their legacy" (35). Another facet of the appeal of narratives about people like the Walker sisters is that they satisfy the descendents of parkland residents, who although they did not live in the park, do not want their families' histories to be discounted as less important than the glory of the park's natural resources. Kemp explains that "[t]he thing that they hate is for some park ranger to talk about what a beautiful wilderness this is with all the animals that live here and stuff. . . . They don't like to be completely forgotten. They don't like to be erased from the scene." Conversely, *The Walker Sisters of Little Greenbrier* commemorates park homesteaders and strengthens ties between the park today and those whose ancestors once lived there.

In addition to *The Walker Sisters*, GSMA has produced a set of booklets about various features of farmers' and others' lives in the park. These are on topics such as churches and worship, log cabins, grist mills, logging, and the Civilian Conservation Corps (or CCC). This group of publications adopts the same rhetorical strategy as Houk's narrative; they help visitors learn the cultural history of the park and show how it was dependent on the biological richness of the mountains. For example, the booklets about logging and the CCC bridge the homesteading era with two later stages that had a great influence on today's physical park. *Logging in the Smokies* (Pierce) recounts the extensive logging inside the park from 1880 to 1939, describing why logging companies were attracted to the steep mountain slopes by choice hardwoods, techniques for cutting and transporting cut timber, the camps that housed loggers and their families, and the environmental effects of logging (such as debris fires, landslides, and ruin of streams and native trout). The devastation alarmed local and regional opinion leaders who led efforts to establish the park. Had the logging been more contained or less destructive, one can speculate that these leaders may not have succeeded in getting the attention of the federal government. Once the park was established, the CCC built much of the current park's infrastructure of roads, bridges, fire towers, buildings, and trails between 1933 and 1942. *The CCC in the Smokies* (Jolley) tells this chapter of park history with details about how the Depression led to the creation of the Corps and about enrollees' lives of long work days followed by evening recreation and educational opportunities in camp. Each era offers its own human stories and connections to the park. We have logging to thank for a powerful lesson about how natural resources may be exploited and nearly lost.

The CCC period and the work and education that it offered young men during the Depression forged important personal, local, and regional relationships between park management and citizens. In addition, CCC workers began important stream and forest rehabilitation projects that helped the land rebound. Although neither endeavor viewed biodiversity as its primary mission, these periods provide important lessons to everyone concerned about the park, biodiversity, sustainable land management, and the roles that people can play in both official and individual capacities to foster them.

From stories that take a historical vantage, it is a short step to telling more recent and contemporary stories that illustrate and foster visitors' personal connections with the park. This notion seems to have guided the design of the *Smokies Life Magazine*, which premiered in the fall of 2007 and is the fullest expression of the strategy of linking cultural and natural history among GSMA publications. This glossy magazine offers a mix of feature articles that use the human-interest strategy for communicating the concept of biodiversity as well as its relevance to a sustainable future.

Articles range from biographical sketches of legendary mountain men (Williams, "Roamin' and Restin', Adventurin' and Philosophisin' with Wiley Oakley"), to stories of the CCC-era (Maynard, "Firetower Lookouts of the Smokies"), articles about local crafts (Waldvogel, "Bark Baskets and Buckets"), fishing tales (Brill, "Fishing the Horseshoe"), profiles of people who are helping to preserve the park (Cantrell, "Amongst the Old Growth: Will Blozan and his Giant Friends"), and pieces overtly about natural history (Hour, "Good Luck Comes in Threes: Trilliums"). Kemp serves as editor of this publication, and his head note to the second issue suggests the kind of associations that the magazine encourages:

> [Readers'] response to the first issue of *Smokies Life Magazine* has been overwhelmingly favorable and for this we are thankful. It is obvious now that the community of people who love the Great Smoky Mountains is very large and very passionate. And it can be no other way. The Smokies and other national parks exist only because we want them to. Every day the land within their boundaries becomes more valuable, as unspoiled scenic places become as rare as diamonds and emeralds.... In 1872, when Americans set aside the world's first national park, many thought it a grand idea that our nation's most beautiful and historic lands not be owned by individuals or institutions, but by the people. So far, this idea has endured. (1)

The article mix of *Smokies Life* casts a broad net to interest many readers and to help them learn about and value the park. It also demonstrates the richness of human interests and activities that have arisen from human engagement with the park, suggesting so many ways that biodiversity matters to people physically, intellectually, psychologically, and spiritually. Although *Smokies Life* articles are rarely didactic, they offer plenty of ideas to help readers understand why the park is important from an ecological perspective. For example, the article about Will Blozan, an arborist who searches out champion trees, contains a passage about the threatened hemlocks: "'It's exciting to find these new record [hemlocks] and sad at the same time,' Blozan said. 'It reveals what we have and what we stand to lose. Eastern hemlock is a vanishing species in the southern Appalachians, but they have a strong will to live'" (Cantrell 50). Just after this statement, readers are told that the champion eastern hemlock, documented by Blozan, lives in the park as well as hemlocks nearly 500 years old. If a reader likes hemlocks, a passage like this one will make an impression.

The many stories about the people of the park—both past and present—are likely to have a cumulative effect on readers. As Shanahan theorized with his notion of how storytelling can cultivate opinions, "repeated exposure to a set of messages is likely to produce agreement in an audience with opinions expressed in those messages" (quoted in Cox 189). Although Shanahan's research has found mixed results of environmental programming on television, where there are many competing sets of messages vying for a viewer's attention, it seems plausible that the varied topics of association publications, each appealing to a subset of park visitors, will, over time, enhance their understanding of and personal connection to the park. Also, the park's rich cultural history renders it a fitting example of the critical link between biodiversity as a good in its own right and as a fundamental component both in philosophical views about the need for a sustainable relationship between humans and the nonhuman world and in public policy that seeks to achieve such relationships. The articles clearly inform and advocate for biodiversity and sustainability through what research finds to be the most successful pathways—the value of stewardship and, separately, connections to self.

A RHETORICAL SPACE FOR BIODIVERSITY MESSAGES

The Biodiversity Project concludes a report chapter about known influences on public attitudes by stating that "[m]essages that wrap species protection within larger arguments for habitat protection are likely to reach a larger audience and be more persuasive" (31). We can extend the scope of this statement, positing that arguments about the value of biodiversity will be more successful if they are wrapped within arguments about its relevance and meaning to humans on physical, economic, intellectual, and emotional levels. This point brings the interplay of GSMA's four rhetorical strategies into focus. First, the strategies are intensely audience-centered, offering readers the information they most need before taking up environmental concerns. When biodiversity and sustainability themes emerge, they appear when and how readers are likely to find them most relevant to their immediate visit or to their own personal interests, following guidelines from park interpretative theory rather than from academic models. Next, these messages are shaped—largely through topic selection and subtle references to critical issues—to elicit appealing, positive associations from readers, rather than guilt, resentment, fear, or dread. Although certainly rhetorical, this shaping fosters a rapport between GSM management and readers because the approach is more understanding than strident, more concerned with a relationship than with (instrumental) dominance. In his article about how a communicative action approach functioned in two instances to preserve the Adirondack Park, Karis states that "[r]hetoric's role in environmental issues should be to help people discover how to synthesize and mesh technical knowledge with human values" (233); GSMA strategies function in just this way, I think.

Because, as Dunwoody says, "Experiences matter more than data" (94), it is acceptable that these strategies are most likely to result in modest intellectual gains on the part of readers. Readers of GSMA publications may not, for instance, reach the third and highest level of environmental literacy as defined by the National Environmental Education and Training Foundation, in which people have a deep understanding of natural processes, an awareness of the human behaviors that affect these processes, and an affinity for protecting or appreciating nature (Coyle xiii–xiv). Perhaps readers will only have a pleasant trip to the mountains, but given the current trend away from nature recreation, that achievement can be significant. It is certainly essential and emerges as the rhetorical space—a visitor's frame of reference—for subsequent messages, information, and experiences. That achievement creates an opportunity for future visits and more reflective reading followed by, perhaps, deeper levels of understanding, engagement, and activity. The possibility of a lasting relationship between visitors and the park qualify GSMA publications as communicative action. Jamieson provides a compelling justification of this tack:

> In general, what we need both to keep our republic and to address slow-onset, long-term problems like climate change is a sense of ownership and identification with the outcomes that our actions produce. It is this sense of ownership and identification that allow us to overcome the alienation from the collective consequences of our actions. (479)

GSMA's rhetorical approach is therefore exquisitely fashioned to suit the challenges of its own ethos, of the subject matter, and of a contemporary tourist audience. This model has been successful for the association, as evidenced from increasing yearly aid to the park, strong sales despite flat visitation to visitor centers, continued membership growth, and awards from the 2008 Association of Partners for Public Lands Media and Partnership competition ("2007 Annual Report Overview"). Equally favorable, long-term results, then, may come from adaptations of this model by other organizations and authors.

NOTES

1. For example, the *Noah 'Bud' Ogle Place* brochure, available for a voluntary donation of a quarter from a kiosk at the site's parking lot, leads a visitor through a self-guided nature trail around the homestead, with stops at the cabin, garden, former cow pasture, mill, cornfield site, and barn. Many like it are available at similar sites throughout the park.
2. For example, the GSMA produces issue folios, which are four-page, color briefing statements about air quality, hemlocks, exotic plants, fire management, black bears, and brook trout, among other topics. The target audience for folios is individuals who hear park employees' public talks, although folios sell in visitor center stores for thirty-five cents. Typically folios describe a problem and species affected, explain how the park is responding to the problem and the limitations of these local remedies, and conclude with a section about what individuals can do to help ameliorate the problem.

WORKS CITED

Barringer, Mark Daniel. *Selling Yellowstone: Capitalism and the Construction of Nature.* Lawrence, KS: U of Kansas P, 2002.

Biodiversity Project. *Engaging the Public on Biodiversity: A Road Map for Education and Communication Strategies*. Madison, Wisconsin: Biodiversity Project, 1998.
Brill, David. "Fishing the Horseshoe," *Smokies Life Magazine* 2.1 (2008) 8–17.
Cantrell, Geoffrey. "Amongst the Old Growth: Will Blozan and His Giant Friends," *Smokies Life Magazine* 2.1 (2008) 46–51.
Chess, Caron and Branden B. Johnson. "Information Is Not Enough," *Creating a Climate for Change: Communicating Climate Change and Facilitating Social Change*. Eds. Susanne C. Moser and Lisa Dilling. Cambridge, UK: Cambridge UP, 2007. 223–33.
Corbett, Julia B. *Communicating Nature: How We Create and Understand Environmental Messages*. Washington DC: Island P. 2006.
Cox, Robert. *Environmental Communication and the Public Sphere*. Thousand Oaks, CA: Sage, 2006.
Coyle, Kevin. *Environmental Literacy in America: What Ten Years of NEETF/ Roper Research and Related Studies Say about Environmental Literacy in the U.S*. Washington DC: National Environmental Education and Training Foundation, 2005. March 30, 2008. www.neefusa.org/pdf/ELR2005.pdf.
DeLaughter, Jerry. *Smokies Road Guide*. Gatlinburg, TN: Great Smoky Mountains Association, 2004.
Dunwoody, Sharon. "The Challenge of Trying to Make a Difference Using Media Messages," *Creating a Climate for Change: Communicating Climate Change and Facilitating Social Change*. Eds. Susanne C. Moser and Lisa Dilling. Cambridge, UK: Cambridge UP, 2007. 89–104.
Farrior, Marian. *Breakthrough Strategies for Engaging the Public: Emerging Trends in Communications and Social Science*. Madison, Wisconsin: Biodiversity Project, 2005. May 29, 2008. http://www.biodiversityproject.org/2008revision/docs/publicationsandtipsheets/breakthroughstrategiesforengagingthepublic.pdf.
Ferguson, Sherry Devereaux. *Communication Planning: An Integrated Approach*. Thousand Oaks, CA: Sage, 1999.
Great Smoky Mountains Association. "About Us." Web page. 2008. May 29, 2008. http://www.smokiesinformation.org/f/aboutus/htm.
———. "Air Quality." Great Smoky Mountains National Park Management Folio #2. Gatlinburg, TN: Great Smoky Mountains Association, 1997.
———. "2007 Annual Report Overview." Web page. 2008. May 29, 2008. http://www.smokiesinformation.org/f/annual_report2007.htm.
———. "GSMA Budgets Nearly $2 Million to Help Park in 2008," *Bear Paw*. (Spring–Summer 2008) 1.
———. "GSMA Budgets Over $1.6 Million to Help Park in 2007," *Bear Paw*. (Spring–Summer 2007) 1.
———. "GSMA Budgets Over $1.5 Million to Help Park in 2006," *Bear Paw*. (Spring 2006) 1.
———. "Hemlock Trees." Great Smoky Mountains National Park Management Folio #7. Gatlinburg, TN: Great Smoky Mountains Association, 2006.
Ingham, Zita. "Rhetoric of Disengagement: Interpretive Talks in the National Parks," *Technical Communication, Deliberative Rhetoric, and Environmental Discourse: Connections and Directions*. Eds. Nancy W. Coppola and Bill Karis. Stamford, CT: Ablex, 2000. 139–47.
"Into the Woods." *Smokies Guide*. Winter 2007–08, 12.
Gove, Doris. *The Smokies Yukky Book: Weird, Creepy, and Completely Gross Stuff that Really, Really Happens Here*. Gatlinburg, TN: Great Smoky Mountains Association, 2006.
Horstman, Lisa. *The Great Salamander Ball*. Gatlinburg, TN: Great Smoky Mountains Association, 1997.

Houk, Rose. "Good Luck Comes in Threes: Trilliums," *Smokies Life Magazine.* 2.1 (2008) 30–35.

———. *The Walker Sisters of Little Greenbrier.* Gatlinburg, TN: Great Smoky Mountains Association, 2005.

Jacobson, Susan K. *Communication Skills for Conservation Professionals.* Washington DC: Island P, 1999.

Jamieson, Dale. "The Moral and Political Challenges of Climate Change," *Creating a Climate for Change: Communicating Climate Change and Facilitating Social Change.* Eds. Susanne C. Moser and Lisa Dilling. Cambridge, UK: Cambridge UP, 2007. 475–82.

Jolley, Harley E. *The CCC in the Smokies.* Gatlinburg, TN: Great Smoky Mountain Association, 2001.

Kareiva, Peter. "Ominous Trends in Nature Recreation," *Publications of the National Academy of Science.* 105.8 (Feb. 2008) 2757–58.

Karis, Bill. "Rhetoric, Habermas, and the Adirondack Park: An Exemplum for Rhetoricians." In *Technical Communication, Deliberative Rhetoric, and Environmental Discourse: Connections and Directions.* Eds. Nancy W. Coppola and Bill Karis. Stamford, CT: Ablex Publishing, 2000. 225–34.

Kemp, Steve. "From the Editor," *Smokies Life Magazine.* 2.1 (2008) 1.

———. Ed. *Hiking Trails of the Smokies.* Gatlinburg, TN: Great Smoky Mountain Association, 1994.

———. Personal interview. February 7, 2008.

———. *Trees of the Smokies.* Gatlinburg, TN: Great Smoky Mountain Association, 1993.

Killingsworth, M. Jimmie and Jacqueline S. Palmer. *Ecospeak: Rhetoric and Environmental Politics in America.* Carbondale: Southern Illinois UP, 1992.

———."The Discourse of 'Environmental Hysteria,'" *Quarterly Journal of Speech.* 81 (1995) 1–19.

Littlejohn, Margaret. *Great Smoky Mountains National Park Visitor Studies: Summer and Fall 1996.* Washington DC: National Park Service, 1997. May 29, 2008. http://www.nps.gov/grsm/parkmgmt/upload/6 %201996GRSMvisitorstudy.pdf.

Maslow, Abraham, "A Theory of Human Motivation," *Psychological Review* 50 (1943): 370–96.

Maynard, Charles W. "Firetower Lookouts of the Smokies," *Smokies Life Magazine.* 2.1 (2008) 52–59.

Moser, Susanne C. "More Bad News: The Risk of Neglecting Emotional Responses to Climate Change Information," *Creating a Climate for Change: Communicating Climate Change and Facilitating Social Change.* Eds. Susanne C. Moser and Lisa Dilling. Cambridge, UK: Cambridge UP, 2007. 64–80.

Muhlbeier, Barbara. Board member, Great Smoky Mountains Association. Personal interview. 7 February 7, 2008.

Noah 'Bud' Ogle Place: Self-guiding Nature Trail. Gatlinburg, TN: Great Smoky Mountains Association, n.d.

Pergams, Oliver R. W. and Patricia A. Zaradic. "Evidence for a Fundamental and Pervasive Shift Away from Nature-based Recreation," *Publications of the National Academy of Science*, 105.7 (Feb. 2008) 2295–2300.

Pierce, Daniel. *Logging in the Smokies.* Gatlinburg, TN: Great Smoky Mountain Association, 2003.

Plevin, Arlene. "Green Guilt: An Effective Rhetoric or Rhetoric in Transition?" *Technical Communication Quarterly.* 6.2 (1997) 125–40.

Reardon, K. E. *Persuasion in Practice.* Newbury Park, CA: Sage, 1991.

"Snow Birds, " *Smokies Guide.* Winter 2007–08, 11.

"Tree I.D. in Winter," *Smokies Guide.* Winter 2007–08, 13.

United States. National Park Service. "Great Smoky Mountains National Park: Amphibians." Web page. July 11, 2007. June 12, 2008. http://www.nps.gov/grsm/naturescience/amphibians.htm.

———. "Great Smoky Mountains National Park: Nature and Science." Web page. January 24, 2008. June 12, 2008. http://www.nps.gov/grsm/naturescience/index.htm.

———. "National Park System Attendance Rises in 2007," News Release. Feb. 26, 2008. June 12, 2008. http://home.nps.gov/applications/release/Detail.cfm?ID=785.

———. "The National Park System: Caring for the American Legacy." Web page. n.d. June 6, 2008. http://www.nps.gov/legacy/mission.html.

———. "New Federal Budget Provides Increases for Great Smoky Mountains National Park," Press release. an. 3, 2008. May 29, 2008. http://www.nps.gov/grsm/parknews/budget.htm.

———. "Study: National Parks Huge Economic Return on Investment," Press release. August 22, 2006. May 29, 2008. http://home.nps.gov/applications/release/Detail.cfm?ID=685.

———. Social Science Program. "FY 2005 Money Generation Model Briefing Statement." Washington DC: National Park Service: 2006.

Waldvogel, Merikay. "Bark, Baskets and Buckets," *Smokies Life Magazine.* 2.1 (2008) 18–21.

Williams, Don. "Roamin' and Restin', Adventurin' and Philosophisin' with Wiley Oakley," *Smokies Life Magazine.* 2.1 (2008) 36–44.

Wilson, Edward O. *The Diversity of Life.* Cambridge, MA: Harvard UP, 1992.

4 The Vision or the View
Cape Wind and the Rhetoric of Sustainable Energy

Kimberly Moekle

On the night of April 27, 2003, a barge carrying oil toward the Cape Cod Canal electric power plant veered off course and struck a ledge that sliced its single hull. Almost 100,000 gallons of Number 6 oil escaped into ocean currents and spread over ninety miles of sandy shoreline at Buzzards Bay just west of Cape Cod. "Number 6 oil" refers to the dregs left over in a refinery after everything else has boiled off. The residual carbon, although too viscous and thick to use as is, still contains energy. Refineries sell it to power plants where these remains are then cut with something more volatile, such as gasoline, in order to make them viable again. The composition of Number 6 oil can vary dramatically from mostly benign to dangerously toxic. The oil that washed up on the shores of Buzzards Bay in 2003 was the latter, killing a variety of endangered animals, ruining shellfish beds, and making the beaches unusable for months.[1]

In the weeks after the spill, as oil continued to lap on the estuary's beaches, residents grew infuriated at the damage. State officials were nowhere to be found, and the governor and attorney general were showing little interest in the spill. But when it came to the Cape Wind project, a field of offshore wind turbines with no risk of oil spill, these same officials cried foul over environmental concerns. In fact, the wind farm proposed for Nantucket Sound would certainly decrease the number of oil barges passing through Buzzards Bay, along with the environmental risks exposed that April night.

The goal of this chapter is to examine the written and visual rhetoric that has characterized the seven-year conflict over the Cape Wind project, and to consider its implications for public debate on energy production in the United States. The mainstream rhetoric of supporters and opponents of Cape Wind demonstrates how these varied dialogues reflect and diverge from traditional patterns of American environmental discourse, and have influenced the long stalemate over the project. This essay traces three binary oppositions that have characterized American environmental rhetoric since the eighteenth century: utilitarian versus romantic, conservationist versus preservationist, and environmental versus developmental. The Cape Wind controversy, however, fails to fit neatly into any of these categories. Instead we find a peculiar inversion of the stereotypical roles that industry and environmentalists in the US have played over the past two centuries. This invites us to question the terms of and conflicts over the development of sustainable energy, as it becomes a more visible component of global economics, politics, and health. Is it possible to measure the value of a scenic vista versus economic output when setting targets for carbon dioxide emissions? How do we define the "public" good? What does it mean to be an "environmentalist"? How does popular rhetoric frame the debate or obscure the facts?

WIND-POWER POLITICS

The Cape Wind project has received an unprecedented amount of scrutiny, study, and opposition. If approved, the wind farm would be a significant marker in our nation's implementation of alternative energy. At a cost in excess of $700 million, the proposed project consists of 130 windmills, spaced one-third to one-half mile apart, less than seven miles off the coast of Cape Cod. James Gordon, the president of Cape Wind, is financing the project himself, along with a few other private investors. There had been talk of government subsidies in the earliest stages of the project, but as of May 2008 the project has received no such funding from government agencies. Embedded in the ocean floor between Nantucket Island, Martha's Vineyard, and the town of Hyannis, each turbine would tower higher than the Statue of Liberty, its three 161-foot blades turning at sixteen revolutions per minute. Optimistic estimates suggest that the wind farm could provide up to 74 percent of the Cape's energy demands, and generate the equivalent of one hundred barges of oil a year (Burkett). The Alliance to Protect Nantucket Sound, an organization opposed to Cape Wind, claims the wind farm will have negative environmental and economic effects, such as damage to the fishing industry, birds, property values, tourism, navigation, and aviation safety. Opponents also argue that the project will drive up electricity costs, rather than lower them. Moreover, they contend that the environmental impact report released by the US Department of Minerals Management Service (MMS) was premature, that crucial information from the US Coast Guard and other agencies was missing from the equation (Brace).

The reality is that reasonable people disagree about the merits of erecting turbines in Nantucket Sound, based on economics, environmental impact, and aesthetics.[2] Advocates often support renewable energy, not for short-term economic gain, but for long-term environmental benefits, whereas opponents worry about both immediate environmental impact and economic viability. In the case of Cape Wind, independent experts and government officials such as the Massachusetts Technology Collaborative, La Capra Associates, the US Army Corps of Engineers, and the MMS have estimated minimal environmental impact during construction and beyond, and have calculated that the wind farm would provide nearly three quarters of the energy needs on the Cape and islands, exerting downward pressure on wholesale electricity markets without emitting any carbon dioxide, nitrous oxide, or mercury—and without burning a single barrel of oil.[3] Opponents often cite the same documents and figures, however, to show that the project will not send its energy to the Cape, thus driving up the cost of electricity for local residents and destroying a "national treasure" in the process.

One can hardly blame the public for its uncertainty about Cape Wind. The rhetoric of wind energy in dominant public news sources has shifted many times in the past decade. In 2003, for example, the *New York Times* argued the following:

> Wind is the world's fastest-growing energy resource, and after a decade of federal and state subsidies kick-starting the industry, [it is now] creating enough power for more than a million American families in 27 states to tap into the breeze when they flick on their light switches. The country's oldest turbines have been part of the landscape on the Altamont Pass, east of San Francisco, for two decades. And Texans zooming along I-10 west to El Paso top a slight rise to the sight of a vast field of turbines stretching across the mesa. (Burkett)

A year later, the *Wall Street Journal* reported that "wind energy is never going to be anything but a bit player in meeting the world's energy needs," and that "the Nantucket tempest is useful mainly as a real-world test of whether some of the world's most privileged liberals wear their ideals all the time, or only when it suits them" ("Wind Jammers"). With such varied rhetoric in the popular media, it's hard for disagreements over the economic and environmental viability of the project to rest solely on scientific data. The average American has neither the time nor the desire to examine a nearly 4,000-page environmental impact statement by the Army Corps of Engineers, but according to a recent report by the Audit Bureau of Circulations, approximately three million readers do glance at the *New York Times* or the *Wall Street Journal* every day.[4]

Disagreement over the economic and environmental viability of Cape Wind is compounded by issues of aesthetics, a subjective but critical externality. Wind farm supporters say, "It's the vision, not the view," and dismiss the visual impact the project will have on residents of the Cape. Opponents argue that property values will drop, tourism will suffer, and a "national treasure" will be lost. The words "vision," "view," and "national treasure" say nothing directly about how tall the wind turbines will appear on the horizon, nor do they describe the likely effects of the project on the roseate tern.⁵ They do, however, make specific arguments that divide audiences based on emotional and ethical appeals, rather than on scientific or economic facts. Whatever one's preference, the Cape Wind chronicle is a persistently awkward story, with no satisfactory conclusion in sight.

POLARITIES IN AMERICAN ENVIRONMENTAL DISCOURSE

The dichotomy between economic progress and environmental preservation has dominated American antienvironmental rhetoric for over two decades, even though it has often proven false. Even today, environmentalism continues to be misconstrued along partisan lines, and falsely depicted as a contest between human and nature (Bruner and Oelschlaeger 211–12). The rhetorical oversimplification of such conflicts, which runs all the way back to the discovery of the New World, obscures fundamental issues about environmentalism. The following section provides a brief historical overview of the three rhetorical dichotomies that have dominated environmental discourse in the US. Considering these binaries will help us to contextualize the Cape Wind controversy and measure how it reflects and differs from previous rhetorical paradigms.

In their article "Tracking the Elusive Jeremiad: The Rhetorical Character of American Environmental Discourse," John Opie and Norbert Elliot give a diachronic account of writings that illustrate American rhetoric used to advance various positions about the environment.⁶ Opie and Elliot explain that, for the Puritan settlers, America stood outside natural science and traditional theology. The wilderness was chaotic and disorderly, but the New World couldn't be abandoned because of its economic importance. Moreover, Puritan culture assumed the unity of church, politics, and the progress of the Kingdom of God (Bercovitch xiv). In this way, the secular and the sacred were already fused as part of the dominant culture, and their mission in the New World was as much religious as economic (Opie and Elliot 11). The contest between human and nature was already well underway as a natural part of a free enterprise structure. In order for the settlers to prosper economically, they would have to "convert the howling wilderness into a domesticated agricultural landscape" (Opie and Elliot 19).

Enlightenment rationalism of philosophers, intellectuals, and scientists in Europe and America did much to advance this position in the late eighteenth century. "According to this view, science was the supreme human activity, legitimate and authoritative because it was grounded in abstract universal principles that transcended any particular human context. Scientific method thus became, as Ramism had before it, the dominant rhetoric of Western Culture" (Opie and Elliot 18).⁷ From an environmentalist perspective, the late eighteenth century was an age of observation. Anthropocentric classification provided a further means of ordering the chaos of nature, allowing humans to know the laws that governed the natural world, and thus possibly to free themselves from nature's grasp. The gradual human conquest of the American wilderness was "a demonstration of civilization's growing mastery of natural resources" and a manifestation of built environments that celebrated human independence from nature (Opie and Elliot 18). Systematically uncovering nature's secrets allowed a practical exploitation of the New World as a commodity, a utilitarian tool in service to humanity (Opie and Elliot 20).

In opposition to the strict techniques of the scientific method came a wave of new Transcendentalists, led by Ralph Waldo Emerson (1803–82), who protested the exacting empirical views of the Enlightenment. Whereas natural historians and scientists of the eighteenth century labeled nature to subdue and then use it to human advantage, the American Romantics "wanted to embrace nature in a holistic, mystical union so as to be ennobled by it.... For Emerson, as for other Romantics, rhetoric became a means of establishing and verifying the vital relationship between humanity and nature" (Opie and Elliot 21). The ambition of such writers was to release, not suppress, the primal forces of nature which Puritans and Enlightenment thinkers sought to control. In "The American Scholar," Emerson argues that the American wilderness might be the source of a new humanity, a place of renewal, an opportunity "to read God directly."[8] In this way, a direct experience of divinity was available to everyone in the unspoiled terrain of the American wilderness.

Later in the eighteenth century, another set of binaries appears to describe people's relationship with nature, one that directly parallels the rationalist versus Romantic conflict. In her essay "Conservationism vs. Preservationism: The 'Public Interest' in the Hetch Hetchy Controversy," Christine Oravec summarizes these opposing viewpoints: "Conservationists, endorsing the utilitarian principle of 'the greatest good for the greatest number,' argued that the material needs of numbers of identifiable individuals represented 'the public interest.' . . . Preservationists, on the other hand, argued that to save the beauty of [nature] served a more generally defined 'national' interest" (444). Here we have a pair of attitudes toward the environment that hinge on concepts of the "public," and of what constitutes "public interest." As Oravec explains, the conservationist and preservationist views corresponded to "two poles of the American self-image that had been linked in uneasy union throughout the later nineteenth century—progressivism, or America as a collective population of individual units, and nationalism, with America viewed as an organic nation, the whole greater than its parts" (444). Conservationists viewed the nation's resources through a politically progressive lens, arguing that natural resources should be used for the highest good of the greatest number of people. Preservationists, on the other hand, approached nature through a nationalistic lens, contending that the remaining bits of American wilderness were a symbolic representation of the nation, and that destruction of natural scenery debilitated the country itself.

For preservationists, the concept of "national" interest obviates any potential conflicts between aesthetics and public utility. In a statement delivered in 1908 at the Governors' Conference on Conservation, for example, J. Horace McFarland, president of the American Civic Association, attributes the "very existence of patriotic sentiment to the physical beauty of the landscape" and "describes the precise sensation of the patriotic-aesthetic response" (445–46). He explains that "it is the love of country that lights and keeps glowing the holy fire of patriotism. And this love is excited primarily by the beauty of the country." He then relates this argument to the words of a familiar hymn:

> My native country, thee,
> Land of the noble free,
> Thy name I love;
> I love thy rock and rills,
> Thy woods and templed hills;
> My heart with rapture thrills
> Like that above.[9]

McFarland's rhetoric parallels the Romantic view espoused earlier by Emerson, in that both Romantics and preservationists argue that humans can have a direct experience of God in nature. McFarland, however, also connects a love of nature with love for one's country, thus rendering the environment valuable not only from an aesthetic perspective, but also because of its potential to elicit patriotism. In this way, the preservationist stance takes the Romantic's relationship to the environment a step farther, moving it out of a sentimental, personal realm into a more political and social one. According to this view, preserving what was left of the American wilderness was thus critical for the health of both the individual and the nation.

Conservationists, by contrast, questioned the character of the "public" that preservationists argued would benefit from the experience of a pristine environment. The conservationist philosophy rested primarily on the notion of "the greatest good for the greatest number" (Oravec 449). In determining whether an area should be developed or protected, early twentieth-century conservationists followed the guidelines laid out in the Division of Forestry's *Use Book* for 1911, which stated that "the welfare of the community or the number of people benefited should be the factor determining a higher use" (McConnell 46). In the controversy over Hetch Hetchy, conservationists argued that San Francisco residents in need of a steady water supply greatly outweighed citizens with enough leisure time and resources to visit the valley. They also pointed out that still fewer of those leisure-class citizens would be hardy enough outdoorsmen to appreciate the wonder of Hetch Hetchy. Oravec notes that those who supported the dam characterized the public as a group that was "numerically strong and materially deserving"; they also accused "the preservationists of sentimentality, idealism, and elitism in their effort to protect the rights of a few mountaineers" versus the needs of "the laboring masses" (Oravec 450). In other words, for the conservationists, the "public good" was best served by making wise use of natural resources for the maximum number of citizens, not for a privileged minority.[10] Marsden Manson, the mayor of San Francisco at the time, makes this point clearly in an address to Congress:

> The highest use of water is the domestic use, and the eight hundred thousand people living in San Francisco [are certainly] entitled to the consideration of the country. . . . By yielding their opposition, sincere lovers of nature will turn the prayers of a million people to praise for the gifts bestowed upon them by the God of Nature, whom they cannot worship in his temple, but must perforce live in sweltering cities. A reduced death rate is a more vital consideration than the discussion of the relative beauties of a meadow or a lake. (quoted in Phelan 340–41)

Here Mayor Manson's rhetoric invokes logical and pathetic appeals, while also courteously undermining the *ethos* of the preservationists. His discussion of the population of San Francisco in terms of concrete numbers makes the argument for the dam being more pressing than the preservationists' formless concept of the national good. Moreover, he stands up for the basic human needs of hard-working Americans, while implying that the preservationists have a moral duty to help those less fortunate wage earners who don't have the time or resources to partake in the beauty of nature. Rather than slighting the average American, Manson's rhetorical strategy reinforces the conservationist allegation that the preservationist stance was elitist and antisocial. Although preservationists soon responded with a positive characterization of the "much maligned nature lover," arguing that the mountaineer of the future would in fact be the typical working-class American seeking to escape the ravages of the city for a "few days of rest and recreation with their families," they nonetheless failed to preserve the valley from which San Francisco still gets its water today (Oravec 450–51).

In recent decades, the preservationist-versus-conservationist binary has become more distinct. Jimmie Killingsworth and Jacqueline Palmer summarize the polarization that characterizes modern American environmental discourse and policy in *Ecospeak: Rhetoric and Environmental Politics in America*. In this text, they identify yet another opposition, environmentalist versus developmentalist, coining the term "ecospeak" as a rhetoric that produces "stark alignment, simplistic dualism, and numbing paralysis along bipolar lines" (Opie and Elliot 29). Killingsworth and Palmer explain:

> On one side are the environmentalists, who seek long-term protection of endangered environments regardless of short-term economic costs. On the other side are the developmentalists, who seek short-term

economic gain regardless of the long-term environmental costs. This analysis oversimplifies the dilemma by projecting the psychological dilemma—the realization that our system produces both economic prosperity and environmental pollution—onto a social background, dividing two stages of liberal consciousness against one another in a kind of allegory of good guys and bad guys, demanding of the observer a value judgment about the goodness or badness of each side. (*Ecospeak* 9)

This binary has its origins in both the romantic-rationalist dichotomy of the eighteenth century and the preservationist-conservationist dichotomy of the nineteenth century, particularly in conflicts over land use in places such as Yosemite Valley and Hetch Hetchy. The environmental-developmental antagonism adds another layer to the continuum of American perspectives about nature as object, nature as resource, and nature as spirit (*Ecospeak* 11). These three binaries and their respective attitudes toward nature persist in today's environmental politics and discourse, and the Cape Wind controversy illustrates and complicates these polarities in a variety of ways.

THE RHETORIC OF CAPE WIND

From a rhetorical perspective, the battle over what could become America's first offshore wind farm illustrates Killingsworth and Palmer's argument that the oversimplification and polarization that occur in such controversies petrify public divisions, prolong conflicts, and defer solutions (8). Indeed, the key players have been deadlocked for years in a series of town-hall debacles, legal proceedings, environmental impact reports, and political red tape.[11] Their rhetoric has perpetuated rather than solved the controversy. As Killingsworth and Palmer argue, the effects of such paralysis are wide-reaching and often counterproductive (10). The majority of residents who would be affected by the project are either confused or completely unaware of Cape Wind's potential economic and environmental consequences, while a vocal and influential minority has largely controlled the public discourse of the debate. A useful example of the rhetorical back-and-forth can be seen in an op-ed by Robert F. Kennedy Jr. for the *New York Times* in December 2005, and the ensuing reply from Cape Wind.[12]

Kennedy's article begins by establishing his ethos as an "environmentalist," and then uses a variety of aesthetic, logical, historical, economic, and emotional appeals to argue against the project. The mixture of these strategies throughout the piece ensures that Kennedy connects with a variety of readers who have differing values and concerns. To reach traditional nature lovers, Kennedy anthropomorphizes the wind turbines as giants "whose windmill arms will reach 417 feet above the water and be visible for up to 26 miles," and whose "hundreds of flashing lights . . . will steal the nighttime stars." In the same paragraph he also touches on aesthetic and environmental concerns by warning that the transformer substation for the wind farm would rise one hundred feet above sea level to house "giant helicopter pads and 40,000 gallons of potentially hazardous oil."[13] For the average working Americans whose money woes outweigh their concern for the environment, Kennedy focuses on the economics of the project, commenting on jobs that will be lost, how the local economy will suffer, and that "offshore wind costs twice as much as gas-fired electricity and significantly more than onshore wind." For the historical preservationists, Kennedy touches on the culture of Cape Cod which he describes as "immersed in history and beauty" and "under consideration as a national marine sanctuary." Kennedy also invokes the fundamental ideal of inclusiveness, referring to "*our* battles for clean water" and inviting critics to investigate closely the wonders of Cape Cod. The sincerity and urgency of his tone seem almost as though he were inviting them personally to the compound for an idyllic afternoon of "netting blue crabs or mucking clams, quahogs and scallops by the bushel on tidal mud flats." He concludes the piece by offering the common-sense alternative of siting the Cape Wind project farther offshore, so that it might achieve the same results "without destroying this national treasure." The article is effective in speaking to a wide range of values, concerns, and priorities, while balancing logical and emotional appeals. Kennedy's record as a successful environmental attorney also enhances his ability to paint a vivid image of this historically and environmentally diverse area.

Cape Wind responds first with a direct attack on Kennedy's *ethos* as an environmentalist, saying that "if anyone should understand the need to maximize the energy output from wind turbines, it is environmentalists—particularly those who live or summer on Cape Cod." From a rhetorical perspective, this statement is loaded and ill-positioned. An obvious assault on Kennedy's professional and personal character, it questions his dedication to the environment and insinuates that his opposition to Cape Wind is nothing more than a case of NIMBY. The response implies that someone as well-educated as Kennedy about the urgency of environmental defense should know better than to block a sustainable energy project like Cape Wind. There is also an implicit accusation of elitism, suggesting that those who are privileged enough to live in a place as beautiful as Cape Cod have an obligation to set an environmental example for others. By attacking a public figure who is generally well-liked by environmental groups, liberals, and conservationists, Cape Wind undermines its intended *ethos* and compromises its ability to convey its information in meaningful and productive ways. For example, the response piece later argues an important point about the potential benefits of Cape Wind in other environmental contexts:

> Groups and high-profile individuals such as Kennedy . . . decry the April breakup of a barge carrying bunker oil to a Cape electricity-generating plant that shut a prized shellfishing area and many beaches.

But they can't see that stopping Cape Wind will subject Buzzards Bay to such oil shipments for decades. Nor does it seem to matter to them that other precious—albeit less prosperous—places, from West Virginia mountaintops to Wyoming sandhills, are sacrificed daily to yield the very fuels that the wind farm would displace.

Cape Wind's point about the ironic juxtaposition of the Buzzards Bay oil spill and Kennedy's opposition to the wind farm is fair, but its ad hominem tactics enervate their argument.[14] Although Kennedy goes out of his way to appeal to a broad audience in his article, Cape Wind runs the risk of alienating an already limited audience by directly attacking Kennedy's character, reducing the possibility of meaningful discussion on key issues of concern. Moreover, because this information is situated on page three of a seven-page document, the casual reader on the Internet may already be skimming at this point, rather than carefully absorbing the details of the response.

This point underscores another significant rhetorical difference between the Kennedy op-ed and Cape Wind's response: the relative authority of the venue of publication. Kennedy's piece was published in the *New York Times*, whereas Cape Wind's point-by-point reply was only made available on its own Web site. A brief letter to the editor from Cape Wind's vice president, Dennis J. Duffy, did not appear in the *Times* until January 4, 2006, a full nineteen days after the Kennedy piece was published.[15] The disparity between the length and location of these publications testifies to the power of Kenneth Burke's concept of "identification" as "the means by which a speaker or writer puts forth an image or character . . . and invites the audience to participate in a consubstantial relationship with that image" (quoted in *Ecospeak* 23). The limited public visibility of Cape Wind's responses, both online and in print, typifies the entire controversy. Ironically the tone of Duffy's succinct response is without aggression or ad hominem attacks, making the brief letter to the editor far more persuasive than Cape Wind's lengthy comeback on the organization's Web site. Moreover, Duffy's measured response makes Kennedy's observations seem overly passionate and factually challenged. The long delay between their publication dates, however, compromises the reader's ability to compare arguments. Furthermore, the fact that Cape Wind published its online reply as an organization, rather than as (or through) an individual of Kennedy's stature and reputation, compromises the effectiveness of their Web response. As a rhetorical strategy, Duffy's individual reply in the *New York Times* is more effective because of his status as the vice president of Cape Wind, but is nonetheless undermined by its late publication.

At first, the Cape Wind controversy seems to fit logically into historical binaries. The rhetoric of supporters parallels the rationalist, conservationist, and developmental positions commonly labeled as scientific, democratic, and concerned with economic growth. Gordon's proposed wind farm favors pragmatism over aesthetics, and views nature as a resource to be used for the common good. From this perspective, "it's the vision, not the view" that matters. For supporters, the long-range goals of reducing carbon dioxide emissions, improving local air quality, and decreasing the number of barges passing through Buzzards Bay outweigh the aesthetic value of the shoal.[16] The rhetoric of opponents aligns with the romantic, preservationist, and environmental positions that are typically characterized as emotional, mystical, and elitist. The Alliance to Protect Nantucket Sound is indeed backed by a wealthy and influential minority who place a high value on aesthetics, and question both the project's long-term economic viability and its environmental benefits.

The rhetoric of supporters and opponents of Cape Wind is complicated, however, because both cross the traditionally polarized boundaries of such debates. Although Gordon's project can be characterized as a conservationist business venture, it also shares certain traits with preservationist thinking. At a philosophical level, the development of all clean energy sources presupposes an inherent value to nature. Wind power off Cape Cod, for example, would benefit the environment by reducing carbon dioxide emissions, improving local air quality, and diminishing the number of barges to pass through Buzzards Bay. In spite of short-term economic and aesthetic externalities, the long-term goals of this developmental project can be interpreted as environmentally responsible. In this way, Cape Wind represents both the utilitarian and environmental viewpoints at once. Opponents to Cape Wind are not strictly aligned with the preservationist position either. On the one hand, the Alliance to Protect Nantucket Sound defends the aesthetic value of the Cape, much as John Muir and other preservationists lobbied to save Hetch Hetchy in the early 1900s. On the other, detractors are also opposing an otherwise "environmentally friendly" project, one which could provide nearly 75 percent of Cape Cod's energy needs, while alleviating strain on the grid that services major metropolitan cities in the surrounding area. The opponents' preservationist stance is further destabilized both by their unwillingness to pay more for clean energy, and by their failure to modify their own patterns of energy consumption which might even obviate the need for a wind farm.[17]

From a visual perspective, many forms of sustainable energy—wind farms, large solar arrays, and wave energy—all impact heavily the landscapes where they are best situated. But these projects represent an undisputed component of a "portfolio-approach" to slowing climate change. In this way the tension between aesthetics and clean energy produces a new category of difficulty in the field of environmental rhetoric: Sustainable energy projects demand that we rewrite the visual rhetoric of our landscapes in order to save them. Whereas early environmentalists like Muir had the relative luxury of fighting to maintain the original integrity of a natural area, we now find ourselves having to sacrifice some of nature's magnificence to preserve it. More importantly, without concerted efforts toward conservation, the value of our aesthetic sacrifice becomes doubtful. If built, Cape Wind's modest benefits will amount to little if its clean energy encourages or justifies higher demand for electricity.

From a rhetorical perspective, the challenge of the Cape Wind controversy is that it blurs the historical binaries of American environmental discourse, causing the key players to ignore the permeability of their own arguments. The polarization of viewpoints in environmental debates is rarely a matter of necessity, but usually a rhetorical device used by each side to mobilize forces against a "palpable villain" (*Ecospeak* 10). Supporters and opponents refuse to acknowledge that they may occupy some of the same ideological territory. Oversimplification is typical of environmental disputes, thus making rhetorical analysis useful. As Killingsworth and Palmer explain, when starkly polarized controversies are

> reported in the news media—where the environmentalist/developmentalist dichotomy has proved immensely attractive and durable, presumably because it provides busy reporters with a ready-made stock of plots and characters—it tends to conceal other sources of solidarity and conflict, which if closely examined, could provide hints toward the kind of social reorganization needed to cut through the environmental dilemma (10).

In other words, the oversimplification of the rhetorical positions in environmental controversies often precludes meaningful analysis. Eventually positions can become so hardened by local communities that they preclude productive debate.

It is interesting to note that since the MMS released its environmental impact report about Cape Wind in January 2008, more than 40,000 individuals and organizations have submitted comments about the review of the proposed wind farm. By contrast, a 2005 report issued by the US Army Corps of Engineers about Cape Wind received one-tenth the number of comments.[18] The unprecedented volume of responses to the MMS indicates that although this controversy will undoubtedly make other energy developers think twice about ventures in New England, the dispute has still managed to break some threshold of confusion and apathy on the part of a broader public. The recent reactions to the MMS report and the rhetorical history of this arduous controversy suggest that opponents and supporters of Cape Wind have at least two beliefs in common: everyone deserves a clean environment and everyone is an "environmentalist."

POLICY, PHILOSOPHY, AND PERSUASION

Killingsworth and Palmer explain that "despite its present status as a household word and its currency in the mass media, *environmentalist* is not an old word nor does it have a distinguished history. As a designation of 'one who is concerned with the preservation of the environment (from pollution, etc.),' it is barely two decades old" (41). The 2006 American Environmental Values Survey found that 44 percent of Americans considered themselves to be "environmentalists," and over 80 percent expressed serious concern for the "environment."[19] A 2007 study by the Yale Center for Environmental Law and Policy found that "Americans want action on global warming and energy conservation—and most agree that they have a responsibility to do their part." Sixty-three percent of Americans agree that our country is "in as much danger from environmental hazards such as air pollution and global warming as it is from terrorists."[20] Although a growing number of Americans seem to be describing themselves as "environmentalists," many leaders in the realm of environmental science and philosophy consider this label weighed down with rhetorical difficulty.

Wendell Berry argued that "the concept of country, homeland, dwelling place becomes simplified as 'the environment'—that is, what surrounds us. Once we see our place, our part of the world, as surrounding us, we have already made a profound distinction between it and ourselves" (22). From this perspective, the ubiquitous term we use to discuss our controversies over nature inherently presupposes our separateness from the environment we value. As a result, we experience a longing to return to the land for a sense of identity. And this longing creates tension for individuals living in a post-industrial society that prides itself on having been *freed* from dependence on the land for a sense of self. Having previously made nature into an adversary to conquer and a resource to exploit, it is no surprise that we feel conflicted about our current separation. The disconnect between a suppressed desire to return to a Romantic sense of unity with nature, and the intrinsic judgment that such a desire is prelapsarian and sentimental produces an irreconcilable pressure. When the innate drive to be in synch with the ecosystem we inhabit is perceived as irrevocably pitted against the ideals of a capitalist society, the need to defend the visual rhetoric of a place becomes a substitute for the true unity desired. In other words, when you can't really connect with the land, the least you can do is save the way it *looks*.

In their book, *Cape Wind: Money, Celebrity, Class, Politics, and the Battle for Our Energy Future on Nantucket Sound*," Wendy Williams and Robert Whitcomb explain that, before the Civil War, Cape Cod was a rarely visited backwater where only adventurous tourists dared to go. The residents considered themselves "a people apart," only going to Boston on business when absolutely necessary. Some left to make a living elsewhere, but those who stayed were so insular that "their version of the English language was barely understandable, even to other Massachusetts residents" (28). Those living on the mainland thought of Cape Cod a bit as though it were a foreign nation, and the Cape Codders themselves took pleasure in their odd-one-out status. After the Civil War, however, the Industrial

Age produced vast fortunes, allowing the wealthy to send their families on seashore retreats during the hot, Bostonian summers. Because Cape Cod's western shoreline was accessible by railroads, this area saw the first wave of nouveau-riche affluence. Many of the family homes built during that time remain in the hands of the same families, some inherited through as many as five generations.

By the early twentieth century, the tone had been set for Cape Cod as a place of beauty and privilege, a place to escape the ravages of the Industrial Age by which the influential and wealthy had made their fortunes in the first place. They spoke of Cape Cod as a kind of paradise, set apart from mainland America, where they could summer without the dirt, misery, and pollution of the smoke-belching, sky-darkening mills that had given them such financial freedom. Sailing was an implicit prerequisite for owning property there, and Cape Cod's image as the "American Riviera" grew (30–31). In this way one can argue that to preserve the visual rhetoric of Horseshoe Shoal is to preserve the identity of the generations of people who have lived on its shores and sailed its waters. To lose the view is to lose their sense of self, their sense of history, their sense of connection to the water and all it represents.

For most environmental rhetoricians, the environment is not a tangible compilation of woodlands and oceans. Rather, as an object of rhetorical study, the environment can be interpreted as an idea, or a set of cultural values, constructed through the way we use language. In this way slogans like "Save Our Sound" and "It's the Vision, Not the View," take on more meaning. As Herndl and Brown emphasize, "the environment about which we all argue and make policy is the product of the discourse about nature established in a variety of powerful disciplines, agencies and discourses" (3). In other words, from a rhetorical perspective, the environment can never be separate from the words we use to represent it. As Killingsworth and Palmer argue:

> Even if we find ourselves in a Babel of discourse communities, each with its own characteristic language, epistemological outlook, and agenda for action, there remains in rhetorical inquiry a need, a mission, and a hope for a generally accessible narrative, the story of how human action reconciles conflicting demands in the search for the good life. Even while stressing caution about claims over the accessibility of information, rhetorical criticism urges continued development of the story of human cooperation. (21)

Analyzing the rhetoric of supporters and opponents of Cape Wind exposes how diverse publics perceive environmental issues and policies, and how rhetoric in a particular context frames social realities (Bruner and Oelshlaeger). Because we are all environmentalists now, debates are entirely about policy, pitting what should be complementary interests against one another. It's less a question of philosophy than one of persuasion, and that makes success or failure a matter of rhetoric.

POSTSCRIPT

On January 16, 2009, the Minerals Management Service released its final environmental impact statement on the Cape Wind project, stating that the wind farm would pose a "negligible" threat to the environment of Nantucket Sound—and a "moderate" impact on the scenery. Barring any further objections from lawmakers and other stakeholders, a final "record of decision" will be issued by the Secretary of the Interior by mid-February. Although Gordon says he hopes to begin construction by the end of 2009, Cape Wind must still obtain several state permits amidst unrelenting political maneuvering against the project. The rhetoric surrounding the debate continues to range from inflammatory to curiously restrained. According to a recent article in the *Wall Street Journal*, for example, "The sort of people who can afford to use *summer* as a verb" are in favor of the project itself, just not the "visual pollution" it would create "within sight of their beachfront vacation homes" ("Blowhards"). On the other hand, the *Washington Post* reported that Cape Wind officials were simply "encouraged" by a recent outpouring of support from President Obama regarding the future of wind energy in the United States (Kravitz). President Obama has indeed made alternative energy a cornerstone of his plan to revive the economy. Whereas the incoming administration must ensure that the project unfolds in a manner consistent with energy, environmental, and safety objectives, the American public will decide whether the soaring wind turbines form a graceful arc of clean lines, or an industrial blight on a national treasure.

NOTES

1. The Number 6 oil from this particular spill was analyzed by scientists Chris Reddy and Bob Nelson (both from the Woods Hole Oceanographic Institution). They found the Buzzards Bay spill to contain a high percentage of naphthalenes—the insecticide in mothballs, and a sub-group of toxic PAH's (polycyclic aromatic hydrocarbons). Reddy found about sixty different types of naphthalenes (which is not an uncommon figure), but there was a greater percentage of the toxic compounds in the oil than expected (Williams and Whitcomb 169). The high percentage caused him to predict, correctly, that a high quantity of sea life would die.

   In the preceding year, the Canal electric plant burned about seven million barrels of Number 6 oil, a figure which translates into somewhere between fifty-eight and seventy oil barges passing through Buzzards Bay (Williams and Whitcomb 169). These estimates are consistent with yearly averages.

2. Though the cost of wind energy has come down to 4.5–5 cents per kilowatt hour (KWH) from 6.1 per KWH in 1999, the technology is still not balancing out as cost-effective for some areas. In August 2007, for example, Long Island withdrew its plans to build a wind energy center in the Atlantic, when

costs were running up toward $800 million. Some projects in Texas have also been abandoned over cost considerations ("Wind Jammers").
3. See, for example, the 3,800-page document released by the Army Corps of Engineers in 2005. This report is a combined Draft Environmental Impact Statement (DEIS), Draft Environmental Impact Review (DEIR), and Determination of Regional Impact (DRI) that represents the results of a coordinated federal, state, and regional review of the Cape Wind project. The document may be viewed in full at http://www.nae.usace.army.mil/projects/ma/ccwf/deis.htm.

Links to all of the Cape Wind project reports from the US Department of the Interior's Minerals Management Service may be located at http://www.mms.gov/offshore/RenewableEnergy/ReportsforCapeWind.htm.
4. These figures include online readership for both newspapers. Richard Pérez-Peña, "More Readers Trading Newspapers for Websites," *New York Times*, Nov. 6, 2007.
5. The roseate tern is a seabird over which there has been much debate in the Cape Wind controversy. Opponents claim that the project will further threaten the birds which are already labeled "endangered" by the US National Biological Service. The Massachusetts Audubon Society, however, has given preliminary support to Cape Wind, after independent studies allayed concerns that the farm's turbine blades would cause significant harm to birds.
6. Opie and Elliot define the jeremiad as a "'ritualistic castigation of the people for having defaulted on their bond with the Lord' (Miller 6). In seventeenth-century New England, such a political sermon was regularly used as what Sacvan Bercovitch aptly calls a 'state-of-the-covenant address' (4). These sermons were delivered at public occasions, most notably on election days. As a rhetorical genre, the jeremiad has left its mark—sometimes explicitly, sometimes implicitly" on a variety of texts (9–10).
7. See also Carolyn R. Miller, "Technology as a Form of Consciousness: A Study of Contemporary Ethos," *Central States Speech Journal* 29 (1978), 228–36; S. Michael Halloran, "Rhetoric in the American College Curriculum: the Decline of Public Discourse," in *Pre/Text* 3 (1982), 245–69; and Charles Bazerman, *Shaping Written Knowledge: The Genre and Activity of the Experimental Article in Science*, Madison: University of Wisconsin Press (1988).
8. Ralph Waldo Emerson, "The American Scholar," orated in 1837 before the Phi Beta Kappa Society in Cambridge; quoted in J. A. Berlin's *Writing Instruction in Nineteenth-Century American Colleges*. Carbondale: Southern Illinois University Press (1984). 58.
9. "Proceedings of a Conference of Governors in the White House," Washington, D.C., May 13–15, 1908 (Washington: Government Printing Office, 1909). 153.
10. Although beyond the scope of this essay, it is noteworthy that the conservationist line of reasoning ignored any consideration of the "greater good" of the Yosemite–Mono Lake Paiutes who inhabited Hetch Hetchy prior to 1850. See Robert W. Righter, *The Battle over Hetch Hetchy: America's Most Controversial Dam and the Birth of Modern Environmentalism* (Oxford: Oxford University Press, 2006); John W. Simpson, *Dam!: Water, Power, Politics and Preservation in Hetch Hetchy and Yosemite National Park* (New York: Pantheon, 2005).
11. The details of these fiascos—which have ranged from media stunts and "filibusters" by the Alliance at town-hall meetings to high-profile demonstrations by Cape Wind—are a story in themselves. One may find detailed descriptions and information regarding these issues in Wendy Williams and Robert Whitcomb's *Cape Wind: Money, Celebrity, Class, Politics, and*

the Battle for Our Energy Future on Nantucket Sound (New York: Public Affairs, 2007). Although Williams and Whitcomb are decidedly in favor of the project, their investigative research and reporting is nonetheless illuminating and well-documented.

12. Although Kennedy himself is not technically a member of the Alliance to Protect Nantucket Sound, his family's involvement in this debate has had notable consequences. Senator Edward Kennedy is listed as a "stakeholder" on the Alliance's home page, and the family has played a significant role in the opposition to the Cape Wind project, in spite of their usual policy to refrain from making public statements about local issues. But as Williams and Whitcomb argue, "On Cape Cod, and particularly in Hyannis, Ted Kennedy is not someone you want to make unhappy.... In a sense, Nantucket Sound [is] accepted by many as the Kennedy clan's private pond" (26–27).

13. Cape Wind's Web site explains that Kennedy's reference to "oil" is misleading here, as the substation would house highly refined *mineral* oil in a triple-containment system. The Web site does not, however, provide any details about the purpose the oil would serve.

14. There is evidence of windmill activity on Cape Cod as early as the end of the seventeenth century, and many real windmills were still in operation during the 1800s (Coogan and Sheedy 170). Eventually what was once considered merely practical became a rhetorical symbol of Cape Cod's national *ethos*. One still finds images of windmills in a variety of contexts on the Cape, such as the elite Oyster Harbors Club which sports an imitation windmill as their club's logo (Williams and Whitcomb 30–32). Ironically, in 1935, the peninsula's oldest windmill was bought and shipped off for display in Henry Ford's tribute to American innovation, sending Cape Codders into an uproar over the loss (Coogan and Sheedy 171).

15. Kennedy's op-ed was 1,007 words, while Cape Wind's letter to the editor was 212.

16. There has been strong disagreement about the visual impact of the wind farm. Cape Wind claims on their Web site that "the slender supporting towers will be painted to blend in with the horizon, making them visible one half-inch above the horizon on clear days." Opponents claim that the wind farm will be far more visible from shore, destroying the view and ruining a "national treasure."

17. The emission of greenhouse gases is the main issue distorting the historical line between conservationism and preservationism in the Cape Wind controversy. What was once an externality has become a measured cost in the face of global climate change, permanently altering the definitions of "utilitarianism" and "preservationism" in the context of environmental debates. Until recently, the "greatest good" in such disputes has been a matter of economics and public welfare. Today the reduction of carbon dioxide emissions (particularly in developed nations) is no longer merely an "environmental" issue, but a pragmatic and ethical one as well. The businessman now treads on the side of preservation when he factors pollution into his cost-benefit analysis, while the preservationist relinquishes his position in rejecting a clean energy project in favor of an unsustainable status quo.

18. As of May 1, 2008, preliminary estimates indicate that approximately three quarters of the responses sent to the MMS are in support of Cape Wind. The period for commenting is scheduled to end on May 2, 2008.

19. Research Summary of "The American Environmental Values Survey," conducted by SRIC for ecoAmerica, October 2006 (5, 14).

20. Global Strategy Group, "2007 Environment Survey—Key Findings," memorandum dated March 7, 2007.

WORKS CITED

Bazerman, Charles. *Shaping Written Knowledge: The Genre and Activity of the Experimental Article in Science*. Madison: U of Wisconsin P, 1988.
Bercovitch, Sacvan. *The American Jeremiad*. Madison: U of Wisconsin P, 1978.
Berlin, James A. *Writing Instruction in Nineteenth-Century American Colleges*. Carbondale: Southern Illinois UP, 1984.
Berry, Wendell. *The Unsettling of America*. San Francisco: Sierra Club, 1977.
"Blowhards: The Fabulous Debate over Wind Power on Nantucket Sound." *Wall Street Journal*, January 24, 2009
Brace, Peter B. "Nantucket to Speak Out on the Wind Farm Tuesday." *Nantucket Independent*, March 5, 2008.
Bruner, Michael and Max Oelshlaeger, "Rhetoric, Environmentalism, and Environmental Ethics" in *Landmark Essays on Rhetoric and the Environment*. Ed., Craig Waddell. New Jersey: Hermagoras P, 1994.
Burke, Kenneth. *A Rhetoric of Motives*. Berkeley: U of California P, 1969.
Burkett, Elinor. "A Mighty Wind." *New York Times*, June 15, 2003.
Cape Wind. "Cape Wind Responds to Robert F. Kennedy, Jr." April 25, 2008 http://capewind.org.
Coogan, Jim and Jack Sheedy. *A Journey through Cape Cod's History and Lore*. East Dennis: Harvest Home Books, 2001.
Duffy, Dennis J. "Wind Power Will Work." *New York Times*, January 4, 2006.
Emerson, Ralph Waldo. "The American Scholar," orated in 1837 before the Phi Beta Kappa Society in Cambridge; quoted in James. A. Berlin's *Writing Instruction in Nineteenth-Century American Colleges*. Carbondale: Southern Illinois UP, 1984.
Global Strategy Group. "2007 Environment Survey—Key Findings," Memorandum dated March 7, 2007.
Halloran, S. Michael. "Rhetoric in the American College Curriculum: the Decline of Public Discourse," in *Pre/Text* 3 (1982).
Herndl, Carl G. and Stuart C. Brown, eds. *Green Culture: Environmental Rhetoric in American Culture*. Madison: U of Wisconsin P, 1996.
Kennedy, Jr. Robert F. "An Ill Wind off Cape Cod." *New York Times*, December 16, 2005.
Killingsworth, M. Jimmie and Jacqueline S. Palmer. *Ecospeak: Rhetoric and Environmental Politics in America*. Carbondale: Southern Illinois UP, 1992.
Kravitz, Derek. "Wind Farm No Threat to Cape Cod, Report Says." *Washington Post*, January 17, 2009.
Massachusetts Technology Collaborative Renewable Energy Trust. September 13, 2008 http://www.masstech.org/offshore/CapeWindFAQs.html.
McConnell, Grant. *Private Power and American Democracy*. New York: Vintage-Random, 1966.
Miller, Carolyn. R. "Technology as a Form of Consciousness: a Study of Contemporary Ethos" in *Central States Speech Journal* 29 (1978).
New England District. United States Army Corps of Engineers. *Cape Wind Energy Project Draft Environmental Impact Statement*. 12 April 2006. September 13, 2008 http://www.nae.usace.army.mil/projects/ma/ccwf/deis.htm.
Opie, John and Norbert Elliot. "Tracking the Ellusive Jeremiad: The Rhetorical Character of American Environmental Discourse," in *The Symbolic Earth: Discourse and Our Creation of the Environment*; eds. James G. Cantrill and Christine L. Oravec. Lexington: UP of Kentucky, 1996.
Oravec, Christine J. "Conservation vs. Preservationism: The 'Public Interest' in the Hetch Hetchy Controversy." *Quarterly Journal of Speech* 70 (1984). 444–58.
Pérez-Peña, Richard. "More Readers Trading Newspapers for Websites." *New York Times* November 6, 2007. Sept. 2008 http://www.nytimes.com/2007/11/06/business/media/06adco.html?partner=rssnyt&emc=rss.

Phelan, James D. "Why Congress Should Pass the Hetch-Hetchy Bill." *Outlook* 91 (February 13, 1909). 340–41.

"Proceedings of a Conference of Governors in the White House," Washington, D.C., May 13–15, 1908. Washington: Government Printing Office, 1909.

Research Summary of "The American Environmental Values Survey," conducted by SRIC for ecoAmerica, October 2006.

Righter, Robert W. *The Battle over Hetch Hetchy: America's Most Controversial Dam and the Birth of Modern Environmentalism.* Oxford: Oxford UP, 2006.

Save Our Sound. Alliance to Protect Nantucket Sound. 8 September 2008. September 13, 2008 http://www.saveoursound.org.

Simpson, John W. *Dam! Water, Power, Politics and Preservation in Hetch Hetchy and Yosemite National Park.* New York: Pantheon, 2005.

United States. Minerals Management Service. Dept. of the Interior. *Cape Wind Energy Project.* 8 September, 2008. Offshore Energy and Minerals Management. September 13, 2008 http://www.mms.gov/offshore/AlternativeEnergy/CapeWind.htm.

United States. National Biological Service. Ed. Jeffrey A. Spendelow. March 1995. *Roseate Tern Fact Sheet.* September 13, 2008 http://www.mbr-pwrc.usgs.gov/mbr/tern2.htm.

Williams, Wendy, and Robert Whitcomb. *Cape Wind: Money, Celebrity, Class, Politics and the Battle for Our Energy Future on Nantucket Sound.* New York: Public Affairs, 2007.

"Wind Jammers," *Wall Street Journal*, August 28, 2007.

5 The Nine Mile Canyon Coalition
Rhetorical Landscapes, Responsible Public Land Use

Lynda McNeil

In response to national security and energy independence concerns following 9/11, President Bush's National Energy Plan, or Federal Energy Initiative, of 2003 set an urgent agenda to develop natural gas and other fossil fuels on public lands throughout the West. This executive order effectively relaxed restrictions on leasing permits for oil and gas development by private corporations on public lands. In one fell swoop, federal policy guidelines governing public lands, deemed impractical in the post-9/11 political climate, became "red tape"—and energy development and independence from foreign resources became the order of the day. In its wake and in conjunction with reductions in federal funding, important protections for public lands were suspended, such as inventorying cultural resources, assessing adverse impacts, vetting alternative proposals, and reaching consensus on what constitutes significant impacts on cultural and environmental resources.

On the West Tavaputs Plateau in eastern Utah (WTP; a glossary of acronyms is available at the end of this chapter), the focus of this case study, the Bureau of Land Management (BLM) granted leasing permits to the Bill Barrett Corporation (BBC) in 2004 and to Gasco Corporation in 2006, both natural gas development companies, to allow natural gas drilling on BLM-administered public lands. Notably the WTP encompasses Nine Mile Canyon (9MC) (actually forty miles long), nominated to the National Register of Historic Places and designated a protected Area of Critical Environmental Concern (ACEC), described as "noteworthy regionally, nationally, and internationally for its prehistoric rock art and other cultural and historical resources" (BLM EIS 2007). In addition to its wealth of irreplaceable cultural resources created over 10,000 years by Native Americans and early settlers, Nine Mile Canyon is still used by tribal groups (including Ute, Southern Paiute, and Hopi) for religiously and ecologically important activities.

As a member of the Utah Rock Art Research Association (URARA) and avid rock art researcher, I was alarmed to read the "Action Alert" in March 2006 posted on the Web site of the Nine Mile Canyon Coalition (9MCC), a nonprofit environmental and cultural oversight and preservation group, informing its members that 9MC in the WTP had been opened to natural gas development. Having visited the canyon to do prehistoric rock art research, I was keenly aware of its natural beauty, and its ecological and archaeological resources, including ancient ruins and over 1,000 rock art panels throughout the canyon, spanning 10,000 years. These cultural resources, heavily concentrated in the canyon bottom along the Minnie Maud and Nine Mile creeks (tributaries of the "wild and scenic"–designated Green River), are now at risk from industrial traffic, dust, and chemical sprays as a direct result of natural gas development by BBC and Gasco Corporation.

Viewed from a broader perspective, the West Tavaputs Plateau Drilling Proposal for eastern Utah serves as a case study encapsulating similar assaults on public lands throughout the American West since 2003. As a result of this "energy initiative," a series of heated debates precipitated between federal agencies and environmental and cultural resource protectionist groups over the meaning and practices of responsible uses of BLM-administered public lands in several western states on public lands.

This chapter focuses on the discursive interplay of rhetorics in the "reticulate public sphere" (Hauser, *Vernacular* 71–72) in relation to the BLM EIS public scoping process, public meetings, and Web-based "Action Alerts." The discursive confrontations, currently being enacted in eastern Utah, involve "radical protectionist" groups, assumed to occupy opposite ends of the political spectrum: anti-drilling, environmental "protectionists" and the pro-drilling, national security "protectionists," seeking independence from foreign oil.[1]

For "radical protectionists" (of the environment and cultural resources), the prospect of *any* drilling occurring in Nine Mile Canyon, especially along the cultural-resource-rich and environmentally fragile canyon bottom of Minnie Maud and Nine Mile creeks, would lead to "significant" negative impacts on cultural and ecological resources. On the pro-drilling end of spectrum, the national security and independence from foreign oil "protectionists" saw no practical alternatives other than increasing domestic production of oil and gas resources on public lands throughout the West.

Based upon the National Environment Policy Act (NEPA) of 1969, the BLM Price Field Office in Price, Utah, was required to prepare an environmental impact statement (EIS) on the impacts of "efficient, orderly, and environmentally sensitive" development of the natural gas and oil resources in the WTP areas on approximately 137,700 acres of public, state, and private lands in Carbon and Duchesne Counties in eastern Utah. Moreover, federal legislation related to "multiple uses" for public lands requires that an EIS public scoping process, whereby the authorized BLM field office solicits letters of the draft EIS (DEIS) from the general public, be conducted before drilling can occur on these lands (119,661 acres of BLM-administered public lands). Consequently the discursive sites of contested meanings and frames that I have chosen to analyze rhetorically include the official discourse of the federally mandated BLM DEIS in 2004 (for BBC) and in 2006 (for Gasco), in conjunction with the vernacular rhetoric of individuals and activist group "diverse publics" expressed in scoping letters and on the

Nine Mile Canyon Coalition Web page's "Action Alerts" to members and other interested publics.

In the WTP drilling case with special regard to Nine Mile Canyon, the BLM initiated a "Notice of Intent" (NOI) to prepare an EIS and to conduct public scoping for the WTP Development Plan. The BLM public scoping process included a thirty-day period during which the affected stakeholders could, as individuals or as distinct groups, participate in a letter-writing campaign to the BLM field offices in Price in 2004 and in Vernal in 2006, and public meetings spanning this period. On a Federal Register Web site for the Environmental Protection Agency, the BLM Price field office posted its NOI to prepare an EIS and to conduct "public scoping," stating: "If you have information, data or concerns related to potential *impacts* of the proposed action, or have suggestions for *additional alternatives*, or have comments on the proposed planning amendment criteria, [please submit them] within 30 days of the NOI [being] published or within 15 days after the last public meeting held" [emphasis added].

By adopting this case study approach, I hope to gain a better understanding of the discursive processes through which the adversarial rhetorics of diverse stakeholders can succeed in opening the space for the emergence of a coalition rhetoric in the "reticulate public sphere" with shared meanings and values. This chapter examines the discursive dynamics of diverse stakeholders identified through the vernacular rhetorics of "public scoping letters" and Web-based "Action Alerts" issued by the Nine Mile Coalition (as a group and by individual members), a cultural and natural resource "radical preservationist" group (see their Web site for their mission statement), as well as through the official discourse of the BLM-Environmental Assessment (EA) and the DEIS in 2008 (Price, Utah, Field Office). The final public scoping process for the West Tavaputs Natural Gas Full Field Development DEIS, recently completed, was conducted from February 1 to May 1, 2008. The summary overview of public scoping comments now appears on the BLM Web site.

Based upon my framing analysis of scoping letters submitted to the Vernal field office in 2004 and "Action Alert" comments posted on March 11, 2008, what initially emerged was an adversarial rhetoric focused on "centered" ("atomized" rather than shared) meanings related to key terms and practices. What would emerge over the course of four years of interaction between activist and official rhetorics between 2004 and 2008 was an increasingly dialogic discourse, moving toward deliberative democracy involved in coalition building with a burgeoning sense of shared meanings and values.

BLM EIS PUBLIC SCOPING

This section examines the shifting power dynamic revealed in the adversarial rhetorics of pro-drilling ("developmentalist") and anti-drilling ("environmentalist," "preservationist," or "protectionist") stakeholders on this

100 *Lynda McNeil*

sociocultural landscape.² The process of the staking out of divergent positions began with the BLM's EIS vetting process (concluded May 1, 2008), whereby federal agents are required by law to solicit scoping letters from the public sphere consisting of multiple users of the public lands. Participants included a range of stakeholders or diverse publics: energy extraction corporations and labor unions; local tourism businesses; chambers of commerce (e.g., in Price and Vernal, Utah) and citizens working for or economically benefiting from energy development in the region; cultural resource and environmental preservation groups (e.g., Nine Mile Canyon Coalition, Utah Rock Art Research Association, Colorado Plateau Alliance; National Trust for Historic Preservation); national and international professional archaeologists and rock art researchers; Native American tribal consultants and groups using the canyon for ceremonial purposes; and a variety of environmental preservationist public land users (hikers, campers, climbers, rafters, and hunters).

With respect to the impact of such public vetting on public policy, Hauser maintains that when vernacular exchanges, in this case public scoping letters, interact with institutional discourse, they serve to "widen the discursive arena" (Hauser, *Vernacular* 89). His assertion raises the question of whether such discursive widening occurs through the public scoping process or alternatively in subsequent face-to-face encounters between antagonists at public meetings. The analysis of Killingsworth and Palmer may more accurately describe the dynamic between institutional (BLM EIS) and vernacular (public scoping letters) discourses.³ They maintain that despite the "democratizing rhetoric of the EIS," the verbatim scoping letters included in the final EIS "indicate their tacit recognition that their voices will have little effect—rhetorical or real" (186).⁴

The ensuing struggle between official (federal, institutional, instrumental) and movement or activist (civic, public) rhetorics, ripe for rhetorical analysis, recalls similar ones currently being played out across the West with respect to the mandated multiple uses of public lands (Travis 28–29). Like the "struggle to control meaning" related to grazing rights in southern Arizona (Stevens 298–300), the BLM EIS public scoping process and Nine Mile Canyon Coalition "Action Alerts" hinged on a complex of contested terms, most notably appropriate or responsible "multiple uses"; "significant impacts" or "adverse effects"; constructive growth or "development;" "reasonable alternatives" to drilling (and related disruptions); and "reliable" (trustworthy) oversight for monitoring mitigation plans.

For the purposes of this analysis, I organized the adversarial rhetorics reflected in the BLM EIS (Vernal field office) public scoping letters from 2004 into three distinct, albeit overlapping, types defined by shared meanings, values, and framing strategies. To foreground the distinctions among adversarial rhetorics, I placed the stakeholders along a continuum defined by degree and duration of adverse impact of drilling on cultural and natural resources. Three groups emerged from the analysis of the letters: for-profit, high-impact/short-term stakeholders; nonprofit, low-impact/long-term stakeholders; and for-profit, low-impact/long-term (the latter taking an emergent, middle-ground position).

Before examining these divergent positions, it is instructive to put the Federal Leasing on Public Lands in the WTP area into legal context. Under the Federal Land Policy and Management Act (FLPMA) of 1976, the Mineral Leasing Act (MLA) of 1920, and the Federal Onshore Oil and Gas Leasing Reform Act of 1987, the federal government has the legal right to grant leases allowing drilling on public lands administered by the BLM and US Forest Service. Moreover, before 1996, Wilderness Study Areas (WSA) in Utah consisted of 3.4 million acres. In 1996–99, the re-inventory of Utah lands designated an additional 2.6 million acres as "wilderness quality," closed to oil and gas leasing. However, in 2003, with the president's energy initiative, the "no more wilderness" settlement agreement between the Department of Interior (DOI) and the state of Utah opened 2.6 million acres of wilderness-quality land to leasing. Since 2003, the Utah BLM has sold oil and gas leases on over 125,000 acres of these wilderness-quality lands.

Under the authority of what Utah preservationist groups referred to as the "no more wilderness" settlement, the BBC in 2004 and Gasco Corporation in 2006 were granted leases to develop (extract) oil and natural gas resources on federal, state, and private lands on the WTP. When they submitted proposals specifying the scope and duration of their gas and oil development plans on the WTP, this prompted the BLM EIS public scoping process required under NEPA.

As identified in these scoping letters, the pro-drilling, for-profit stakeholders tended to place a high priority (value) on high-impact/short-term positions. These groups based their arguments on shared meanings and framing strategies with respect to energy independence and financial security. They included the energy production corporations (BBC and Gasco), the oil and natural gas extraction labor unions, and the Price and Vernal chambers of commerce. The latter pro-drilling civic groups anticipated an increase in the local tax base, with resultant benefits to businesses, public schools, and municipal infrastructure. For these stakeholders, pro-drilling arguments were infused with pathos and framed in terms of economic revitalization and growth, as well as national security concerns post-9/11.

The pro-drilling letters referred to protection of national interests, our "way of life" (i.e., energy consumption, material comforts, and/or Christian values), and our children's futures. These stakeholders tended to frame the act of drilling on public lands as a reasonable response to national security fears associated with America's energy dependence on hostile states abroad, conceptually "tagged" to patriotism ("proud to support national interest"), and long-term economic security and growth. Here are some direct quotes from high-impact/short-term positions (all quotes from scoping letters were provided by the BLM Vernal field office; emphasis added):

- "*Our future depends* on new [fossil fuel/energy] production."
- [We need oil and gas production] "*to protect our children and grandchildren.*"
- "*We are proud* to earn our living by natural resource production."
- "Energy production is an important part of *protecting our national interests.*"
- Economic growth will help prevent the Uintah Basin from suffering "*economic devastation.*"
- Development is important for "*protecting our [economic] way of life.*"

Notably these pro-drilling advocates fail to address the concerns of anti-drilling, "radical protectionist" stakeholders related to "significant (adverse) impacts" on cultural and environmental resources, including reliable (trustworthy) monitoring of mitigation to ensure federal compliance with cultural and environmental resource protections.

In contrast, the anti-drilling, nonprofit stakeholders tended to place a high priority (value) on low-impact/long-term issues to frame their arguments. The groups with these shared values include the Nine Mile Canyon Coalition, the Colorado Plateau Alliance, the Wilderness Society, the Southern Utah Wilderness Alliance, the Utah Rock Art Research Association, and the Western Wildlife Conservancy, as well as Native American tribal organizations and other nonprofit citizens' groups who have challenged these leases and the "no more wilderness" settlement in court. Here are some quotes from low-impact/long-term positions (emphasis added):

- Oil and gas development should not drive "the *public lands management process* a the expense of other priorities."
- "These *lands are sacred to Native American peoples* whose ancestors inhabited the canyon for thousands of years."
- "The BLM are *custodians of the public lands* and should do a thorough *inventory* of cultural sites and rock art in the region."
- "*Preserve Desolation Canyon for our children and their children* and their children."
- "Drilling would be a *bargain with the devil* that tosses science and spirit on the dust heap of social and corporate greed."

Under federal laws, these stakeholders have the argumentative advantage of several long-standing congressional acts: the National Environmental Preservation Act (NEPA), the National Historic Preservation Act (NHPA), the Antiquities Act, the Archaeological Resources Protection Act (ARPA); and the Native American Graves and Repatriation Act (NAGPRA) (1990). They also have in their court, the congressionally chartered National Trust for Historic Preservation (NTHP), a nonprofit, advocacy, fund-raising organization that oversees cultural resource management policies and practices.

For these cultural and environmental protectionist stakeholders, anti-drilling arguments are based on shared meanings and framed in terms, similarly infused with pathos, of federal agents' primary role as "stewards of the land" and the right of diverse public land users to experience a "pristine" environment with protected endangered species (such as the Mexican spotted owl) and rare plant species. This includes the rights of Native Americans to have access to traditional, "sacred" tribal territories and ecological resources; for academic researchers and avocationists to study ancient ruins and rock art; and for tourists, campers, climbers, rafters, hikers, and hunters to have an unspoiled wilderness experience. Their shared values, antithetical to drilling, centered on maintaining a "pristine wilderness" experience and "the preservation of wild places against the intrusion of civilization" (Killingsworth and Palmer 32–33 on transcendentalism). In the case of the WTP EIS, this included preserving archaeological ruins and prehistoric rock art; their preservationist values discounted arguments centered on economic growth and development or on national security fears.

To conclude this section, I took a closer, more nuanced look at the polarized stances so far represented in the reticulate public sphere. In doing so, I found a previously overlooked group of "middle ground" stakeholders, whose definitions, frames, and values overlap those of the antithetical high-impact/short-term and low-impact/long-term positions. This newly recognized group of "radical centrist" stakeholders (my label) reflect values that overlap unexpectedly with the two antithetical groups previously discussed, thereby adopting a for-profit, albeit low-impact/long-term position. In so doing, they succeed in challenging the facile categories of dominant ("official" government or corporation) and marginalized ("vernacular" social or activist movements) agents and resources.

In this category of diverse publics, we find scoping letters written from a "radical centrist" (middle ground) perspective representing the following groups: recreational businesses (river rafting, biking, hiking, off-roading); ecological and cultural (archaeological and rock art) tourism; outdoor education organizations and institutions; and hunting, fishing, and birding organizations and businesses. Clearly it is in the long-term economic interests of these stakeholders to lobby for "low impact" on cultural and environmental resources in order to protect both their businesses, as well as the rights of the customers, who are multiple users of the public lands. Here are some quotes from the emergent middle ground, for-profit, low-impact/long-term positions (emphasis added):

- "The Olympics opened peoples' eyes to *the value of tourism in the state.*"
- "Multi-use must consider *all stakeholders.*"
- "Consider the impact (of development) on *wildlife, rock art, and tourism for future generations.*"

104   Lynda McNeil

- The Western Wildlife Conservancy "acknowledges the necessity of developing new natural gas resources, as well as of *developing new, clean environmentally- friendly energy technologies.*"
- "Public lands management requires *balance. Only drill in the buffer zone.*"
- "*New technology* has made it possible for *gas production to be compatible with almost all other activities on public lands.*"
- "*The BLM can call on partner groups* in preserving and protecting the canyon" (NTHP, "Nine Mile Canyon at Risk").

In the past, a rhetorical power dynamic exerted itself in situations where marginalized individuals or groups (social activist, small businesses, recreational, or educational organizations) failed to gain access to authoritative resources (Giddens 137, cited in M. Goggin 88–89), such as powerful or knowledgeable individuals, groups, or social alliances (governmental, legal, academic institutions), as well as access to empowering allocative (technological) resources. The emergent middle-ground stakeholders in this case study show how this changed for the better.

In addition to gaining access to empowering (authoritative and allocative) resources, we find burgeoning coalition building between formerly marginalized and dominant groups and the resulting discursive interaction that also challenges the dominant-marginalized rhetorical polarities. In the case of the 9MCC (2004–2008), this nonprofit activist organization formed close partnerships with dominant groups, marshaling both authoritative (congressional legislation, academic research, and NTHP advocacy and funding), as well as allocative resources (new, low-impact drilling technologies, alternative fuels) that support their values *and* bolster their arguments either against drilling or in favor of restricted drilling and less invasive practices, like alternative routes (Goggin 88–89; Kaufer and Carley 137, drawing on Giddens; Kress 191). As a result, the 9MCC has been able to gain a persuasive advantage due to the redistribution of authoritative and allocative resources, resulting in the nomination of Nine Mile Canyon to the National Register of Historic Places (to be decided in June 2008) and the concomitant protections to its cultural and environmental resources.

In closing this section, the BLM EIS public scoping process proved to be productive in that it opened an interactive rhetorical space for emergent "middle-ground" stakeholders who would become involved in subsequent public forums to deliberate and explore common ground. Unfortunately, in practical terms it functioned unidirectionally and hierarchically from the marginalized to the powerful, from grassroots publics to federal officials. As a result, one could accurately argue that the public scoping process is an inherently flawed rhetorical tool for a deliberative democracy, because it tends to "atomize" stances (Billig 65), thereby fostering "centered meaning-making," rather than a socially interactive meaning-construction process (Stevens 303–4).

9MCC: "ACTION ALERTS"

In contrast to the institutional control over public opinion enacted through the EIS drafting and scoping process, social activist groups' Web-based "Action Alerts" appear to have fostered "centered meaning-making" in a couple of ways: first, through "white paper" analyses of the DEIS and, secondly, through public meetings involving BLM administrators, a diverse group of stakeholders comprised of individual public land users, and social activist groups like the 9MCC.

On February 1, 2008, the BLM posted the WTP DEIS on its Web site to officially solicit public scoping letters and public meetings until May 1, 2008. In the 9MCC Spring 2008 online newsletter, the Impact Research Committee provided a "white paper" analysis of the DEIS, focusing on several contested issues: the "major impact of industrial traffic" through Nine Mile and Cottonwood canyons (the location of the highest concentration of cultural resources); their counterargument to BBC's claim that the drilling company would not be able to "mitigate the impacts of industrial traffic," by proposing that the BLM consider "Alternative C: the Transportation Impact Reduction Alternative" (which they dismissed without a reasonable investigation), that is, "alternative access routes" to the wells; and their counterargument to the BLM proposal that the BLM and BBC select a "company to monitor the project for compliance with the stipulations and mitigation directives agreed to, and approved in the EIS." In addition, "The monitoring company would report to the BLM and BBC."

The 9MCC "Action Alert" in their Internet newsletter, March 11, 2008, appeared in direct response to the BLM DEIS, February 1, 2008, position taken regarding three areas of critical concern with respect to adverse effects on cultural resources. First, regarding industrial traffic through Nine Mile and Cottonwood canyons (the location of the highest concentration of cultural resources), the DEIS reported a "Finding of No Significant Impact": "Pursuant to Section 106 of the National Historic Preservation Act, it is concluded that the project will not adversely affect districts, sites, highways, structures, or other objects listed in or eligible for listing in the National Register of Historic Places, nor will it cause loss or destruction of significant scientific, cultural, or historical resources."

Next the BLM and BBC asserted that the drilling company would not be able to "mitigate the impacts of industrial traffic" by implementing "Alternative C: the Transportation Impact Reduction Alternative," that is, by seeking "alternative access routes" to the wells. And finally the DEIS proposed that the BBC, acting in partnership with the BLM, select a "company to monitor the project for compliance with the stipulations and mitigation directives agreed to, and approved in the EIS."

In response to the BLM DEIS, the 9MCC's Impact Research Committee urged its members to respond to the BLM scoping process by addressing these high-priority agenda items. On March 11, 2008, Ivan White, a member of the 9MCC Impact Research Committee, posted his comments in the form of an e-mailed "Action Alert" to the 9MCC membership list, asking them to "please, remember these points as you attend the various public meetings and compose your comments" (due May 1, 2008) regarding the BLM DEIS for the BBC's proposed West Tavaputs Drilling Project. A framing analysis of Ivan White's argument reveals how an initial adversarial rhetoric softened over several years (2004–2008) as a result of the discursive interaction among BLM administrators, public land users of all kinds, and local businesses and laborers impacted in some way by energy extraction in the region.

BEYOND ADVERSARIAL RHETORICS

In "Activist Rhetorics and the Struggle for Meaning: The Case of 'Sustainability' in the Reticulate Public Sphere," Sharon M. Stevens explains how adversarial rhetorics can be instrumental in creating "the possibility for the types of deliberative public spheres" in which contesting groups, in this case pro-drilling and anti-drilling "radical protectionists," "feel the need to engage one another face to face" (311). In contrast to individual scoping letters, which tended to reflect "atomized" meaning-making (Billig 65) and related egocentric emotional appeals, four years after the first DEIS in 2004, the 9MCC e-mail "Action Alerts" relied upon more socially constructed, committee-generated discourse. Moreover, they tended to make more persuasive arguments by extensively researching authoritative legal and historical precedents, comparable BLM EIS processes, and empirical data, and such allocative resources as new lower-impact drilling technologies, and photographic and video recording of cultural resources (Goggin 89–90).

In Ivan White's "Action Alert" argument, March 11, 2008, mentioned above, he initially couches the BLM's past actions in the language of adversarial rhetoric and distrust: BLM "consistently refused to admit that they are responsible" for mitigating "significant impacts"; and "the BLM assured those attending (a public scoping meeting in 2005) that there would be no surface occupancy allows on Federal public lands in Nine Mile Canyon." However, in "all of the alternatives in the Draft EIS, including the Agency (BLM)'s Preferred Alternative, (they) proposed two pump stations to be located in very scenic and archaeologically rich areas of the Canyon, one on federal public land and one on private property (not BBC's property). By doing so, the BLM is violating another public commitment they made in their Draft Resource Management Plan (DRMP) that there would be no surface occupancy allowed on Federal public lands in the bottom of Nine Mile Canyon." White then attributes "bad faith" to the timing of the BLM's DRMP, asking, "Could it be coincidence that the final decision of the DRMP has been timed to allow for some industrial surface occupancy to be approved in the canyon prior to the decision?"

White prioritizes the "major impact" of the West Tavaputs Gas project as "the industrial traffic that goes through Nine Mile Canyon and Cottonwood Canyon (areas of highest concentration of cultural resources, notably ancient ruins and rock art such as "the hunters" rock art panel; see figure 5.1). Furthermore White frames the problem in global and aesthetic terms: We have been recording the impact of the gas drilling on *"the world's longest art gallery,"* using an aesthetic frame by defining the profusion of ancient rock art cultural resources in the canyon as an "art gallery" and "irreplaceable treasure." Moreover, it uses a legal frame by foregrounding 9MC's World Heritage Site status as one of the world's eleven most endangered cultural sites.

SOCIAL MOVEMENT FRAMING STRATEGIES

While relying in part on scripted adversarial rhetoric promoted by various environmental and cultural resource protectionist groups, White transcends the polemic by demonstrating a deeper rhetorical awareness of alternative stakeholders' positions, honed over four years of scoping and public meetings. In this section, I revisit White's "Action Alert" argument, applying what Stevens refers to as the "central tenets of framing theory" in relation to rhetorical analysis (302). Useful to the 9MCC case study, Stevens bases her analysis of "anti-grazing on public lands" rhetoric on "two seminal articles from the late 1980s that "establish the primary structure and vocabulary of framing theory" (302). The first article by David Snow and coauthors, "Frame Alignment Processes, Micromobilization, and Movement Participation" (1986), defines "frames" in the context of social movement scholarship as: "largely cognitive structures that organize meaning and guide interpretation (464).

Figure 5.1 "The Hunters' Panel" in Cottonwood Canyon of Nine Mile Canyon, impacted by industrial traffic, dust, and chemical spray, in Fremont Style, ca. A.D. 500–700. Photo by J.A. McNeil.

According to Stevens, framing functions as a persuasive strategy that reveals "ways that social movement actors and organizations seek to share meanings with the potential actors in their audiences" (302).

In their second article central to Stevens's analysis, "Ideology, Frame Resonance, and Participant Mobilization," David Snow and Robert Benford "focus more explicitly on features that make social movement frames effective, arguing that social movement mobilization often relies on frames needed in order to persuade people to act as part of a social movement collective" (Stevens 302). To build my case for the increased effectiveness of White's persuasive strategies relative to the initial scoping letters of 2004, I focus on three core framing strategies, used in his "Action Alert" comments in March 2008, which Stevens describes as "particularly important in persuasion": (1) diagnostic framing, "interpreting sociomaterial conditions as problems" (302), which means in the 9MC case, the impact of industrial traffic in the canyon on irreplaceable cultural resources; (2) prognostic framing, "inventing and articulating solutions to those problems" (302), which means, in the 9MC case, identifying alternative routes in order to bypass rock art panels and creating an oversight committee to monitor compliance to mitigation procedures; and (3) motivational framing, "giving speakers and their audiences hope that their actions can advance solutions" (302), which means comparing the 9MC and the Pinedale, Wyoming, cases in terms of reliable oversight of compliance to BLM EIS directives.

First, with regard to diagnostic framing, White amplifies and extends the frames related to the destructive impact of industrial traffic on the canyon's cultural resources (ancient ruins and rock art) by asserting that the rock art has already been damaged by dust and chemical dust-suppressant sprays (frame amplification). Moreover, he notes the contingent negative economic impacts on cultural and eco-tourism: "driving sightseers out of the Canyon" (frame extension) and notes that "the Coalition counts of sightseer traffic show a steadily decreasing number of people coming into the Canyon to see the rock art and it is clear that the word has spread about the industrial traffic and the dust." Here White uses appeals to public lands' multiple users with respect to the canyon's pristine and quiet setting, as well as to health concerns related to the documented heavy dust particulates and dust-suppressant toxic chemical spray inhaled by canyon visitors.

By pointing out the negative impact of industrial traffic and dust on tourism in the canyon since 2005 ("when we started to receive reports from sightseers about *dust and industrial traffic* in the Canyon"), White's tacit audience analysis of diverse publics recalls Snow and Benford's emphasis on "frame resonance to account for the effectiveness of particular framing strategies" (Stevens 303, citing Snow and Benford). In this instance White rejects adversarial rhetoric in favor of framing his argument in economic terms, thereby targeting both "for-profit" and "non-profit" stakeholders who share economic interests in preserving the ecology and cultural resources in the canyon.

As my earlier analysis of the scoping letters revealed, middle-ground, for-profit/long-term stakeholders with shared "protectionist" values were ripe for appeals to coalition-building strategies despite divergent motivations to protect the cultural resources in the canyon. Sensitive to the need to cultivate common ground, White adopts a more balanced type of "coalition rhetoric" that speaks to the values and interests of otherwise polarized groups: responsible (sustainable) public land development practices that balance economic interests with environmental and cultural stewardship. By focusing on the impact of "reduction of tourism" (thereby adopting a pro-tourism frame), White shows a tacit awareness of this "middle ground" (economic "protectionist") audience, as well as sensitivity to the concerns raised by Utah citizens regarding their depressed local economies. In doing so, he departs from the atomism of adversarial rhetorics reflected in the 2004 scoping letters, to reflect the "cultural resonance" that results from "the interpersonal dynamics of framing" (Stevens 303). In this vein, Rhys Williams and Timothy Kubal maintain that "movement frames are shaped by, and in turn shape, their cultural environment" (227). As a result of White's exposure to the diverse rhetorics of the scoping process in public meetings, meaning making has become "dialogic" (Bakhtin) and "decentered, taking place in relationships rather than in individual consciousness" (Williams and Kubal 227).

In addition to using diagnostic framing with a heightened audience awareness, White also engages in prognostic framing when proposing that the BLM consider "Alternative C" in the DEIS, that is, alternative routes that bypass rock art panels, and that it look to policy precedents (Pinedale, Wyoming) to monitor compliance with the EIS mitigation directives.

In proposing "Alternative C," White first frames the problem of the adverse effects of industrial traffic, dust, and chemical suppressants (diagnostic framing) by blaming the BLM for failing to accept responsibility "for seeing . . . all significant impacts no matter where they occur or who does the impact." Next, using the authority of legal precedent, he compares the BBC drilling in Nine Mile Canyon case of 2004–2008 (pending) to that of the *Calvert Cliffs' Coordinating Commission, Inc. v. United States Atomic Energy Commission* of the 1970s whereby "the federal lead agency (BLM) was required to see that all significant impacts were mitigated.[5] If the impacts cannot be mitigated then the proposed action cannot be carried out."

White uses this legal precedent as evidence in support of his claim that in the Nine Mile case involving the Dry Canyon Compressor Station pollution (visual, sound, or chemical), the BLM is "refusing to admit that they are responsible" for mitigating the station's negative impacts on the cultural and ecological resources in the canyon bottom. He extends this legal frame to include the BLM's responsibility to mitigate all (negative) impacts, which "applies not only to the Dry Canyon Compressor Station, but also to the traffic impact on the Gate Canyon, Nine Mile Canyon, and Cottonwood

Canyon Roads, as well as the impact on any of the cultural resources of the area the West Tavaputs."

While failing to acknowledge the problem of underfunding and understaffing from the BLM perspective, White again blames the BLM DEIS for "offering less protection for Nine Mile Canyon cultural resources" than they currently enjoy. He goes on to point out that "one alternative offers lip service to have the county construct pull-outs and working with BBC to do signs and trails at the identified sites from the Special Recreation and Cultural Area Management Plan." Despite the very real problem of BLM funding cuts, he argues that "this is only one-third of the proposed plan, which should also include a full-time archaeologist, full-time recreation planner and staff 'to teach proper etiquette' while around cultural resources during the visitor season, and full-time law enforcement in the canyon."

With a more effective framing strategy than the playing the "blame game," White posits a "reasonable" alternative" in his counterargument to the BLM's claim that they are unable to adopt "Alternative C" (alternate routes). His complaint lies in the fact that "unfortunately, the BLM has eliminated the alternative access routes in EIS Section 2.8.6 (See DEIS "Alternative Access Routes," chapter 2, section 2–149).

White argues in favor of a bypass route, suggesting that there is no acceptable level of industrial traffic in the canyon bottom: "In reality, the only way to save the canyon from the traffic is to use bypass roads that will keep traffic away from the Nine Mile and Cottonwood Canyons." In a counterclaim, he proposes using Trail Canyon as an "alternative Access Route," actually a win-win solution, allowing for gas drilling while virtually eliminating the destructive impact on the dense concentration of rock art in the canyon bottom along Minnie Maud and Nine Mile Creeks.

Again, using the authority of legal precedents, he argues that this option was illegally eliminated from the BLM EIS Section 2.8.6. He writes that "Trail Canyon is a feasible and reasonable alternative, in fact, having gotten its name from the time when it 'was the access route in and out of Nine Mile Canyon.'" In fact, Trail Canyon "comes to Nine Mile Canyon opposite the entrance to Harmon Canyon Road which is the main access to the west side of the gas field on the Tavaputs," thereby lending itself to a bypass road system.

In addition to his persuasive use of diagnostic and prognostic framing strategies, White offers a hopeful solution to the problem of establishing reliable oversight for compliance to BLM EIS directives. According to the BLM DEIS, February 2008, the federal agency together with the BBC would select a company to oversee the mitigation and monitoring process. Clearly White, the 9MCC, and other "protectionist" groups found this proposal unacceptable.

Evoking the specter of corruption and broken promises associated with the BLM Pinedale Field Office Resource Management Plan (RMP) in Pinedale, Wyoming, White affirms the polarization and distrust between "radical protectionists" and "radical development" (corporate, federal) groups. At the same time, however, the Pinedale case serves as a positive model for reliable (trustworthy) oversight of the mitigation and monitoring process. Functioning as a motivational frame, White uses the Pinedale solution as a counterexample to the suspect BLM-BBC offer to select their own oversight company. Like the Pinedale case, White offers his audience hope that reliable oversight can be achieved:

> What is required is an oversight committee like the one set up in Wyoming because of the corruption in the Pinedale BLM office. The members should include stakeholders like BLM, hunters, property owners, the Nine Mile Coalition, Carbon County, the State Historic Preservation Office and others. The monitoring company would report to the oversight committee to ensure compliance with mitigation requirements (White).

Cause for optimism in the WTP development case, the company that the BBC selected, Preservar, Inc., conducted a study of the possible effects of the industrial traffic dust and found that "the kick-up dust that lands on the rock art panel creates a very serious conservation problem" (Stark).

Looking back over the EIS scoping process and resulting 9MCC (activist movement) "Action Alerts" spanning 2004 to 2008, I found the tendency to engage in "centered meaning-making" and atomized concerns. These, however, gradually gave way to more nuanced, middle-ground positions and burgeoning social alliances. If Ivan White's interactive meaning-making (extending the meaning of "significant impacts" on the cultural resources to appeal to a wider audience) and persuasive framing strategies are any indication, then palpable progress had been made toward enacting the ideals of a deliberative democracy. We are left with the sense that coalition building is in progress, that legal resources can be marshaled to preserve the cultural resources on our public lands, and that an oversight committee will represent the diverse users of 9MC.

As Gerald Hauser and Chantal Benoit-Barne aptly point out, "the grassroots resources of civil society are the major cultural resource for deliberative democracy to thrive provided we nurture its rhetorical inflections" (261). In the end, the resolution to the issue of responsible public land use hinges on the public trust. Hauser and Benoit-Barnes identify "the central problem a deliberative democracy must meet if it is to flourish under conditions of political pluralism: the problem of trust" (261). In the context of the 9MC case, "trust" is a multivalent term, referring to an action (to trust), an agent or agency (one who is trustworthy), and an object (a treasure trust) with which we are entrusted for future generations.

CONCLUSION

In closing we must ask: Is the BLM EIS public scoping process an effective deliberative tool by which to explore socially constructed meanings of responsible public land use? This research revealed a discursive progression over a four-year period (2004 to 2008), beginning with the stridently adversarial rhetorics of numerous stakeholders expressed in the public scoping letters. However, from these adversarial rhetorics emerged an increasingly nuanced and deliberative perspective, as well as a more "centrist" voice from the heteroglossic voices of the diverse public land users. Possible solutions also emerged from this deliberative process, including forming an oversight committee composed of diverse publics invested in the use and preservation of 9MC. In addition, new partnerships between federal agencies and activist and advocacy groups (e.g., 9MCC, URARA, and NTHP) aspire to assist with the daunting task of inventorying cultural resources on public lands. Current technological innovations in rock art recording, such as URARA Education Chair Diane Orr's Web-based "Visionscape," a 360-degree Hulcherama camera for documenting rock art images in the canyon, promise to expedite an overwhelming inventorying process.

Finally, in response to Killingsworth and Palmer's question, "Can a truly democratic public discourse emerge among conflicting traditions and interests?" (191), my answer would be cautiously optimistic. In the discourse of public scoping letters we see an emergent "narrative paradigm" as public land users challenge the "objectivist prose" of the EIS instrumental discourse by "reasserting their own stories against a discourse that . . . violates what might be called the narrative structure of their lifeworlds" (191). Although inherently adversarial, the WTP EIS public scoping process appears to have provided the kairotic condition key to opening the rhetorical space wherein contested meanings concerning public land use practices could be vetted, examined, and negotiated, thereby cultivating deliberative alternatives across the rhetorical landscape necessary to promote responsible (sustainable) public land use policies.

GLOSSARY OF ACRONYMS

ACEC:	Area of Critical Environmental Concern
ARPA:	Archaeological Resource Protection Act
BBC:	Bill Barrett Corporation
BLM:	Bureau of Land Management
DEIS:	Draft Environmental Impact Statement
DOI:	Department of the Interior
DRMP:	Draft Resource Management Plan
EIS:	Environmental Impact Statement
FLPMA:	Federal Land Policy and Management Act
MLA:	Mineral Leasing Act
NAGPRA:	Native American Grave Protection and Repatriation Act
NEPA:	National Environmental Policy Act
9MC:	Nine Mile Canyon (Utah)

9MCC: Nine Mile Canyon Coalition
NTHP: National Trust for Historic Preservation
NOI: Notice of Intent
RMP: Resource Management Plan
URARA: Utah Rock Art Research Association
WSA: Wilderness Study Area
WTP: West Tavaputs Plateau (eastern Utah)

NOTES

1. See Killingsworth and Palmer 2000, 31–36, on the evolution of the "environmental" movement, from its neo-Romantic (transcendentalist) "wilderness protectionist" roots to the "reform environmentalists" of the Sierra Club and the problematic use of these labels.
2. I have adopted the labels "developmentalist" for pro-drilling advocates and "preservationist" for anti-drilling from Killingsworth and Palmer 2000, 38–40.
3. For a syntactic and stylistic analysis of the EIS "objectivist prose" in contrast to scoping letters as a narrative form, see Killingsworth and Palmer 172–74, 181–86.
4. This debate centers on whether the conflicting values and interests polarizing institutional and vernacular discourses can create a democratic "discursive arena," as Hauser claims (89). Whereas Killingsworth and Palmer suggest that the EIS is a form of "instrumental discourse" that tends to silence or marginalize public dissent (168–69), my research reveals an alternative outcome. In the case of WTP EIS, the scoping process in isolation did fail to foster a dialogic exchange of views; however, over time it initiated coalition building in the context of social activist groups' "action alerts" and public meetings between the BLM and public land users.
5. *Calvert Cliffs' Coordinating Committee, Inc. v. United States Atomic Energy Commission* is described as " a seminal case in the area of environmental law; it played a crucial role in furthering the goals of the burgeoning environmental movement of the 1960s and 70s (D.C. Cir. 1971). It represents the first time that the courts interpreted the National Environmental Policy Act (NEPA) as creating a cause of action against federal agencies that do not comply with the Act's directives" (Sally Horton, http://www.kentlaw.edu).

WORKS CITED

Bakhtin, Mikhail M. "Discourse in the Novel." *The Dialogic Imagination*. Ed. Michael Holquist. Trans. Caryl Emerson and Michael Holquist. Austin: U. of Texas, 1981. 259–422.

Billig, Michael. "Rhetorical Psychology, Ideological Thinking, and Imagining Nationhood." *Social Movements and Culture*. Ed. Hank Johnson and Bert Klandermans. Minneapolis: U. of Minneapolis P, 1995. 64–81.

Bureau of Land Management, Price Field Office. Draft Environmental Impact Statement, Oct. 20, 2007 http://www.blm.gov/ut/st/en/fo/price/energy/Oil_Gas/Draft_EIS.html.

Bureau of Land Management, *Uinta Basin Natural Gas Development Project* (2006), Oct. 20, 2007 http://www.blm.gov/utah/vernal/gasco/index.htm.

Bureau of Land Management, Vernal Field Office. "Gasco's Well Drilling Project: Riverbend Unit Public Comments." UT-080–05-322, May 2007.

Bureau of Land Management, "Volunteers," 20 Oct 2007 http://www.blm.gov/co/st/en/BML_Resources/volunteers.print.html.

Bureau of Land Management, West Tavaputs Drilling Proposal (2004), Oct. 20, 2007 http://www.ut.blm.gov/westtavaputs/fonsidecision.htm.

Bureau of Land Management, "What are the Public Lands?" Oct. 20, 2007 http://www.blm.gov/nhp/info/whatare.html.

Environmental Protection Agency (EPA), "Federal Register Environmental Documents: Notice of Intent to Prepare an Environmental Impact Statement (EIS) and to Conduct Public Scoping for the West Tavaputs Natural Gas Full Field Development Plan, Carbon and Duchesne Counties, UT," Mar. 10, 2007 http://www.epa.gov/EPA-IMPACT/2005/August/Day/i16953.htm.

Environmental Working Group (EWG), "Who Owns the West? Oil & Gas Leases in America's West," Oct. 20, 2007 http://www.ewg.org/oil_and_gas/printer-friendly.php.

Giddens, Anthony. "Structuralism, Post-Structuralism and the Production of Culture." *Social Theory Today*. Ed. Anthony Giddens and Jonathan Turner. Palo-Alto: Stanford UP, 1987. 195–223.

Goggin, Maureen Daly. "Visual Rhetoric in Pens of Steel and Inks of Silk: Challenging the Great Visual/Verbal Divide." *Defining Visual Rhetorics*. Eds. C. Hill and M. Helmers. Mahwah, NJ: Earlbaum, 2004. 87–110.

Hauser, Gerald A. "Rhetorical Democracy and Civic Engagement." *Rhetorical Democracy*. Eds. Hauser, Gerald and Amy Grim. Mahwah, NJ: Earlbaum, 2004. 1–14.

———. *Vernacular Voices: The Rhetoric of Publics and Public Spheres*. Columbia: U of South Carolina P, 1999.

Hauser, Gerald A., and Chantal Benoit-Barne. "Reflections on Rhetoric, Deliberative Democracy, Civil Society, and Trust." *Rhetoric and Public Affairs* 5.2 (2002): 261–75.

Horton, Sally. On *Calvert Cliffs' Coordinating Committee, Inc. v. United States Atomic Energy Commission*, May 18, 2008 http://www.kentlaw.edu.

Kaufer, David S., and Kathleen M. Carley. *Communication at a Distance: The Influence of Print on Sociocultural Organization and Change*. Hillsdale, NJ: Earlbaum, 1993.

Killingworth, M. Jimmie, and Jacqueline S. Palmer. *Ecospeak: Rhetoric and Environmental Politics in America*, Carbondale: Southern Illinois UP, 1992.

Kress, Gunther. "Multimodality." *Multiliteracies: Literary Learning and the Design of Social Futures*. Ed. B. Cope and M. Kalantzis. New York: Routledge, 2000. 182–202.

National Trust For Historic Preservation (NTHP). "Cultural Resources: On the Bureau of Land Management Public Lands: An Assessment and Needs Analysis." Prepared by T. Destry Jarvis, May 2006, Mar.10, 2007 http://www.nationaltrust.org.

National Trust For Historic Preservation (NTHP). "Nine Mile Canyon at Risk," 10 Mar. 2007 http://www.preservationnation.org/take-action/advocacy-center/action- alerts/nine-mile-canyon.html.

Nine Mile Canyon Coalition, May 18, 2008 http://www.ninemilecanyoncoalition.org.

Orr, Diane "Visionscape," Mar. 10, 2007 http://www.dianeorr.com/index.html.

Snow, David A., et al. "Frame Alignment Processes, Micromobilization, and Movement Participation." *American Sociological Review* 51 (1986): 464–81.

Snow, David A. and Robert D. Benford "Ideology, Frame Resonance, and Participant Mobilization." *International Social Movement Research* 1 (1988): 197–217.

Stark, Mike. "Drilling may imperil petroglyphs." *Boulder Camera*, May 29, 2008, 6B.
Stevens, Sharon M. Activist Rhetorics and the Struggle for Meaning: The Case of 'Sustainability' in the Reticulate Public Sphere." *Rhetoric Review*, 25 (2006): 297–315.
Travis, W. *New Geographies of the American West: Land Use and the Changing Patterns of Place.* Washington, DC: Island P, 2007.
Utah Rock Art Research Association (URARA), May 18, 2008 http://www.utahrockart.org.
Vestiges, monthly newsletter of URARA, the Utah Rock Art Research Association, May 18, 2008 http://www.utahrockart.org/pubs/index.shtml#vestiges.
Williams, Rhys, and Timothy Kubal. "Movement Frames and the Cultural Environment: Resonance, Failure, and the Boundaries of the Legitimate." *Research in Social Movements, Conflicts and Change* 21 (1999): 225–48.

6 From Oral Tradition to Legal Documents
Words to Protect the Headwaters of the San Antonio River

Sally E. Said

When modern Coahuiltecans, descendents of Native Americans who lived in southern Texas and northern Mexico before the arrival of the Spanish, mention in song or ritual the name Yanaguana, they are calling from ancestral memory a story linking them to the springs at the headwaters of the San Antonio River. In the words of Keith H. Basso, author of *Wisdom Sits in Places,* they also engage in place-making:

> Long before the advent of literacy, to say nothing of "history" as an academic discipline, places served humankind as durable symbols of distant events and as indispensable aids for remembering and imagining them—and this convenient arrangement, ancient but not outmoded, is with us still today. If place-making is a way of constructing the past, a venerable means of *doing* human history, it is also a way of constructing social traditions and, in the process, personal and social identities. We *are,* in a sense, the place-worlds we imagine. (7)

As the name Yanaguana (up-flowing water of the spirit) spread to the songs of other native groups, sometimes memory of the location was lost, but recent retellings have given new life to the myth, and thus to the identity that the myth engenders (Pérez).

Place-making is one strategy to assure sustainability, to create a relationship between a people and a place that allows for continuance of a culture in collaboration with the natural world. If we are, as Basso suggests, "the place-worlds we imagine," then keeping these place-worlds intact is essential to the continuity of a people who imagine them. It requires mutual care: in this case, the headwaters will make life possible for the people, but the people must respect the water and use it wisely. Place-making is a synchronic process, one that erases the time elapsed in favor of a present connection, and it exists through story.

In contrast to the Native Americans, for whom the land was a part of their identity, a series of subsequent occupants—the Spanish, the Anglo-Texans, the Sisters of Charity of the Incarnate Word—did not engage in place-making. They viewed the headwaters of the San Antonio River primarily as instrumental to their goals of empire, economic expansion, or religious service, respectively. Each successive group rewrote the history of events, in a diachronic view, linear and analytical, selecting a chain of cause and effect to explain each change as inevitable and flowing naturally from the circumstances that preceded it. The Spanish were destined to find this land and expand their empire; the Anglo-Texans laid claim to it as part of a manifest destiny of westward expansion; and the Sisters of Charity were called from France to help the poor, and they purchased this land to further their mission. The selective lens allowed the author to distance readers from events and to experience them as object, something to be viewed and understood. It is this diachronic habit of mind in which events take precedence over attachment to place, that renders place-making difficult for Euro-Americans.

In the present, we have come full circle, to a need to reestablish a connection to the land in order to save it and our relationship to it. Noting the danger that development posed to the remaining urban forest and headwaters springs, a small group of faculty at University of the Incarnate Word (UIW) initiated the Headwaters Project in 2002 to "restore our connection to the land" (logo, Headwaters Coalition Web site). Yet despite a common purpose, the faculty members, the Sisters of Charity of the Incarnate Word, and a small number of community individuals who came to be involved, found themselves having difficulty defining the problems and planning to solve them because our approaches came from different academic disciplines and cultural perspectives. That is, we belonged to different discourse communities, used to the presuppositions and background information that we shared with like colleagues, and using particular frames to approach the land and decision making concerning its future (Little, Jordens, and Sayers 73). We found we were engaged in something of a language war (Lakoff 50), each group insisting on the terminology and procedures of its discourse community. This chapter examines differences in language employed historically to memorialize the San Antonio River headwaters and surrounding land in story, to depict the land as seen by newcomers, and to protect and control it through legal documents. It also traces the process of weaving a common narrative necessary to the renewed place-making activities of the Headwaters Project.

Although this chapter is primarily an account of how one place has been treated rhetorically through time, it also raises theoretical questions concerning the hybridity of approaches in the present. Carl G. Vaught observes in his *Metaphor, Analogy, and the Place of Places*:

> One of the most obvious features about the concept of place is that it displays temporal, spatial, and eternal dimensions. Places are to be characterized in terms of the past they presuppose, the present they instantiate, and the future toward which they are oriented. . . . It is

also important to notice that time has taken precedence over space and eternity in modern and contemporary philosophy. (8–9)

The dominance of diachronic over synchronic views of the land historically is accompanied by a third element, the blending of approaches by academic disciplines and involved communities to the question of the future of the headwaters. The integrated (synthetic, synchronic) relationship to the environment more typical of the arts and humanities opposes the analytical (distanced, diachronic) methods of scientists, whose praxis (albeit caring and hands-on) is an application and a testing of theory. The required observational distance limits the experience of the land to those (largely physical) aspects important to the theory. Between these two perspectives we have that of the Sisters of Charity of the Incarnate Word, whose view of the land has changed over time from instrumental use to stewardship, and who have acted as intermediaries between the two academic positions. We also have Native American voices that have begun to inform our discussions. A hybrid form of place-making is at hand: in Vaught's terms, the process of recovering the sense of connectedness in the present which we instantiate, to incorporate the eternal sacred, while blending these considerations with the practical aspects of scientific ecological restoration to assure the future of the headwaters.

The headwaters of the San Antonio River include the Olmos Creek stream system and its catchment basin of thirty-four square miles. (Halstead). The lowest portion of the headwaters is the main spring complex known as the Blue Hole, situated in the Olmos Basin in San Antonio, Texas, on land adjacent to the University of the Incarnate Word and deeded in 2008 by the Sisters of Charity of the Incarnate Word to a conservation nonprofit, the Headwaters Coalition. Locally the Blue Hole springs (sometimes including Olmos Creek) are referred to as "the headwaters," thus the name given to the coalition. In this essay, "headwaters" will retain this local meaning. The creation of the Headwaters Coalition is only the most recent in a series of actions throughout history to use words (in this case a legal document) to protect the springs and to honor their centrality and importance to a people. When the springs flow, all is well. When they do not, there is concern. It is then that sacred words are spoken, legal words are written, to bring about change, if not in the Blue Hole directly, then in the ways of the people who have endangered its flow by excessive water use or other imbalance.

The Blue Hole is the ecological centerpiece of the Olmos Basin, and was the site of Native American encampments as early as 11,000 years ago. The headwaters were the origin of the water sent by *acequia* to the Spanish missions downriver, and the main source of water for the city of San Antonio until the late 1890s, when artesian wells tapped the Edwards Aquifer directly. The Blue Hole has been the focus of concern as a reflection of the ecological health of the area in more recent times. The emergence of this special site began some 300 million years ago, with the collision of the North American landmass with another to the south, forming the Ouachita Mountains along the line of contact. Visible as mountains in Arkansas and Oklahoma, the Ouachitas in Texas were worn down by erosion and pressed downward by the weight of the limestone deposited in the Gulf Coast Basin (Harrigan 138), leaving the Balcones Escarpment to rise above the Balcones fault zone, extending from Waco in the northeast to Del Rio in the southwest. Blackland Prairie to the southeast, at about 700 feet above mean sea level (MSL), abuts the limestone escarpment and the Edwards Plateau, at around 1,100 feet above MSL. The Balcones Escarpment is a climatic and cultural divide, marking "the boundary between the cotton economy of the Old South and the cattle economy of the Old West" (Abbott and Woodruff, preface). The Olmos Basin, where the Olmos Creek crosses the Balcones Fault, is the location of many springs, including the Blue Hole. Because the Olmos Basin lies in a geographical and biotic transition zone, the area has been called "the biological hub" of the northern half of this hemisphere (Stothert 3).

The earliest humans to wander across this land and, in the end, decide to stay, were the Native Americans, as reported by Karen Stothert in her 1989 survey of the archaeology and early history of the area (7). Artifacts, including Clovis, Folsom, and Plainview projectile points, have placed Paleo-Indians in the region at least as early as 11,000 years ago (Chandler 11–19). The first hunter-gatherers came to hunt the plentiful bison, deer, bear, and occasional mammoths that lived in the area at the end of the last ice age. Several Paleo-Indian archaeological sites have yielded stone projectile points, tools, and lithic debris; scattered deer and bison bones; and burned hearth stones. Other excavations nearby have revealed remnants of settlements and burials from later periods, up to the time of Spanish occupation. Because of the many sites in the Olmos Basin, identified and excavated by archaeologists from Incarnate Word and the University of Texas at San Antonio, the "Source of the River Archeological District, Bexar County, Texas" was entered in the National Register of Historic Places in 1978, placing the cultural resources under the protection of the 1966 Historic Preservation Act. The district is also registered as State Archeological Landmark #108, under the Antiquities Code of Texas (Stothert 82).

The value placed by ancient native peoples on the headwaters was probably in keeping with a native integration with the natural world. In general, for native peoples, all beings (including themselves, plants, animals, rocks, streams, clouds, and mountains) are sentient, interdependent, and spiritually connected. Native American scholar Vine Deloria Jr. explains about the elders whose stories he tells in *The World We Used to Live In*:

> By observing the behavior and growth of other organic forms of life, they could see that a benign personal energy flowed through everything and undergirded the physical world. They understood that their task

was to fit into the physical world in the most constructive manner and to establish relationships with the higher power, or powers, that created and sustained the universe. They sought to learn a way of living that would most efficiently accomplish these tasks. This posture was not unique to any tribe; it was generally the way Indians of all tribes described the mysterious reality that affected their lives. (xxv)

In Deloria's view, traditional Native Americans made decisions regarding the land from a philosophical standpoint of integration with their surroundings. The environment wasn't a "wild" place to them; it was sacred, it was mysterious, it was home.

The type of involvement of a native people with the land is a form of praxis. The connectedness is primary, and learning that follows from it is encoded in the form of oral tradition that allows others to participate in the reality of historical events recast in narrative mode. Acoma author Simon Ortiz observes through the words of a character in his short story "What Indians Do":

The storyteller participates in the story with those that are listening. In the same way, the listeners are taking part in the story. The story includes them in. You see, storytelling is more like an event. The story is not just a story then. It's occurring; it's happening; it's coming into being. (130)

Thus, the time frame is shifted, and the audience's view becomes synchronous with the time of occurrence.

The stories of the native people that we have begun to hear in relation to the springs are from the Coahuiltecans, who arrived late in the prehistoric period and whose descendents still live in the region. The Coahuiltecan people, a cover term for small, related bands, spoke a language isolate, possibly a sister language to Hokan, spoken in California, according to a report by the National Park Service, which oversees four of the five Spanish colonial missions in San Antonio (Thoms 1–2). A simplified version of their founding story, "Yanaguana" was given by local Coahuiltecans to Theatre Arts Department faculty member Margaret Mitchell (also part of the Headwaters Project) to serve as the basis of a play she was writing. In this narrative a woman had been traveling across the scrublands of southern Texas for some time with her band, without sufficient water. She went ahead purposely, searching for water because her people were dying. Three times she collapsed and gave up. Three times she heard a whistle, which was the great Creator telling her to rise, and giving her further direction. She was led to a limestone rock, and from the rock an anhinga sprang into flight. Water poured from the rock, the bird flew some distance, and the river formed as the bird flew. The woman drank, then went to get her people. The people were sustained, and traveled further and found peyote.

At the time of the woman's death, the bird returned and flew through her body, so that she became the spirit of the water (Mitchell). Her name, Yanaguana (up-flowing water of the spirit), was given to the springs and to the river, and she was thought to reappear occasionally as "the Blue Lady." For the Coahuiltecans, the water of the springs in the region became essential, and they developed a special ceremony performed by women and used to this day, to take water from the springs for religious use (Pérez). Until the 1920s other native groups, such as the Poncas in Oklahoma, would visit the Headwaters (Stothert 73–76), one of several stops in their pilgrimage to the peyote gardens at Mirando City near Laredo (Pérez).

It was Coahuiltecan reverence for the water known as Yanaguana that has passed into the tribal lore of many indigenous groups who traveled through the area, including the Mescalero Apache, and that can be found in Native American Church songs today. One such chant shared by native healer Masauki includes some Spanish (to be repeated four times):

Yanaguana hey, yana yana, wi ana.
Yo y tú, Yanaguana hey, yana hey, hey ney.

Whereas the native inhabitants of the headwaters identified closely with the land and water, the utility of the headwaters to the Spanish was to enable empire, religious conversion, and commerce. The headwaters permitted New Spain to protect its northern frontier from incursions by the French, to convert local Indians to Christianity and make of them a labor force for the five missions, and to develop a profitable agricultural trade. Cabeza de Vaca visited the region between 1528 and 1535 and described the natives' varied diet, movements in search of food, and trade goods. In 1691, Don Domingo Terán de los Ríos and Father Damian Massanet were the first Spaniards to visit the headwaters of the river. Bison were abundant in the area, and it was an old buffalo road that first afforded the Spanish passage through the wooded Edwards Aquifer area to the north and east. Massanet remarked that all Indians spoke a common language, presumably Coahuilteco, thought to have served as a lingua franca as far northeast as the Guadalupe River, where the language switched to dialects mutually intelligible with the language of the Chomas or Jumanes. By the end of the seventeenth century, one Coahuiltecan group, the Payayas, were still living in temporary camps, although they, like the other bands, were in the process of being absorbed into the missions located further south, including San Antonio de Valero, now known as the Alamo (Stothert 45–53).

Serious Spanish colonization did not begin until the early eighteenth century, and it depended on the availability of plentiful water. The headwaters area served as a secure campsite for soldiers pushing the Spanish frontier further north and east to counter French expansion from Louisiana into East Texas. A story from those times, similar to that of the story of Yanaguana, tells of a group of conquistadors accompanying Father Antonio Margil de

Jesús and other priests. All suffered from thirst. They saw a vision of green in the distance and rode toward it, where the priests prayed for water. Their prayers were answered as they pulled at the roots of a wild grapevine and "to their great marvel, there came a bold flow of pure water," thus in legend establishing the Blue Hole springs (Stothert 55).

The Blue Hole and other area springs continued to provide water to the Spanish. As described in I. Waynne Cox's *The Spanish Acequias of San Antonio*, *acequias* (stone-lined ditches) and aqueducts were built to take the pure water for drinking, household use, and irrigation from the Blue Hole springs and the nearby San Pedro Springs to the civilian community, the presidio, and the five missions. For more than 150 years, San Antonio depended for water on this fifty-mile network of irrigation ditches designed by Spanish engineers using Roman and Moorish technology. One of the *acequias*, irrigating lands near Mission Espada, remains in use to this day. Limestone quarried just to the south of the Blue Hole provided stone to line the *acequias*, and the nearby grassland was declared an *ejido* (commons), or publicly held land for common grazing. A network of *acequias* that brought the waters of life to their homes and partitioned agricultural lands allowed Spanish presence, making San Antonio habitable for them. Laws were constantly being revised to protect the purity of *acequia* water, requiring regular cleaning of the channels and prohibiting the disposal of sewage, garbage, or other debris into irrigation ditches (Cox 38–51).

After the ending of the Texas War of Secession from Mexico in 1836 placed the headwaters in the hands of the city of San Antonio, controlled by Anglos and Tejanos (Texans of Mexican descent), there was still great fear of Indians—Comanches and Apaches—raiding from the north and west. The land and its springs served to sustain the defensive effort. In the 1840s, Texas Army troops were stationed on this ground to protect the city, both from Indians and from a feared attempt by Mexico to retake the territory. Troops included mounted militia and later the newly formed Texas Rangers, which replaced the Texas Army in 1841 (Stothert 59–60). In 1849 a cholera epidemic, abetted in part by contaminated *acequia* water, killed some 600 San Antonians, including many soldiers. In 1869 it was another cholera outbreak that brought the first Incarnate Word Sisters to San Antonio from France, heeding the call of Bishop Claude Dubuis to provide medical assistance to the poor, as described in Sister Margaret Patrice Slattery's history of the Sisters of Charity of the Incarnate Word, *Promises to Keep* (1–10).

If Spain had used headwaters land and water as a means to establish empire, convert the native peoples, and protect boundaries, under the new republic, then state, of Texas, San Antonio leaders saw the potential for amassing individual wealth through sales of the land and a fee charged for providing water to the citizens. The headwaters passed from the public to the private domain, and the water it produced became a commodity. In 1852, money-strapped San Antonio sold the headwaters, sole source of the city's drinking water, to city alderman J. R. Sweet, who built a house on adjoining property and acquired more land. Sweet sold the springs and land to businessman George W. Brackenridge in 1869. After several years of public controversy over private ownership, Brackenridge tried to sell the headwaters back to the city, but they could not agree on price. He then purchased the nearby pumping station and waterworks, and acquired more riverfront property, establishing the first closed-system water distribution network in 1878, taking water from the headwaters and conveying it to a holding tank. Another innovation that helped to meet the city's increased demand for water due to post–Civil War immigration and the arrival of the railroads in 1877 was the drilling of artesian wells in 1895, lowering the water table and making the question of spring ownership less critical. After the death of his mother in 1886, for whom he had built an addition to the Sweet house, Brackenridge had decided to relocate (Slattery 79). He finally sold about 283 acres that had become his Head of the River Estate to the Incarnate Word Sisters in 1897, and two years later conveyed to the city 320 acres for Brackenridge Park, situated south of the Incarnate Word property. According to Dick McCracken, in his article "Rip Van River: From Springs to Riverwalk," Brackenridge sold his home because he could not bear to watch the drying up of the river, which he assumed was permanent: "I have seen this bold, bubbling, laughing river dwindle and fade away. . . . This river is my child and it is dying and I cannot stay here to see its last gasps. . . . I must go" (33).

By the time the Incarnate Word Sisters acquired the rural property, the spring flow had resumed, and the land served them as home to their motherhouse and academy. Beginning in the early 1900s, San Antonio expanded northward to surround the headwaters land and the nearby suburb of Alamo Heights. Yet the Blue Hole and adjacent acreage remained a park-like preserve for much of the twentieth century. Part of the land was cleared for farming activities, which were mostly abandoned by mid-century, and in the early 1960s the last rural remnant, a dairy, was closed (Ryan). Through the years, parcels of the land were sold: in 1923 for building of the Olmos Dam, in 1966 for Highway 281 right-of-way (after bitter opposition by the Sisters), and for commercial development on the margins at various times, the money being needed to support the Sisters' work. These sales left about 155 acres, including the main campus of the University of the Incarnate Word, property belonging to the Sisters' retirement community, a few acres reserved for future development, and some fifty-three acres of urban forest, deeded to the Headwaters Coalition for a nature sanctuary in 2008.

Drought has always plagued the area, and it may have been temporary dormancy of the springs that allowed the miracles recorded by Coahuiltecans and Spaniards to stimulate spring flow where none was visible at the time. According to McCracken, the longest period in recorded history during which the springs were dry began in the 1950s. Water remained at 612 feet above MSL, well below the 678 feet necessary for the headwaters springs to flow, while deep wells downriver kept water in the downtown Riverwalk tourist attraction. It was not until the early 1970s that rains brought back the springs at the Blue Hole (McCracken 30).

After the arrival of President Louis J. Agnese Jr. at Incarnate Word College (later University of the Incarnate Word) in 1985, there began a program of expansion, although undertaken with care for archaeological and environmental concerns (McCracken 34). However, it was not unusual for environmentalists on and off campus to question the wisdom of the development. An example of opposition, two articles by Bryce Milligan appeared in the *San Antonio Express-News* in 1986. In the first, a feature article on December 7, a detailed record of his walk through the property, Milligan describes the headwaters area as a nearly pristine urban forest. One puzzling photo bears the caption "Bulldozer fells forest near downtown" (G1). One might have assumed it was a misplaced photo, as Milligan had mentioned no forest felling. However, in a subsequent article on December 17, he explains that the part about the "30–50 acres, depending on who you talk to" that had been bulldozed flat and covered with fill dirt to provide for sports fields, had been cut from his original article and that he was "personally horrified by what many consider to be the rape of a much treasured natural resource" (B6).

In the mid-nineties, with the water table lowered by drought and overuse, the springs again went dry. In 2000, representatives of the Coalhuitecan tribal group performed a ceremony beside the Blue Hole, so that the springs might resume flowing and restore the land. They had just shared their ancient myth of Yanaguana with the UIW Theatre Arts Department for enactment in a series called *Land Dreamings,* performed near the Blue Hole. After their ceremony, rains came, and the springs began to flow and continued flowing for six years. It was during this green time in 2002–2003 that our small group of activists on campus worked to organize the Blue Hole Project, later the Headwaters Project.

When worldviews exist in temporal sequence, it seems as if the newest might replace the one before it, but in reality older layers remain, sometimes marginalized, sometimes invisible for a while. We find members of the wider community holding values in keeping with those of Native Americans, individuals who see the land and water as part of their rich Hispanic cultural heritage along with the *acequias* and missions, Texas "patriots" who view 1836 as the year "we took it all," developers concerned with economic sustainability through expansion, and more recently, environmentalists of various persuasions seeking to restore and preserve the land. The last to acquire the land through purchase, the Sisters of Charity of the Incarnate Word, have arrived at a new understanding of their responsibility for the care, or stewardship, of the headwaters, reflected in their sponsorship of a nature sanctuary.

On February 1, 2008, fifty-three acres, including the Blue Hole, were placed under the protection of the Headwaters Coalition, "a non-profit, sponsored ministry of the Congregation of the Sisters of Charity of the Incarnate Word, dedicated to spreading an ecological ethic" (Headwaters Coalition Web site). This was the culmination of a multiyear effort to form the Headwaters Project, to define its mission and plan of action, and to create the nonprofit Headwaters Coalition, accomplished in 2006. The earlier Blue Hole Project, initiated by faculty in 2002, had drawn up plans centering on the Blue Hole, to include ecological restoration, historical preservation, and cultural and spiritual interpretation. The group planted trees for Earth Day 2002, but lacked funding to carry out larger projects. In December of 2002, as one of the Blue Hole Project organizers, I discussed our plans with a biology faculty member, Ben McPherson, who had a dream of creating an arboretum, and we decided to collaborate. On Earth Day of 2003, Dr. Bob Connelly, a philosopher who was then acting dean of science, mathematics, and engineering, assumed leadership of the efforts and brought three interest groups together: science faculty who were conducting water quality surveys, GPS mapping, and other class-related activities on the land; arts and humanities faculty who were interested in incorporating spiritual, historic, and cultural elements in restoration and documentation efforts; and the Sisters of Charity of the Incarnate Word, represented by Sister Helena Monahan, congregational coordinator. Members of the wider community were also invited to join. The development of the Headwaters Project is further described in a 2004 article, "The Birth of the Incarnate Word Headwaters Project" (Connelly et al.).

The article weaves together contributions reflecting the diverse views and academic backgrounds of the six coauthors, but also reveals an issue that had divided the Headwaters Project group in early meetings: a separation of the spiritual, cultural, and historical interests from the scientific, downplaying the former in favor of restoration ecology as the primary methodology and an arboretum as the major outcome. The two main goals are summarized: "to restore the land around the Blue Hole as a special gathering place, and to create an arboretum on the rest of the undeveloped land" (Connelly et al. 66). According to the article, "a major portion of the undeveloped 55 acres [sic] will be preserved and returned to its 'original condition,' following the tenets of Restoration Ecology" (69). Other points of view become "different rationales for restoring the land" (70–75). The University of the Incarnate Word is a very interdisciplinary environment, and one in which community is highly valued. For this reason, I was surprised to find discussions so difficult, because the people around the table were ones I had worked with for years, and I had assumed we held similar attitudes and values concerning the Blue Hole and surrounding land.

I came to understand that we belonged to different discourse communities. As described by Miles Little, Christopher F. C. Jordens, and Emma-Jane Sayers, discourse communities are "groups of people who share common ideologies, and common ways of speaking about things" (73). While facilitating internal communication, these groups—be they defined by affiliation with academic disciplines, religious denominations, or political parties—colonize their members, making heteroglossic discourse suspect, if not impossible. In the case of the Headwaters Project, the necessary task, while writing mission statements and outlining plans, was to forge a common discourse that honored all traditions present. As a linguist trained in conflict resolution, I became interested in the process of our interactions, which seemed to involve a "language war."

In a book by that title, *The Language War,* linguist Robin Lakoff presents the notion of frames. In the Headwaters Project, among the ten to twelve of us who met together regularly, there were at least three subgroups, or discourse communities, represented: arts/humanities, science, and religion, although with much overlap (Sister Helena holds a PhD in English; Bob Connelly is a philosopher who, as mentioned, served as dean of science, mathematics, and engineering). It seems as if the conflicting frames used by the three discourse communities as makers of meaning were at the center of our misunderstandings. Frames, like academic disciplines or worldviews, provide us with a set of expectations and a body of shared knowledge within which interaction can occur according to rules of the frame. In the Headwaters Project we were seeking to bring about change, as is often necessary in the maintenance of a place-making relationship. The headwaters land surrounding the Blue Hole was being abused by trash dumping and use of vehicles off-road, leading to erosion; old-growth trees were in danger; historical ruins and archaeological sites lacked proper identification and protection; the university was considering building on sites that could damage the environment further; excessive pumping from the aquifer threatened the springs.

According to Lakoff, "Change always entails struggle, often . . . taking the form of a 'language war,' because we defend old frames, and create new ones through language" (50). What is within a frame is "normal," taken for granted by those who share it, and thus invisible. Only when required to step outside our accustomed frames can we name the invisible, because we can imagine a world in which it does not exist (Lakoff 50). She continues, "When bias is made explicit . . . it can be identified and criticized. But when it's implicit, hiding behind a frame that renders it invisible, it is impervious to critique or change" (52). Attempts to make frames visible or to change them often bring derision. "Othering" is the common name given to the process, and Edward Said in his *Orientalism* notes that for a dominant discourse to succeed, it must appear neutral, impartial, academic, despite the impossibility of separating scholars from their contexts (10). In our group there was a bit of a struggle to have one's own frame accepted as neutral or normal, with "other" opinions listened to as uncomfortable, or relegated to support for the dominant view, which had come to be a scientific model of restoration ecology.

In early Headwaters meetings, two subgroups tended to differ first according to their understanding of the task at hand. For the arts/

humanities group (my own perspective, although I will use third person) the task was ideological change. Familiar with the language of deep ecology, the interests of native peoples were important, as well as the notion of interconnectedness to the earth in a spiritual way. They also valued the human history of the place, and looked for the stories of the people attached to this land and water. Some saw the Sisters' notion of stewardship of the land to be hegemonic. Some also held a bias of seeing modern science as dogmatic, distanced, mechanistic, positivistic. They wrote position papers, drafts of mission statements, filled with lofty language. The arts/humanities group looked at the history of the ecological movement and pointed out how it had developed from viewing nature as a resource and trying to manage it with more careful stewardship, to recognizing the place of humans in the biosphere as not one of duality (subject, context), but rather one of full participation and membership. They pointed out that praxis leads to further learning, as we grant agency to the land and the living terrestrial order as self-healer and teacher, and open ourselves to deeper understanding. At the point of discussing actually working on the land, the scientists began to listen.

Science advocates viewed the project as primarily a practical matter, within the purview of restoration ecology, with a set of procedures, which, if followed to the letter, would produce the desired outcome, an ecologically intact urban forest, an arboretum. They were the most active in making lists of concrete tasks, taking photographs, conducting tours, and organizing clean-ups. They recommended the guidelines of the Society for Ecological Restoration (SER), as delineated in *The SER Primer on Ecological Restoration*. Surprising to the arts/humanities group, the primer not only sets out the steps for restoration of the environment, as expected, but also allows for restoring a cultural landscape or ecosystem "that has developed under the joint influence of natural processes and human-imposed organization" (4). A final section is labeled "Integration of Ecological Restoration into a Larger Program" (9). This is the point at which further discussion became possible, a view that ecological restoration could be combined with cultural, historical, and spiritual concerns, a frame that could contain us all.

Despite our differences, we tried to reach those across academic and ideological divides, especially the Sisters, who would take the lead in formation of the Headwaters Coalition. They felt particularly responsible for the process, and often called for more civil dialogue. They distributed copies of the congregation's position on stewardship and the *Earth Charter*. As the article on the birth of the Headwaters Project points out, the understanding of stewardship has evolved in Catholic thinking, from a traditional concentration on a God-given dominion over the earth, to the first papal document devoted entirely to ecology in 1990, calling for care of the earth, elimination of poverty, and just distribution of wealth (Connelly et al. 72). In discussion, what was clearly obvious to each subgroup (and thus invisible to them) was called into question, yielding hurt feelings, and resulting in us-them divisions among the members, which the Sisters tried to heal. Through the able facilitating of Bob Connelly, we survived our early meetings, and still speak to each other.

Two additions to the group made for more open exchange. First, in 2006, a member of the local Coahuiltecan community was invited to add a different voice. At first we were mystified by Gary Pérez's presentation of lengthy personal stories of connection to the waters of Yanaguana. His patience in retelling and our willingness to listen to a style more suited to the oral tradition, rather than to our schedule-driven and bookish ways, have allowed us to include more native perspectives in the design phase of the project, now in progress. The second addition was the hiring of former conservation planner for the Texas chapter of the Nature Conservancy, Lacey Halstead, to work full-time as executive director of the Headwaters Coalition, beginning in August of 2007. Trained also as a meeting facilitator, she is polyglot in terms of discourse communities, and has assisted us in creating a more inclusive frame for the project, now termed a nature sanctuary.

Protection of the headwaters has a good start at Incarnate Word and in the surrounding community. The new, inclusive frame is visible in the following portion of the mission statement of the Headwaters Project:

> Acting with the endorsement of the Coalition, the Headwaters Project intends to honor the unique nature of the place: fragile, rich in history, spirituality, and ecological diversity. By learning lessons embodied in the land—its ecology, history and pre-history, and inherent spirituality—the Headwaters Project aims to preserve and restore native biodiversity, to understand historical and pre-historical human valuation of the site, and to make areas within the location available to members of the three groups participating in the Coalition (the CCVI, the University of the Incarnate Word, and the wider San Antonio community) who wish to experience and study its complexity and changing reality. (Headwaters Project Mission Statement)

The Headwaters Coalition now has a Web site and a promotional video (*Headwaters Coalition Overview*) that emphasize the teaching mission of the Coalition. The process of place-making continues, as groups outside the Headwaters Project link their identity and destiny to the Blue Hole. On July 14, 2005, the "Third Annual Global Ceremony of Love and Thanks to the World's Water in the Interest of World Peace" was celebrated at the Blue Hole. On June 29, 2007, at the United States Social Forum meeting in Atlanta, Georgia, the Fuerza Unida group of San Antonio presented a two-hour workshop, "Waters of Yanaguana: Native Peoples' History and Organizing to Protect Water for all of Creation."

Perhaps, as suggested by director Lacey Halstead, the Headwaters Project and Coalition are also engaged in place-remaking, as old stories are remembered, and the people again learn to listen to the land: "The land (which of course, includes the waters) is the constant, that entity that has been, is, will be here to see generations of lives (human and otherwise) pass through, watching us learn the same lessons over and over. That repetition and reinvention link us together across cultures and time, as the land links us together" (Halstead).

A concept of the blending of time and space, movement and constancy, is symbolized in the Aztec (Nahua) notion of *ollin*. According to Miguel León-Portilla in his *Aztect Thought and Culture,*

> space and time, combining and interpenetrating, made possible the harmony among the gods (the four cosmic forces) and, consequently, the movement of the sun and the existence of life. . . . The Nahuas therefore believed that movement and life resulted from the harmony achieved by the . . . spacialization of time. (56)

A shimmering element, a form of cosmic energy, *ollin* was embodied by the butterfly and the hummingbird. It is perhaps this ephemeral reality that we try to bring into being with our combining of diachronic and synchronic perspectives, with our blending of approaches to the land and water emerging from our different discourse communities. The frame that contains us all may well be ancient, linking science, art, and spirituality to a timeless place.

POSTSCRIPT

In October 2008, after a brief summer hiatus, the springs began to flow, only to dry up again with little rainfall through the autumn and winter. Headwaters Coalition work has continued. A landscape engineering firm has completed mapping the area, marking possible trails and areas for restoration. With the assistance of newly formed Science and Cultural Heritage committees, Lacey Halstead has assembled a fifty-page master plan for restoration and programming at the Headwaters Sanctuary. Sister Helena has written the educational goals for the plan; in summary: to involve university faculty and students in multidisciplinary research and curricular redesign related to the headwaters, to host educational programs for K–12 schools and the Incarnate Word Sisters' retirement center, to work with the Witte Museum of Natural History and other community institutions to produce programming related to the headwaters, and to invite scholars from other institutions to collaborate in identifying additional archaeological sites, resuming the archaeological work left off in the early 1980s.

The Headwaters Coalition has reached out to the community for help. A Native American archaeologist has offered her services to the effort. Consultants in restoration ecology, forestry, and landscape engineering have volunteered time to identify invasive species, to establish priorities in the restoration effort, and to develop a plan to abate damage from run-off related to nearby construction. We await an important visit from members of a Native American group in Oklahoma who plan a stop by the Blue Hole on their way to Mirando City in southern Texas, resuming their old practice of taking water from the sacred springs to offer to the parched lands of their destination. We also await another miracle of rain to restore the springs in time for their visit.

WORKS CITED

Abbott, Patrick L., and C. M. Woodruff Jr., eds. *The Balcones Escarpment*. Geological Society of America (Santa Fe Springs, CA: Comet Reproduction Services): 1986, Dec. 28, 2008 http://www.lib.utexas.edu/geo/balcones_escarpment/balconesescarpment.html.

Basso, Keith H. *Wisdom Sits in Places: Landscape and Language Among the Western Apache*. Albuquerque: U New Mexico P, 1996.

Chandler, C. K. "Paleo-Indian Projectile Points from the Olmos Basin in San Antonio, Texas." *La Tierra: Journal of the Southern Texas Archaeological Association* 21.1 (1994): 11–19.

Connelly, Robert, Rebecca Cross, Ben McPherson, Margaret Mitchell, Helena Monahan, and Sally Said. "The Birth of the Incarnate Word Headwaters Project." *The Eclectic Edition*. Eds. Philip E. Lampe and Julie B. Miller. San Antonio, TX: University Incarnate Word, 2004. 66–76.

Cox, I. Waynne. *The Spanish Acequias of San Antonio*. San Antonio, TX: Maverick, 2005.

Deloria, Vine, Jr. *The World We Used to Live In: Remembering the Powers of the Medicine Men*. Golden, CO: Fulcrum, 2006.

The Earth Charter. San Jose, Costa Rica: University for Peace: 2000.

Fuerza Unida. "Waters of Yanaguana: Native Peoples' History and Organizing to Protect Water for all of Creation." Workshop at the United States Social Forum, Atlanta, Georgia, June 29, 2007.

Halstead, Lacey. E-mail to the author. May 22, 2008.

Harrigan, Stephen. "Texas Primer: The Balcones Escarpment." *Texas Monthly Magazine* December 1987: 138–39.

Headwaters Coalition. Web site. May 13, 2008 http://www.headwaterscoalition.org.

Headwaters Coalition Overview. Dir. Lacey Halstead. DVD. San Antonio: Bauhaus Media Group, 2008.

Lakoff, Robin Tolmach. *The Language War*. Berkeley: U of California P, 2000.

León-Portilla, Miguel. *Aztec Thought and Culture: A Study of the Ancient Nahuatl Mind*. Trans. Jack Emory Davis. Norman, OK: U Oklahoma P, 1963.

Little, Miles, Christopher F. C. Jordens, and Emma-Jane Sayers. "Discourse Communities and Discourse Experience." *Health* 7.1 (2003): 73–86.

Masauki. "Yanaguana hey." Personal communication, Nov. 11, 2007.

McCracken, Dick. "Rip Van River: From Springs to Riverwalk." *Palo Alto Review* 13.1 (2004): 29–35.

Milligan, Bryce. "Basin's Treasure Lost." *Express-News* [San Antonio] Dec. 17, 1986: B6.

———. "Walk on the Wild Side." *Express-News* [San Antonio] Dec. 7, 1986: G1+.

Mitchell, Margaret. "The Yanaguana Story." Personal interview. Mar. 14, 2008.

Ortiz, Simon. "What Indians Do." *Men on the Moon: Collected Short Stories by Simon J. Ortiz*. Tucson: U Arizona P, 1999. 129–39.
Pérez, Gary. The Coahuiltecan water ceremony. Personal communication. Nov. 17, 2007.
Ryan, Eilish. Personal communication. May 13, 2008.
Said, Edward. *Orientalism*. New York: Vintage-Random, 1979.
Slattery, Margaret Patrice. *Promises to Keep: A History of the Sisters of the Incarnate Word of San Antonio, Texas*. Vol. 1. San Antonio: Sisters of Charity of the Incarnate Word, 1995.
Society for Ecological Restoration. *The SER Primer on Ecological Restoration*, Nov. 1, 2004 http://www.ser.org/content/ecological_restoration_primer.asp.
Stothert, Karen E. *The Archaeology and Early History of the Head of the San Antonio River*, Archaeology Series, no. 3. San Antonio: Incarnate Word College, 1989.
Thoms, Alston V., ed. *Assessing Cultural Extinction: Change and Survival at Mission San Juan Capistrano, Texas (Part 2)*. San Antonio, TX: San Antonio Missions National Historical Park, 2001. May 5, 2008 http://home.nps.gov/applications/parks/saan/ppdocuments/san%20juan%20cultural%20study2.htm.
Vaught, Carl G. *Metaphor, Analogy, and the Place of Places*. Waco, TX: Baylor UP, 2004.

7 Acquiring Biospheric Literacy
Discursive Tools, Situated Learning and the Rhetoric of Use

Anne Faith Mareck

A human being is a part of the whole called by us "the universe," a part limited in time and space. He experiences himself, his thoughts and feelings, as something separate from the rest. This delusion is a kind of prison for us. Our task must be to free ourselves from this prison by widening our circle of understanding and compassion to embrace all living creatures and the whole of nature in its beauty.

—Albert Einstein

A technological society has two choices: first, it can wait until catastrophic failures expose systemic deficiencies, distortions, and self-deceptions. Secondly, a culture can provide social checks and balances to correct for systemic distortion prior to catastrophic failures.

—Mohandas Gandhi

The change in global climate is not caused by financial or technological factors alone and will not be solved just through financial or technological solutions. Global climate change results from the realities of Western post-industrialist, capitalist culture. It is embedded in unsustainable lifestyles.

—Wilfred Wang

You must change your life.

—Rainier Maria Rilke

The stage for this chapter is set in late modernity, a time when the grim reality of global climate change is dawning on humanity. In 2007 the Intergovernmental Panel on Climate Change (IPCC) warned that total global greenhouse gas emissions must peak and begin to drop by 2015 if humanity wishes to avoid the most dangerous warming scenarios. In the US, "environmentalists" are working to raise their voices above the hubbub of exuberant consumption. Determined activists and scientists, like NASA's atmospheric physicist James Hansen, persist in a constant drumming of the message, a message becoming faintly audible above the din of the marketplace. *Global warming is real. We must gear up immediately and respond all-out, as if for a war.*

Yet despite the science and the warnings, US citizens are deeply split as to whether or not humans are responsible for climate change (Pew Research), and all the while greenhouse gas emissions continue to rise. As they rise, new terms are beginning to enter the common lexicon, terms like "phenology"—the natural timing of how pollinators (insects and birds) and the blossoming of plants occur in concert, "trophic mismatch"—"trophic" being an organism's location within a food chain (what it eats and what eats it), "locavore"—a person who subsists on locally grown foodstuffs, "walkshed"—the area within manageable walking distance of one's home, and "three-fifty"—the "optimal" level of the greenhouse gas CO_2 being 350 parts per million. We are currently at 385 and rising. Some fear that we are close to a climactic "tipping point," that we may face a cascading change in ecosystems that will change life on earth as we know it (Hansen). With only 4.6 percent of the global population, the US is responsible for 25 percent of total global greenhouse gas emissions (EIA [Milbrath]).

Why, with all that we know about climate change, do we in the US collectively persist in unsustainable environmental practices?

One reason may be that the implicit ordinary discourses in support of the ideologies that constitute the "dominant social paradigm" (Pirages and Ehrlich) of unlimited market growth, exuberant consumption, and laissez faire exploitation of ecological domains far outweigh the more explicit elevated discourses in support of biospheric stewardship.

Thus this chapter considers discourse and the rhetoric of use. Not the elevated discourses of public policy making, but the ordinary, everyday ocean of unremarkable material discourses in which we are daily immersed, such as the *packaging* in which we receive groceries, tools, toys, fast food, entertainment items, personal care products, and sundries; the *disposables* such as cameras, throw-away cell phones, diapers, tableware, cutlery, paper towels, razors, and batteries; and the *electronic media* such as e-mail, cell phones, iPods, marquees, video games, and Web sites—the common discourses of common material artifacts. One biospherically interesting thing about packaging is that great resources of energy and material go into creating technological artifacts that are intentionally designed as waste. Disposables are equally interesting technologies, as the immense energy and materials invested in their creation is intended for only brief use. And electronic media use not only vast energy and material resources, but toxic e-waste significantly contributes to ecosystem compromise. These common material artifacts—packaging, disposables, electronic media—are identified as *discursive tools* (Owens). In particular, this essay draws upon on my recent ecocritical analysis of an electronic media discursive tool, the Weather Channel Desktop.

"Discursive" here implies the inherently ideological nature of any communicative artifact (Fairclough). And "tool" implies the hands-on *use* of that material discourse and thus the agency, realized or not, of its user. Unlike the elevated discourses of public debate, wherein the audience can consciously choose to receive or rebuff the argument and then move on to other concerns, ordinary material discourses fly under the cognitive radar. Because the repetitive use of a discursive tool is not commonly perceived as a rhetorical situation, the cumulative rhetoric of such use can be a significant conveyor of what Pirages and Ehrlich in 1974 defined as the "dominant social paradigm"—the DSP:

> The collection of norms, beliefs, values, habits, and so on that form the worldview most commonly held within a culture and transmitted from generation to generation by social institutions. . . . The prominent worldview, model, or frame of references through which individuals, or, collectively, a society, interpret the meaning of the external world. . . . Different societies have different DSPs. . . . It is an essential part of the cultural information that is passed from generation to generation as it guides the behaviour and expectations of those born into it . . . the common content of the paradigms shared by most individuals, although . . . not . . . all views of all citizens. (42)

Social researchers Dunlap and Van Liere suggest that the DSP now functioning in the US arose during a long historic period of "ecological abundance," and that its characteristics include "private property rights, faith in science and technology, individualism, belief in future prosperity, economic growthism, and a view of nature as something to be subdued" ("Cognitive" 333). These characteristics were amplified during the great synthesis of federal government, corporate capitalism, and technological development during and after World War II, a time during which the US technological ability to dominate the earth was suddenly magnified many times over (Miller), domination which continues to this day.

To investigate the notion that values in the US were beginning to shift as a sense of ecological degradation grew—Rachel Carson's best seller *Silent Spring* was published in 1962 and the first Earth Day was celebrated in 1970—Dunlap and Van Liere developed a testing instrument to measure public attitudes concerning both the DSP and a growing alternative perspective more appropriate to our current age of "ecological scarcity," which they labeled the "new environmental paradigm" ("The New"). They describe the new environmental paradigm (NEP) as an "emerging challenge to the DSP," a paradigmatic challenge that includes environmental stewardship, limits to growth, and awareness of problems with wide-scale human modification of the natural environment ("Cognitive" 333).

According to the IPCC—the World Meteorological Organization and United Nations Environment Program entity established in 1988 as the clearinghouse and assessment body for global climate change research—humanity's best-case global warming scenario calls for global greenhouse emissions to peak and begin dropping by the year 2015 (IPCC 4AR). Whereas even the "minimal" increase of 3–4°F inherent to this scenario will trigger widespread ecological and social disturbance, it is believed to be within an "adaptable" range (Pachauri). Thus, not only is human civilization challenged with the necessity of making massive changes in consumption and habitation patterns in order to safeguard ecological stability, but it is challenged with the necessity for immediate fast change. Thinkers such as Arne Naess and David Orr have suggested that for such deep change to come about, our fundamental understanding of what it means to inhabit a planet must change as well.

This chapter explores relationships between the *use* of everyday discursive tools and the systemic acquisition of literacy about the planetary environment. It suggests that the intentional redesign of ordinary discursive tools may work to foster a biospheric literacy—a literacy that represents the human animal as just one of the myriad members of the vast biotic community graced by the richness of our biosphere—the sphere of life, the interconnected global system of ecosystems that supports life on the planet (Lovelock; Merchant).

To accomplish this discursive investigation, I undertook to critically analyze an ordinary material artifact in hopes of discerning the natures of its discourses, whether DSP or NEP or some combination of the two. I chose a free, unremarkable electronic artifact, the Weather Channel Desktop, and developed an analytical method to unpack its discourses about the planetary environment. The purpose of the study was twofold. First it would investigate the nature of the discourses conveyed by the artifact and to consider how these discourses function as tacit rhetorical conveyors of literacy about the planetary environment—the particular way in which these discourses invite us to read our planetary environment. Do they urge us more toward a DSP literacy of consumption—teaching us to view the planet as a limitless renewable resource? Or do they urge us more toward an NEP literacy of biospheric stewardship—teaching us to view the planet as a balanced ecological system with inherent limitations? Second, the study would investigate the particular way in which the artifact's interface and its associated computer hardware teaches these discourses to its users (Mareck).

The essay proceeds in three sections: (1) description of the artifact, (2) overview of methods and findings, and (3) situated learning and the rhetoric of use.

1. DESCRIPTION OF THE ARTIFACT

In my search for an artifact through which to investigate the DSP-NEP discursive natures of ordinary material texts, I had four aims: First, I looked for an artifact that purported to teach its users how to "see" and "read" and "write" the planetary environment. As well, I looked for an artifact that could select for a socioeconomic class of individuals who might reasonably be asked to voluntarily change their consumption patterns, an artifact that presented a mainstream perspective to a wide audience, and an artifact that was small enough to analyze thoroughly. The artifact I chose is an online weather information tool, the Weather Channel Desktop.

The Weather Channel Desktop (TWC-d), a computer desktop accessory, is available free for downloading from its parent, the Weather Channel at weather.com. The accessory automatically loads when the user starts her computer, and the opening display features weather data relevant to a local area identified by zip code, and includes temperature, visibility, wind direction, humidity, and UV index. Also available are links to a ten-day forecast, a selection of weather-related maps, a traffic conditions feature, a hurricane-reporting feature, and a lifestyle feature that offers information relative to business, leisure, and health interests. Other features include photographs, weather videos, and a weather-trivia game, and many features link back to the parent site, weather.com.

2. OVERVIEW OF METHOD AND FINDINGS

Analysis of TWC-d sought to answer two questions: First, what are the natures of the discourses circulating in the tool? And second, how does the tool teach those discourses to its users?

In order to unpack the tool's implicit and explicit discourses about the planetary environment and to explore the particular way in which TWC-d functions as a learning tool, I devised a tri-faceted analytical approach that considers the artifact from three discursive vantage points. The first vantage point considers TWC-d as a *map*, a discursive tool whose implicit ideological arguments are naturalized so that they appear as transparent, obvious fact—a *finding* tool. The second vantage point considers TWC-d as an *advertisement*, a discursive tool bearing an intentionally constructed argument—a *selling* tool. The third vantage point considers TWC-d as a *situated active learning environment*, a tool through which the discourses of the map and the advertisement are taught in the course of the hands-on use of the interface and associated computer apparatus—a *learning tool*.

To facilitate analysis, I segmented the Weather Channel Desktop Web page into seven component parts or *metasigns*. Each metasign was analyzed in turn following a five-step sequence: a description of the metasign, a reading of the metasign as a finding tool (Wood; Barthes, "Image" and "Mythologies"), a reading of the metasign as a selling tool (Williamson; Barthes, "Image" and "Mythologies"), a reading of the metasign as a learning tool (Gee; Lave and Wenger), and observations based on the readings (Wood and Fels). The metasign readings included following menu and tab links. Then I compiled, open-coded, and focused the observations into six broad themes (Emerson, Fretz, and Shaw).

Themes 1–5 provide an answer to the first research question: "What are the natures of the discourses circulating in the tool?"

Theme 1: Radical Simplification of the Planetary Environment. This theme is concerned with the way in which the displays serve to dissect the physical environment—the atmospheric, oceanic, and terranean systems of the planet—and present them as simple to understand and easy to manage through the application of science and technology. In effect, the immense complexity of the interactive global biospheric system is masked; the physical context of the system has been stripped and its meaning rewritten in terms of human desire.

Theme 2: Inversion of Conceptual Mass. This theme is concerned with the way that the planetary environment is diminished through representation to the point where myriad human concerns loom conceptually larger than the actual physical planet and its associated biospheric systems.

Theme 3: Corporate Appropriation/Assimilation of a Natural Phenomenon. This theme is concerned with the way in which a natural atmospheric phenomenon has been appropriated by a corporate entity and reimagined as a value-added product. Through the progressive, synecdochic expansion involved in constructing a retail "weather product," a corporate entity claims the atmosphere, the oceans, geographic space, botanical life, and the human body as commodities.

Theme 4: Corporate-Government-Science-Technology Synthesis. This theme has to do with the blurring together of for-profit business, federal government, and their respective scientific research and technological systems. Whereas a Memorandum of Agreement (Ban and Kelly) allows the Weather Channel to use the raw meteorological data gathered by NOAA/National Weather Service scientists and technologies, that fact is masked: the data appears as a product of the corporation.

Theme 5: Circulation of Prominent Cultural Myths. This theme has to do with what seems to be an effort to "add value" to the weather in order to create a marketable weather-product that in turn develops a marketable audience-product. Here, the Weather Channel Desktop is shown to reflect a medley of common cultural myths:

- the expert word of science and technology (from a biospheric literacy perspective, this encourages a broad passivity in the general public)
- a sublime Romantic nature, picturesque and terrifying (biospherically this presents an appealing yet distorted concept of the planetary environment)
- the cult of the car as the American icon of freedom (biospherically, the widespread use of fossil fuels drives climate change)
- the sport of golf as the icon of mogul deal making and its relation to idealized landscapes (biospherically, unlimited quantitative market growth is incongruent with sustainable practices; maintenance of such idealized landscapes is energy-intensive; and local ecosystems are compromised through runoff of herbicides, pesticides, and fertilizers)

138 *Anne Faith Mareck*

- The American ideal of "happiness" is conflated with a DSP valuation of consumption and thus can be achieved through the consumption of material goods.

Each of these first five broad themes can be identified as roughly congruent with a DSP founded upon "private property rights, faith in science and technology, individualism, belief in future prosperity, economic growthism, and a view of nature as something to be subdued" (Dunlap and Van Liere, "Cognitive" 333).

When I began analysis of TWC-d, I did expect to find a predominance of DSP discourse. Yet I was surprised to find exactly how pervasive it was. I had expected that because TWC-d conveys weather information, there would be at least some examples of NEP discourse. I reasoned that by learning about the weather the user would become more familiar with the planetary environment overall, and that as a result the user's biospheric literacy would develop. However, as the five themes above suggest, the deep discourses of the site are tightly interwoven with the epistemic matrix of the DSP. This interlacing distorts the environment so thoroughly that the development of a biospheric literacy by the user seems unlikely. Instead these discourses seem more likely to appeal to a consumer literacy and thus stimulate consumption.

The sixth and final broad theme provides an answer to the second research question: "How does the tool teach these discourses to its users?"

Theme 6: Enactment, the Rhetorical Nature of Repetitive Use. The last discursive theme is a consideration of the actual electronic interface and associated hardware through which the Weather Channel Desktop content is made available to the user. The interface is designed as a game-style approach to the delivery of weather-related information, and in combination with the computer screen, keyboard, speakers, and mouse, proffers the user a sense of active control over that delivery.

The video game has been described as a near-perfect learning tool (Gee), a phenomenon demonstrated in the game-style interface of the Weather Channel Desktop. The learner takes command of the "weather game" using the centrally located control panel, which enables the learner to click through the various options on the site. The learner is in charge of her own experience and is motivated by the site's structure to take action, action that is immediately rewarded with sensory feedback. Tactile reinforcement comes through the fingers in the process of manipulating, pointing, and clicking the computer mouse; visual reinforcement comes from the identification of hyperlinked choices and the mouse-click-based change of display; auditory reinforcement comes from sound of the keyboard keys being depressed, the click of the mouse, and audible embellishment of the content conveyed through the computer's speakers. Through repeated use of the high-immediate-reinforcement and low-risk-of-failure interface, the learner both becomes familiar with the content and develops a "weather-insider" identity (Gee). This sort of experiential engagement is an example of "situated learning." Where traditional classroom lessons can be abstract and decontextualized, a situated learning environment is one in which the "lesson" to be learned is organically acquired during the learner's active participation in and identification with a specific, related, concrete context (Lave and Wenger; Brown, Collins, and Duguid).

In sum, the first five themes are congruent with the epistemic vantage of the current DSP. This vantage is proffered to the user from within the situated learning environment of a video-game-like interface. Thus, in the example of the Weather Channel Desktop we see a situation in which the biospherically problematic DSP of exuberant consumption is being silently taught to the user during her or his uncritical, repetitive *use* of a weather-information interface that employs "the best theories of learning in cognitive science" (Gee 7).

Whereas an analysis of a single ordinary discursive tool cannot be broadly generalized to the class of all ordinary discursive tools, it can suggest the potential for rhetorical influence by this class of material discourses. If the discourses inherent in ordinary electronic media technologies like TWC-d and other ordinary technologies like packaging and disposables do indeed tend to conform to the current DSP, then our uncritical, repetitive, hands-on use of these common technologies may be a factor in widespread retention of the biospherically problematic epistemic vantage of the DSP. Conversely, an intentional discursive redesign of these technologies could serve to foster the acquisition of a biospheric epistemic vantage.

3. SITUATED LEARNING AND THE RHETORIC OF USE

Technology is an aspect of late modern life to which we in the US have become habituated, and we may rarely recognize the extent to which our lives are supported and mediated by our technologies. For example, the term "technology" is often associated with computers. Yet a simple lead pencil is a complex technology in its own right. Glossy yellow pigmented enamel paint, specialized softwood, varying hardnesses of lead, a metal cylinder compressed to one end of the stick to hold a rubber eraser. The materials from which the pencil is composed are acquired in various parts of the world through various means, and are transported to various sites to undergo manufacturing transformations, and the end products are transported to distribution points, where the consumer provides the final transport to the location of end use. A pencil thus involves a technological complex of extraction, manufacturing, and transportation. The concept of technological determinism identifies *technology* as the primary shaping force of human society and thus human history (Winner, 2001; Williams, 2003). Plato was especially concerned with this idea.

I return to the ancients as we are in a time when we seek to socially construct first principles as to how global human community might exist in harmony with the biosphere. Plato was concerned with first principles and his model may provide topics useful to our search for the means to construct a sustainable human society. According to philosopher John Wild, the notion of *techne* (art)—the human ability to *make*, to bring into existence that which did not exist before—holds a central position in Plato's philosophy. Where Kant asked, "How is science possible?" Plato asked "How is technical procedure possible?" (255). To Wild's Plato, because of its very nature as productive, techne holds the potential to endanger society. Continuing on with Wild, in Plato's four-part hierarchy of science, techne was carefully governed. Lowest in the hierarchy were the acquisitive arts, those which gathered matter—then understood as forms of divine life—for use by humans: mining, logging, hunting, fishing. Next were the productive arts, techne, those which crafted divine matter to bring into existence that which did not exist before. Governing techne were the directive arts, statesmanship, which followed and enforced the guidance given by the highest and ruling art, philosophy. Philosopher-kings intuited eternal first principles and communicated them to the statesmen that they might govern wisely.

Through this structure Wild's Plato sought to restrain the possibility of an inversion of power, one in which the immense power of the productive arts was left unchecked by higher philosophic reasoning and artifacts were created without consideration of final telos for the good. As further safeguard against an inversion of power, Plato's techne was rigidly structured, consisting of five necessary, ordered elements:

1. the useful end, telos, because of which the techne (art) exists
2. the work or concrete achievement of the techne, which serves the telos
3. the form or structure that every work must exemplify to realize the telos
4. the technical procedure by which this form is imposed on divine matter
5. the concrete divine matter on which the form is imposed

Thus in Plato's hierarchy, the *telos* of technical production was of primary consideration whereas *technical procedure* was far down the hierarchy, in quaternary position. Wild's Plato was concerned that 1, 2 and 3 might lose primacy, resulting in a degeneration of techne into a simple technique enacted for its own sake, rather than for the higher good. Indeed, Wild's closing remarks, written in 1941 in the midst of World War II, ring starkly true today:

> The general materialization of *techne* . . . is no less characteristic of modern society. When the guiding arts of philosophy and statesmanship become weakened and confused, the productive arts chafe at the

leash, and set up the cry for autonomy and *laissez faire*. When this is achieved, the sheer production of various goods and articles no longer submits to the control of a distribution *planned* by the statesman to meet the *real* needs of the whole community, but is regarded as an end in itself. Hence essential needs are overlooked, and vast energy is consumed in the manufacture of articles which meet only accidental or apparent needs.

Art [techne] is regarded as the mere ability to *produce* articles. . . . The world is flooded with useless goods poured forth by unplanned productive activity. This leads at home to the vast waste involved in the huge industry of competitive advertising, which seeks to dispose of unnecessary goods, and, abroad, to the competitive struggle for markets which leads to imperialism and war. Unguided production thus causes "almost all the evil in states, private as well as public." (293)

Whereas Plato's insistence on intuitively received eternal truth is rightly feared as a philosophical loophole through which tyrannical rule might enter society, his insistence upon the need for guiding principles and the importance of governing techne in accordance with those principles appears sharply pertinent in this age of looming climate change brought about by laissez faire technological development.

Philosopher of technology Langdon Winner seems to extend Plato's concern about the potentially disruptive nature of techne. Arguing in "Do Artifacts Have Politics?" that technologies are inherently linked to structures of power, Winner explores the social consequences of a widespread change of energy source, a job we have immediately before us today. Writing in 1991, Winner identifies two likely alternatives to fossil fuel: solar power and nuclear power. He characterizes locally produced solar energy as an implicitly democratic energy source. It is freely available to all, it is at its most efficient functioning as a localized source, and its production involves no great inherent danger. In contrast, the political structure necessitated by a move to a large centralized nuclear energy source is characterized as authoritarian. The production of nuclear energy is inherently dangerous, the by-product of fusion can be used to create nuclear weapons, and the problem of a lethal waste product with a 25,000-year half-life defies solution. Thus, concludes Winner, a society can safely embrace nuclear power only if it enacts rigorous surveillance of its citizens.

In this way, Winner illustrates how the actual material presence of any particular technology is in essence a discourse bearing substantial rhetorical force—a force that over time can shape the sensibilities of individuals. One of the many examples Winner gives of the inherently rhetorical nature of technologies is startling. He relates the intentional activities some years ago of a New York builder who did not want poor people or racial minorities to use his streets and parks. Reasoning that such groups use public transportation, the builder designed the bridges linking his system with low overhead clearances, thus making it impossible for busses to travel his byways. This steel discourse of discrimination argues his convictions to this day. Yet when I speak with students who have seen these low bridges, they remark that "overheads must have been lower then," or "the cost of materials must have been higher then," or "cars were smaller then." Thus are ideologies silently incorporated into the fabric of our daily culture and their fundamental social shaping influence rendered invisible in the passage of time. Whereas this particular builder's intentionality may be extreme, the example affords high contrast to the discursive nature of material artifacts.

It seems to me that everyday small technologies function in a fashion similar to the monumental technologies that Winner describes. Thus an ordinary online weather tool such as TWC-d can represent the world in such a way as to make reliance upon unlimited growth and consumption appear as a commonsensical aspect of normal human existence. The implicit rhetorical force wielded by ordinary technologies, discursive tools, is tied to their repetitive use over time. Such use can be seen as a situated learning environment, an environment in which one can implicitly acquire a literacy about the planet constructed from the discourses conveyed by the technology.

In *Situated Learning*, Lave and Wenger use the example of traditional craft apprenticeship to demonstrate the effectiveness of pedagogical approaches that situate the learner in a hands-on environment in which they learn by trial-and-error practice over time. They stress the importance of "legitimate peripheral participation," and the way that situated learning environments are most effective when the learner produces products that are of real use to their immediate community. Rather than classroom exercises that may appear to have little real-world value, situated learning products contribute to the actual task at hand and offer the new practitioners entry to the particular social environment in which the practice occurs. Through scaffolded progression the learner is protected against failure, while the product of her labor is valued. Brown, Collins, and Duguid emphasize that the concepts of "learning" and "enculturation" can be understood as two sides of the same coin. People are "enculturated" through the hands-on, real-life reinforcement of the "situated learning environment" of their daily lives; thus, learning might be better understood as a "cognitive apprenticeship" (37). Rather than mental retention of abstract principles, a cognitive apprenticeship affords the learner meaningful social practice. Further, Clancy emphasizes that knowledge is not abstract. He defines situated learning as a sensory process during which humans develop their knowledge base "in the course of activity . . . dynamically constructed as we conceive of what is happening to us, talk, and move . . . not a thing or a set of descriptions or a set of facts and rules" (49).

Following these descriptions, our daily life engagement with ordinary discursive tools such as packaging, disposables, and electronic media can be understood as situated learning environments whose DSP discourses we have over time come to see as normal. For example, the manufactured paper wrapper that holds a fast-food flavor-engineered cheeseburger is a tool necessary to convey the burger from maker to user. The cheeseburger itself is a tool used to provide fuel for human work. These tools represent a global industry that uses vast resources, including agriculture and its associated reliance upon pesticides and herbicides; transportation and its associated reliance upon roads, airlines, and fossil fuel; manufacturing and its associated reliance upon cheap "natural resources" to which "value" can be added; and advertising, with its reliance upon research in psychological and social understanding of human behavior used to "market" "fast food" to "consumers." The use of both tools—the wrapper and the burger—necessitates a physical engagement. The immediate reinforcement afforded by use of the tool (the soft crinkle of the wrapper, the warmth, aroma, and taste of the burger, the satiety), the physically reinforcing engagement with these tools, situated use, engaged in repetitiously over time reinforces the ordinary normalcy of the discourses inherent to their materiality (Shafer).

TWC-d, despite its lowly status as a rather humdrum, free computer desktop accessory, is in fact a sophisticated electronic interface reliant upon global satellite technology that makes database information garnered from around the world instantly accessible for use (Batten; Monmonier). Thus, "cognitive apprenticeships," such as those enabled by TWC-d or a fast-food burger can be understood as situated learning environments that teach the DSP literacy of consumption.

Sensory engagement, *use*, is a potent rhetoric. Michael Calvin McGee offers the perspective that rhetoric is not an elevated, abstract art wielded by gifted rhetors. Instead, it is material—a permanent function together with human communication in all its guises. Rhetoric arises amid the catalytic gestalt of human communicative action and as such it must be broadly conceived. "The whole of rhetoric is "material" by measure of human *experiencing* it. . . . Rhetoric is "object" because of its pragmatic *presence*" (29). Rhetoric is expansively inclusive, "exist[ing] on a continuum from the absolutely specific experience of being persuaded to the absolutely general experience of having been conditioned to a pattern of social and political opinions" (31).

> "Speakers" do not have to be single individuals; "speeches" do not have to be words uttered in one place and at one time; "audiences" need not be present immediately; "occasion" is not restricted by time or space; and "change" may occur gradually over centuries as well as immediately in the presence of a single "speaker." (31)

McGee argues that all discourses function as communicative events within the larger state of rhetoric: "There is no type of discourse which cannot function as "speech" in a material rhetoric" (39). An ordinary discursive tool such as the Weather Channel desktop, then, can be understood as fundamentally rhetorical in nature. It argues the ideologies implicit to its discourses, but not in an abstract fashion. Instead it is an actual, material tool through the hands-on use of which the user physiologically *experiences* the sensory-based suasive appeals of the tool.

If, after McGee, "the whole of rhetoric is material by virtue of human *experiencing* it" (29), then a function triangle for *use* such as that shown in Figure 7.1 can be constructed that reflects the interaction of three elements: a *user* makes *use* of an *artifact*. The in-the-moment synthesis of these three generates the rhetoric of the situation. It is the application of *use* that provides the catalytic action uniting user and artifact that gives rise to the rhetoric of the occasion. The persuasiveness of a situation depends upon *use*. Thus, discursive tools like TWC-d slowly and quietly enculturate their users toward conformance to a DSP that is biospherically untenable. Such enculturation is a rhetorical argument whose transaction occurs over time during the repetitive user-use-artifact synthesis reflected in Figure 7.1.

Use is a simple, unremarkable aspect of living. We are so familiar with *use* that we may not really notice our myriad daily sensory interactions with discursive tools. In reimagining the context of daily life as a situated learning environment, use then becomes unmistakable as a rhetoric in its own right. If rhetoric is indeed not abstract, but instead material (McGee; Gonzalez; Marback), a material occurrence arising from a constellation of material contingencies, then rhetoric and use are inextricably bound. It is in the situated use of the material object that the user becomes the co-generator of its rhetoric. Is any argument rhetorical if that argument is not "used"

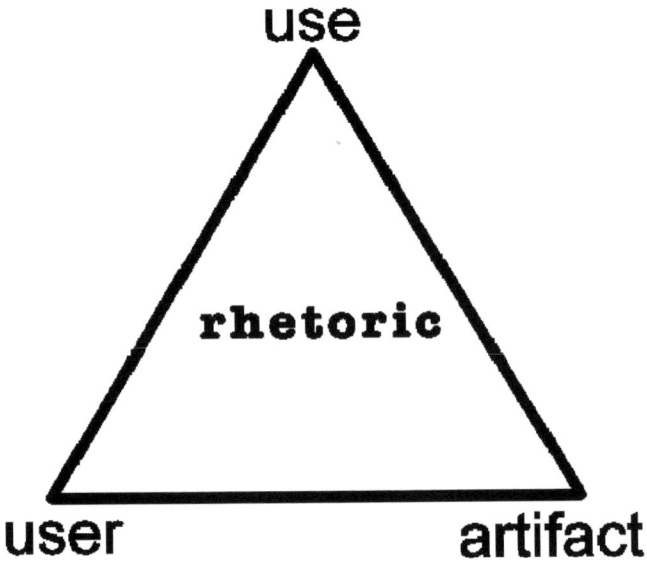

Figure 7.1 Use function triangle.

by the audience? Is a speech persuasive in and of itself, sans audience? Is TWC-d persuasive without someone at its game-style controls?

It is informative to invert the rhetorical concept of "audience" and reenvision that individual as a "user" (Johnson). In this figuration, a "passive" audience, said to be stimulated to take specified action simply by auditing a rhetor's intentional construct, instead becomes an individual active agent of change who *makes use* of the rhetor's construct. Along with *use* comes all the cognitive force inherent to situated practice—whether that situatedness be the familiar, time-honored, formal tradition of a craft apprenticeship or the less-familiar yet just as formally constrained engagement with online media. The *use* of the implicitly ideological artifact is the catalyst whereby the rhetoric of the situation arises.

To further explore this relationship between rhetoric and use, I return once again to the ancients. For Wild's Plato, the final telos of a manufactured artifact must aim to serve the good. He argued that it was essential that *techne*, the ability to make that which might or might not exist, be governed lest an "inversion" occur—a socially disruptive condition in which the guiding wisdoms are subverted and material goods are brought into existence for their own sake. However, Plato excluded *rhetoric* from classification within the scheme of intellectual virtues. He believed that the knowledge of how to speak effectively was an in-born aristocratic trait. Thus, rhetoric, as taught by sophists like Gorgias, Plato rejected out-of-hand as a false techne.

In contrast, Aristotle seemed to understand the epistemic nature of rhetoric and chose to govern it by locating it within the hierarchy of intellectual virtues he detailed in *The Nicomachean Ethics*:

> *Sophia*: Philosophic wisdom: highest and most finished wisdom; *nous* + *episteme*
>
> *Nous*: Intuitive wisdom: knowledge of first principles
>
> *Episteme*: Scientific wisdom: knowledge of the unchanging; acquired through *nous*
>
> *Phronesis*: Practical wisdom: knowledge of how to act in accord with the good
>
> *Techne*: Productive wisdom: knowledge of how to make in a true, reasoned way

The inclusion of techne in this hierarchy is interesting. Sophia is the highest philosophical wisdom, a synthesis of Nous, knowledge of first principles, and Episteme, knowledge of that which could not be otherwise. These three virtues are abstract, ideal forms of wisdom, far from the common life of humans and apprehensible only through the gifted intuition of the contempletative philosopher. The fourth wisdom, Phronesis, enters the realm of human action as a knowledge of how to act in accord with the good.

In contrast, Techne seems to be a different sort of wisdom altogether: a knowledge of how to make, to produce material goods, whether houses or hamburgers. By placing Techne in the company of the higher wisdoms, all of which carry expectations of action for the good, Aristotle may have attempted to place moral governance on Techne. Seeming to support this governance, Dunne's Habermas finds a techne/phronesis relationship in Aristotle's work. Here we find the noun *techne*, knowledge of how to make, and its companion action verb *poiesis*, to make. Habermas marries these with *phronesis*, knowledge of how to act for the good, and its companion action verb *praxis*, to take right action. The result is a compound of complimentary pairs: *techne-poiesis–phronesis-praxis*. Thus techne and poiesis are understood as action, and action is governed by phronesis.

By so embellishing techne with an underlying expectation of right action, Aristotle addresses Plato's concern with inversion. While Plato dismissed rhetoric as a false art, Aristotle instead seemed to recognize rhetoric as a peculiar form of making that held great potential for social destructiveness: the making of new knowledge. Thus he classified rhetoric as a techne—thereby constraining it to the realm of intellectual virtue. By doing so, he effectively placed an expectation for phronetic action on the rhetor-maker (Dunne). Any speech-artifact the rhetor might construct should thus aim in its final telos to serve the higher good. Such a governance of techne was in effect governance of the human actor—the maker, whether the carpenter or the rhetor, whether constructing a house or constructing discursive tools such as TWC-d.

This governance of the maker, it seems to me, is an effort to govern the *use* of inanimate technological artifacts. Once an artifact with its implicit ideologies has been constructed, then the opportunity is there for any random user to *make use* of that artifact, providing the catalytic action that generates the artifact's rhetoric. As Mary Shelley suggested in her 1818 novel *Frankenstein: Or, the Modern Prometheus*, once an artifact has been constructed and deployed through *use* it takes on a social life of its own. Aristotle could not govern *use* itself, but he could attempt to govern the maker of artifacts in hopes that artifacts that did not serve the common good might therefore not be brought into existence.

Indeed, our current predicament of climate change might be seen as the cumulative telos of 250 years of ungoverned technological development. Yet ordinary discursive tools like TWC-d, given the steady pressure of their under-the-radar repetitive material rhetoric, hold an unrealized potential to convey biospheric literacy to a wide audience. Such a steady conveyance of biospheric vantage, realized through a redesign of our mundane discursive tools, might assist with our vast project of fast adaptation to climate change.

At the beginning of this essay I shared my original motivating question: "Why, with all that we know about climate change, do we in the US collectively persist in unsustainable environmental practices?" It occurs to me that we may persist, at least in part, because we are epistemically bound by a matrix of everyday DSP discourses, perhaps similar to the way in which Gulliver was taken captive by the Lilliputians, held down by a thick, criss-crossing network of tiny threads (Swift). Any one, or even dozens of those Gulliver could have easily broken, but held by thousands on thousands of tiny threads, he was rendered helpless. So may we, collectively, be held captive by the myriad mundane discourses of our current DSP.

WORKS CITED

Aristotle. *The Nicomachean Ethics*. Trans. David Ross. New York: Oxford, 1988.

Ban, Raymond and John Kelly. "Renewal of Memorandum of Agreement between The Weather Channel, Inc. and The National Oceanic and Atmospheric Administration." NOAA-NWS. June 5, 1998.

Barthes, Roland. *Image, Music, Text*. Trans. S. Heath. New York: Hill & Wang, 1977.

———. *Mythologies*. Trans. A. Lavers. New York: Hill & Wang, 1972.

Batten, Frank. *The Weather Channel: The Improbable Rise of a Media Phenomenon*. Boston: Harvard Business School P, 2002.

Brown, John, Allen Collins, and Paul Duguid. "Situated Cognition and the Culture of Learning." *Educational Researcher*, 18.1 (1989): 32–42.

Carson, Rachel. *Silent Spring*. Boston: Houghton, 1962.

Clancy, William. "A Tutorial on Situated Learning." *Proceedings of the International Conference on Computers and Education (Taiwan)*. J. Self, ed. Charlottesville, VA: AACE. 49–70, 1995.

Dunlap, Riley and Kent Van Liere, "Cognitive Integration of Social and Environmental Beliefs." *Social Inquiry*, 53.2–3 (1983): 333–341.

———. "The 'New Environmental Paradigm': A Proposed Measuring Instrument and Preliminary Results." *Journal of Environmental Education*, 9 (1978): 10–19.

Dunne, Joseph. *Back to the Rough Ground: Practical Judgment and the Lure of Technique*. Notre Dame: U of Notre Dame P, 1993.

EIA, Energy Information Association: Official Energy Information Statistics from the US Government. What is the Prospect for Future Emissions? "Greenhouse Gases, Climate Change, and Energy." May 18, 2008 http://www.eia.doe.gov/oiaf/1605/ggccebro/ chapter1.html.

Emerson, Robert, Rachel Fretz and Linda Shaw. *Writing Ethnographic Fieldnotes*. Chicago: U of Chicago P, 1995.

Fairclough, Norman. *Language and Power*. Edinburgh Gate: Pearson, 2001.

Gee, James. *What Video Games Have to Teach Us about Learning and Literacy*. New York: Palgrave, 2003.

Gonzalez, Jennifer. "Rhetoric of the Object: Material Memory and the Artwork of Amalia Mesa-Bains." *Visual Anthropology Review*, 9.1 (1993): 82–91.

Hansen, James. "Target CO_2: Where Should Humanity Aim?" Final draft of paper submitted April 2008 to *Science*. Retrieved May 16, 2008 from http://www.columbia.edu/~jeh1.

IPCC-4AR. *Fourth Assessment Report* (summary). Intergovernmental Panel on Climate Change. September 20, 2007 http://www.ipcc.ch.

Johnson, Robert. "Audience Involved." *Computers and Composition*, 14.3 (1997): 361–76.

Lave, Jean, and Etienne Wenger. *Situated Learning: Legitimate Peripheral Participation.* NY: Cambridge, 1991.
Lovelock, James. *Gaia: A New Look at Life on Earth.* Oxford: Oxford, 1979.
Marback, Richard. "Detroit and the Closed Fist: Toward a Theory of Material Rhetoric." *Rhetoric Review,* 17.1 (1998): 74–91.
Mareck, Anne. *Climate Change, Technology, and the Rhetoric of Use: An Ecocritical Study of the Weather Channel Desktop.* Diss. Michigan Technological University, 2008. Ann Arbor: UMI, 2008.
McGee, Michael. "A Materialist's Conception of Rhetoric." In R. McKerrow (Ed.) *Explorations in Rhetoric: Studies in Honor of Douglas Ehininger,* 23–48. Glenview, IL: Scott, Foresman, 1982.
Merchant, Carolyn. *Radical Ecology: The Search for a Livable World.* New York: Routledge, 1992.
Milbrath, Lester. "Culture and the Environment in the United States." *Environmental Management,* 9.2 (1985): 161–72.
Miller, Carolyn. "Learning from History: World War II and the Culture of High Technology." *Journal of Business and Technical Communication,* 12.3 (1998): 288–315.
Monmonier, Mark. *Air Apparent: How Meteorologists Learned to Map, Predict, and Dramatize Weather.* Chicago: U. Chicago P, 1999.
Naess, Arne. "The Shallow and the Deep." *Inquiry,* 16 (1973): 95–100.
Orr, David. *Earth in Mind.* Washington, D.C.: Island, 2004.
———. *Ecological Literacy.* Albany, NY: SUNY P, 1992.
Owens, Derek. *Composition and Sustainability: Teaching for a Threatened Generation.* Urbana, IL: NCTE, 2001.
Pachauri, Rajendra. "Acceptance Speech for the Nobel Peace Prize Awarded to the Intergovernmental Panel on Climate Change (IPCC)." Delivered by R. K. Pachauri, Chairman, IPCC. Oslo, December 10, 2007. May 12, 2008 http://www.ipcc.ch/graphics/speeches/nobel-peace-prize-oslo-10-december-2007.pdf.
Pew Research Center for the People and the Press. "A Deeper Partisan Divide Over Global Warming." Survey Reports. News Release, May 8, 2008. May 17, 2008 http://people-press.org/reports/display.php3?ReportID=417.
Pirages, Dennis, and Paul Ehrlich. *Ark II: Social Response to Environmental Imperatives.* New York: Viking, 1974.
Plato. *Gorgias: Complete Works.* Ed. Jonathan Cooper. Indianapolis: Hackett, 1997. 791–869.
———. *Phaedrus: Complete Works.* Ed. Jonathan Cooper. Indianapolis: Hackett, 1997. 506–56.
Shafer, William. "Social Paradigms and Attitudes Toward Environmental Accountability." *Journal of Business Ethics,* 65 (2006): 121–47.
Shelley, Mary. *Frankenstein.* Mineola, NY: Dover, 1994 [based on 1831 third edition].
Swift, Jonathan. *Gulliver's Travels.* Baltimore: Penguin, 1967.
Wang, Wilfried. "Sustainability is a Cultural Problem." *Harvard Design Magazine,* Spring/Summer, (2003): 1–3.
The Weather Channel Desktop. Downloads. May 17, 2008 http://www.weather.com/services/downloads/index.html?from=hp_tool.
Wild, John. "Plato's Theory of Texnh: A Phenomenological Interpretation." *Philosophy and Phenomenological Research,* 1.3 (1941): 255–93.
Williams, Rosalind. *Retooling: A Historian Confronts Technological Change.* Cambridge, MA: MIT, 2003.
Williamson, Judith. *Decoding Advertisements.* London, UK: Marion Boyars, 1994, 1978.

Winner, Langdon. "Do Artifacts Have Politics?" In *The Whale & the Reactor: A Search for Limits in an Age of High Technology*. Chicago: U. Chicago P, 1986, 19-39.

Wood, Denis. "Pleasure in the Idea: The Atlas as a Narrative Form." *Cartographica*, 24.1 (1987): 24-45.

———. *The Power of Maps*. NY: Guilford, 1992.

Wood, Denis, and John Fels. "Designs on Signs: Myth and Meaning in Maps." *Cartographica*, 23.3 (1986): 54-103.

8 Alone on the Ark
Al Gore Reconstructed in *An Inconvenient Truth*

Jeff Bergin

> Documentary realism aligns itself with an epistephilia . . . a pleasure in knowing, that marks out a distinctive form of social engagement. The engagement stems from the rhetorical force of an argument about the very world we inhabit. We are moved to confront a topic, issue, situation, or event that bears the mark of the historically real.
>
> —Bill Nichols, *Representing Reality*

DOCUMENTARY FILM: STORY OR ARGUMENT?

Scholars have long defined documentary film as inherently rhetorical (see Bruzzi, Finnegan, Foss, Nichols, Plantinga, and Winston). Although they are often labeled "nonfiction" films, documentaries are a hybrid of journalism, ethnography, and art, "designed to portray reality artistically for the purposes of influencing public thought" (Foss 51). Moreover, documentaries are rhetorical vehicles, conveying sophisticated, well-crafted messages that are free from the disciplinary constraints of scientific objectivity and journalistic balance. Indeed, they seek to influence thought and manifest action—what rhetoricians know as agency—through scripted narration; interviews with carefully selected experts, scientists, and citizens; decontextualized and reordered sound bites; thoughtfully sequenced visual images; and the use of music and sounds. Together these elements provide "multiple forces that interact to produce meaning" in which "images become inventional resources for public argument" (Finnegan, 39, 40).

Bill Nichols, author of *Representing Reality: Issues and Concepts in Documentary*, has written extensively on documentary film. He believes that an argument, rather than a narrative, lies at the heart of documentary film. Nichols writes that "documentary presents us with an image of the world as if for the first time; we see things anew, in a fresh light, with associations we had not consciously realized or attended to" (113). Often the world portrayed in documentary film is one of social injustice, danger, and peril. Nichols notes, "The recurring focus for the great majority of documentaries . . . is the ways in which our bodies and mortality are placed at risk" (109, 111). Increasingly filmmakers are turning their attention to global crises such as climate change and its affects on weather patterns, food production, and local communities. Climate change itself is a hot topic due to the debate over whether global warming, as a phenomenon, exists, and, if so, to what degree it is caused by human action.

One of the most pertinent and widely distributed examples of environmental documentary film is *An Inconvenient Truth*, which won Best Documentary at the 2007 Academy Awards, providing the issue of global climate change with an unprecedented platform of visibility. The film focuses on the central, catastrophic issue of global warming, but to do so, ties together seemingly isolated incidents into a chain of causality. Many of the incidents that the film discusses—storms, diseases, droughts, floods, and temperature increases—don't seem necessarily connected when examined locally or individually. For instance, isolated films about Hurricane Katrina tend to focus so closely on that particular storm or one of its outcomes that they often fail to examine broader storm patterns and the associated climate changes. Through the broader lens of *An Inconvenient Truth*, however, individual incidents become evidence for the argument that the earth's climate is changing. According to Nichols, the notion that "'this happened' . . . only becomes meaningful as more than an isolated incident when it is placed within a narrative or expository frame" (117). *An Inconvenient Truth* provides such a frame for local weather conditions to be meaningful as part of a global climate crisis. Events that one might see on the news, such as a hurricanes or floods, take on new meaning in the context of this larger frame.

M. Jimmie Killingsworth and Jacqueline Palmer, authors of *Ecospeak: Rhetoric and Environmental Politics in America*, might well concur with this notion. They note that something doesn't become news until it "tells readers something they don't already know, something they haven't already heard or become accustomed to"—that "something" is the broader context for the isolated incidents that are familiar from the nightly news (134). This chapter explicates how a particularly popular environmental documentary, *An Inconvenient Truth*, uses rhetorical proofs—namely logos and ethos—to create the notion of truth in a tacit effort to create agency. This essay draws on Bill Nichol's theorizing about documentary film as highly rhetorical and M. Jimmie Killingsworth and Jacqueline S. Palmer's theorizing about environmental rhetorics as appropriations and interpretations of science.

AN UNCONVENTIONAL DOCUMENTARY

An Inconvenient Truth is an anomaly among documentary films. Documentary films have long been contentiously defined as ethnographic—stemming from anthropological work. However, *An Inconvenient Truth* is based on a well-rehearsed presentation and slideshow and relies heavily on a direct address rather than multiple-interview sound bites that documentaries have adopted from journalism. Indeed, its emphasis on a nearly solitary narrative voice places it nearer to a speech than a documentary. Yet, its status as documentary brings with it the entire truth-bearing schema—that of the "fly-on-the-wall" anthropologist—that the association with ethnography provokes (Lucaites & Hariman 2001, Plantinga 1997, Selig 1989, Winston 1995). Based on its title alone, the chief goal of the film is to persuade viewers about the nature of an undesirable truth. One of the ways that the filmmakers go about this task is to employ classical rhetorical proofs—logos, pathos, and ethos—to buttress arguments and privilege points of view. Yet, the filmmakers concurrently construct the ethos of the film's star performer—former vice president Al Gore—by casting him as a character of biblical and patriotic proportions. The term "concurrent" is an important one, for the construction of the concept of truth and the construction of Gore's character are intertwined so closely in the film's arrangement that they become one seamless effort.

Nichols writes, "At the heart of documentary is ... an argument about the historical world" (111). Yet the documentary format is narrative; thus, the argument is presented as a story and, in the case of *An Inconvenient Truth*, part of the story is global warming and part of the story is Gore's life. To tell these stories, the filmmakers shift between two primary formats: the slideshow for which the film is known and short vignettes called "little films" focusing on Gore's life, mission, and motivation. The former are largely devoted to building a logical argument for the scientific truth of global warming, whereas the latter are focused on constructing Gore's ethos (which, of course, reinforces the former).

THE PERFORMANCE: GORE ON STAGE

An Inconvenient Truth is a performance of a performance; the first being the film itself and the second being the performance of Gore *within* the film. Nowhere is Gore's performance more explicit than in the "slideshow" segments of the film; that is, those segments which show Gore addressing his audiences (both live and through the camera) in front of two plasma screens and an enormous background screen. Here Gore performs by being on a stage, using props such as the screen and the "man lift," and speaking, gesturing, and joking. Yet Gore also performs in what director Davis Guggenheim calls the "little films." These are ten short vignettes in which Gore seemingly discloses pivotal points in his personal journey. Here his tone shifts to the quiet, confessional tone of a confidant, yet these vignettes are performed. Some, such as Gore taking a phone call, are clearly staged. Others, such as Gore describing the river that runs through his family's farm, are made to seem authentic through the use of older cameras and post-production techniques ("the idea," according to the director, "is to *feel* his memory"). Nevertheless, the narration that Gore provides is generated for public consumption, and carefully paced and sequenced in the film.

Stella Bruzzi writes, "These broadcasts serve as reminders that to try to enforce the distinction between the 'real' person and the performance is futile, the politician is necessarily performative" (127). Yet, is Gore performing as a politician, an environmentalist, or both? Unlike many of the politicians profiled in Tarla Rai Peterson's *Green Talk in the White House*, Gore doesn't seem to co-opt the environment to further his political agenda; rather, he seems to do just the opposite: co-opt his political career to further his environmental agenda (if we allow that these two agendas can be separated). Although his subject position as a politician is inescapable, it is only one of the subject positions he assumes throughout the film, the others being activist, student, father, son, and brother. These subject positions are explored in five of the ten little films, whereas his political career (although tacitly referenced throughout the film) is only explored in two of the little films. The intent to cast Gore as first and foremost a humanist, and secondarily a politician, is clear. Therefore Gore performs this role throughout the film. While not denying his political self, he seeks to diminish it.

Assuming a humanitarian role allows Gore to be portrayed (as opposed to "portraying himself" which would deny the involvement of the director and producers) as a Noah figure: a solitary, struggling hero, urging others to heed his warning. In the opening of the film, we hear Gore's voice juxtaposed against disaster footage: "I've been trying to tell this story for a long time and I feel as if I failed to get the message across . . . the moral imperative is inescapable." Gore's solitariness in the film—for the film lacks testimony from friends, family, scientists, scholars, or politicians—casts him as a lone voice in a (foreboding) wilderness of near-biblical proportions. Indeed, Gore nearly says as much: "The only way I know how to do it is city by city, person by person, family by family . . . and I have faith that pretty soon enough minds will change that we'll cross the threshold." The imagery of a traveling missionary, whose "faith" will bring believers across "the threshold," connotes biblical themes and a values-based argument.

Gore adopts what Plantinga calls the "formal voice." It "is relatively omniscient, assuming complete knowledge of relevant high-level aspects of its subject; it knows more than the people represented in that world" (112). Plantinga believes that all films of the formal voice "imply an ideological position" and "proselytize . . . since their function is to teach and explain" (123). Yet Gore is hardly presented as the deep ecologist or stereotypical "tree-hugger" environmentalist. Dressed in a suit, carrying his laptop, standing amidst plasma screens, conveying data (numbers, statistics, and graphs), Gore conveys logic, reason, and rationality. Shots of him traveling, driving, using his telephone and computer all show that Gore embraces technology and progress, despite his leveled criticism of its misuses. He even declares, "I went under that ice in a nuclear submarine," illustrating that our ability to use technology to resolve natural problems supersedes any risk the technology may pose to the environment in the first place—a view that is not too dissimilar to that espoused by liberal environmentalists who see "science" and "scientifically informed government" as a "necessary evil" and who "put their faith in technological solutions" (Killingsworth and Palmer, 88, 159).

THE SLIDESHOW: DRAWING LOGICAL PROOFS

The slideshow segments of the film rely heavily on logos to persuade the viewer that global warming is *true*. In these segments, Gore's pleas take a turn toward the scientific via photos taken of Earth from space (connoting the power of science and technology) that are ultimately morphed into a map of Earth. This image is used to advance a story from Gore's childhood wherein a classmate asks the teacher if South America and Africa were ever part of the same land mass and the teacher derides the student. Gore notes that this position "reflected the conclusions of the science establishment at that time." By first emphasizing the technology that has allowed us to photograph Earth from space, and then stressing that science is mutable, Gore sets an important precedent: new science is better than old science. Likewise he shows how science today, illustrated through beautiful digital photographs, is not the science of one's youth, represented by an old map attached to a blackboard in a classroom. In doing so, Gore is turning *textbook science* into *Hollywood science*; this is a critical move if he is to keep his audience engaged.

According to Plantinga, "Nonfiction films of the formal voice . . . perform two significant operations: (1) they pose a clear question or a relevant and coherent set of questions (or they elicit such questions on the part of the spectator) and (2) they answer every salient question they pose" (107). Gore begins by answering the question that is central to the film: What is global warming? The question, however, is implied, and he assumes a conciliatory tone: "I'm not going to spend a lot of time on this because you know it well." Yet, according to the director's commentary, Gore would not allow this portion to be omitted because of its importance. Indeed, it's followed by a cartoon that reinforces the key points. Gore is doing two things: providing the core for his argument and, perhaps more importantly, building consensus among what Nichols calls "decent people." By accepting the obvious to the degree that it's unnecessary to repeat it, he "articulates the shared response of decent people everywhere" (135). According to Killingsworth, Gore's "position represents a particular communal outlook that points toward agreed-upon values and invites the audience to join (or return to) the community" (252). Thus the filmmakers are continuing to build upon their notion of truth while simultaneously advancing Gore's ethos.

Although the primary rhetorical purpose of the slideshow is to use *science* to create truth, Gore does divert from this path to directly build his ethos (a task that is primarily handled through the little films). He briefly recounts a long history of environmental activism. He "kept having" hearings with Congress, "wrote a book," had "science roundtables," ran for president in 1988 "partly for this issue," and signed the Kyoto Protocols in 1998—forty-one years after the onset of Dr. Revelle's global climate study—giving Gore nearly a half-century of environmental knowledge. With this aside, he becomes the locus of knowledge, just as he's the locus of the film, locus of the slideshow, and locus of the set (i.e., the auditorium).

The slideshow features four types of visuals: animations, photographs, video clips, and cartoons. Chief among these is the animation, which provides a pulsating (and personified) Earth "breathing" once a year; a variety of bar charts and line graphs, which show increasing levels of carbon dioxide, increasing temperatures, and increasing storms; and the memorable 650,000-year history of ice ages, newly released: "This is the first time that anybody outside of a small group of scientists has seen this image." Thus, new science meets ancient ice ages, to illustrate to the skeptics that the current climate patterns are not part of a routine natural cycle. Here Gore uses a "contraption" to rise to the point of current and projected carbon dioxide levels which are "off the charts." This bit of theatrics is worth attending to. This is not only an example of Gore as a hesitant technophile, but, more importantly, as a performer. According to the director's commentary, this scene took three takes and they cut Gore's descent as it was anticlimactic.

In addition to animation, the slideshow also employs photographs, which "[bear] the imprint of science that demands and receives reverential acquiescence by the 'public' due to their 'weighty epistemic force' and 'scientific veracity'" (Plantinga, 33). The film presents photographs that are difficult to refute: barren mountains, trees stripped of their bark, and cracked landscapes. To see these images is to see fact itself; yet, despite the strength of the images, they need the textual context to fill in the gaps in meaning. They do not tell us distances and proportions, seasons and variations, and from whom, when, and with what negotiated restrictions they were acquired. "Visual information often misses subtle, unseen elements of an event, and cannot account for human motivation or causal relationships" (Plantinga, 57). We see photographs of Kilimanjaro, Glacier National Park, the Columbia Glacier, the Himalayas, and the Italian, Swiss, Peruvian, and Patagonian Alps, first with snow and then without. Yet, we don't see a steady deterioration; we see only what is presumably "before" and "after." Gore talks about ecological niches (for example, the connection between caterpillars and chicks), showing an image of a baby bird with its mouth open and its mother, with no food for it. This photo "operates as a political aesthetic . . . that provides crucial social, emotional, and mnemonic resources for animating the collective identity and action" (Lucaites and Hariman, 38).

Photographs are often paired with numerical data: "The change from conditions like we have here today to an ice age took place in perhaps ten years time." Gore's slideshow stresses numerical data in rapid-fire succession: the ten hottest years on record, 35,000 people dead in Europe, 122 degrees in India, 200 cities in the West setting heat records, and thirty new diseases in the last twenty-five years. The slideshow gives Gore a platform, but it also gives him something more: the persona of a meteorologist (which one might liken to a modern-day Noah), which is fitting, as he's talking about jet streams, storms, and climactic shifts. In short, he becomes as familiar and authoritative as a television weathercaster, an ethos most viewers are familiar with. This is particularly effective during the animations that show Florida, San Francisco, the Netherlands, Beijing, Shanghai, Calcutta, Bangladesh, and Manhattan flooding. One could speculate on the selection of cities, states, and nations represented. They are low-lying population centers, certainly, but they are also places of cultural, economic, and historical significance. When, after a pause, Gore describes Manhattan flooding, he focuses not on the island, but on the site of the World Trade Center memorial, saying, "We said 'never again,'" as though we had already reneged on a promise.

Although the majority of the slideshow builds a progressively stronger logical argument for global warming, the animations and cartoons also provide pivotal points of pathos. The polar bear animation shows a solitary polar bear swimming in a vast ocean, with no sign of ice in sight. The frog cartoon, although humorous, illustrates the third of Gore's three factors affecting our relationship with the earth: population growth, the technological revolution, and ways of thinking. This last one can be changed; because climate change has seemed gradual to us we've gotten used to it, but we need to adjust our thinking and "save the frog," implying that we must save ourselves. The *Futurama*-esque cartoon of a small girl asking her teacher about global warming allows Gore to react with humor (as opposed to being mired in fatalism or fanaticism), without *being* humorous. The cartoon represents "politicians" coming up with the solution of dropping a big ice cube in the ocean. It satirizes politicians and creates a sense that, by appreciating the satire, the audience is tacitly agreeing that the problem cannot be fixed easily or by political means alone. They make the little girl (and, by power association, the audience) smarter than the teacher and, by power association, the politician.

THE LITTLE FILMS: BUILDING CHARACTER

Bruzzi writes, "What has been revealing through the decades has been the way in which different [politicians] have negotiated the interaction with the camera, for it is at that moment that the politician comes into being" (152). Gore negotiates his interaction with the camera in two manners: performing onstage during the slideshow and performing offstage during the "little films" (so named by director Davis Guggenheim). Throughout these ten segments, Gore shifts from didactic exposition to reflective commentary.

"Commentary guides our grasp of the moral, political view of the world offered by the documentary text" (Nichols 129). Gore's commentary, quieter, slower, and more personal, is portrayed as confessional and revealing. Nichols writes, "Like trained actors, social actors who convey a sense of psychological depth by means of their looks, gestures, tone, inflection, pacing, movement, and so on become favored subjects" (120). Although the information he shares is within the public record, he adopts the tone of a confidant. The shift between the two voices oscillates the viewer between being a member of his public audience, seated in the auditorium, movie theatre, or at home in front of the television, and his private audience, listening to his confessions. Of course, both are public performances. Nevertheless, the rhetorical effect—the constant shift between logos and ethos—propels the viewer through the rhetorical argument with ever increasing velocity.

The little films, in order of appearance, focus on Gore's days at Harvard, an accident that nearly killed his son, Hurricane Katrina, the confusion surrounding Florida going to George W. Bush in the 2000 election, growing up on a ranch, traveling to share his message during the Reagan and Bush presidencies, Chinese efforts to fight global warming, Gore's sister dying from lung cancer, the influence on science of oil and auto lobbyists, and Gore's giving more than 1,000 presentations.

The little films focus on Gore's motivation; they answer the question "Why is global warming important to you?" The film answers that question by re-creating Gore's son's hospital room, with black-and-white photographs that signify lifelessness, stillness, and waiting. Watching his son struggle to recover, Gore reflected, "How should I spend my time on this earth?" Amid shots of him looking out an airplane window, Gore comments, "I really dug into trying to learn about it much more deeply. I went to places scientists could help me understand parts of the issue that I didn't really understand in depth." This equates almost losing one's child to almost losing the earth. It creates a paternal relationship between Gore and the earth, and shows that he went to the geographic, scientific, and epistemic sources of the problem to become the earth's steward. This paternal relationship works well with the Noah motif, as Noah became the biblical steward for all of Earth's creatures.

Another little film describes Gore's youth, spent partly on a cattle farm, where his father was "Breeder of the Month." Gore says, "Learning it from your dad on the land, that's really something special." This creates an image of him as a utilitarian American, who, according to Killingsworth and Palmer, is connected with his opponents in his appreciation for land "in terms of possession, consumption, or personal experience" (40). The grainy, authentic-looking footage creates nostalgia, foregoing any allusion to the damage that we now know cattle ranching causes to the environment. Yet Gore does accept responsibility and regret for his family's tobacco farming, to which he attributes his sister's cigarette smoking and eventual death. "That we had been part of the economic pattern that produced the cigarette, the cancer, is so painful." The subtext suggests that we cannot let our culpability excuse us from action.

One of the most intriguing little films focuses on Gore's trips to China. He notes, "Every time I've visited China, I've learned from their scientists. They are right on the cutting edge." Although China has been known for its human rights violations, pollution, overpopulation, diminished resources, and authoritarianism, Gore casts it as scientifically advanced. During the slideshow, he points out that China won't even buy US-manufactured cars because they don't comply with Chinese emissions laws. Why does Gore single out China as heroic in a world in which it has long been vilified? Perhaps he does so simply to invoke a sense of the competitive American one-upping.

Finally, one of the little films focuses on scientists. Gore asserts, "Scientists have an obligation to present the truth as they see it." He relates the "bad science" reported in the Soviet Union to the work of American scientists who, like the "whipping boy of environmentalist critics" (89) that Killingsworth and Palmer reference, have been "persecuted, ridiculed, deprived of jobs, income . . . because facts they discussed led them to an inconvenient truth that they insisted on telling." Thus scientists who will confirm the empirical veracity of global warming are martyrs of biblical proportions.

AN ITERATIVE ARRANGEMENT OF APPEALS

An Inconvenient Truth arranges its rhetorical proofs in a sophisticated layering that attempts to take the audience down a persuasive path. As Killingsworth writes, "Appeals . . . are directed from an author to an audience by way of an established position of value. The aim is to align the three positions: author, audience, and values. The success of the appeal depends upon the movement of the audience toward that of the author." (262). This path, according to Killingsworth, is analogous to leading a ship into port: "Implied in the navigational metaphor is the idea of moving through something and the idea of resistance. Authors and audiences occupy stances of positions and must be set into motion against the resistance of inertia" (255). In order to move through this fog of inertia, *An Inconvenient Truth* uses sophisticated transitions between the various media of which it is comprised. That is to say, the slideshows, with their didactic presentation, numerical data, and animations, are not randomly mixed together with the little films. The pieces are carefully composed into a cohesive whole. The film is arranged in two ways: the "stacked" layering of images over narration and the "sequential" transitions from slideshow to little films.

The latter are evidenced throughout the little film that describes the consequences of Hurricane Katrina. The film makes a string of causal links between increased carbon dioxide, higher temperatures, ocean warming, and more storms, that culminates in Katrina. Gore connects the abstract (carbon dioxide) to the concrete (Katrina) and states only, "There are no words to describe it." This is followed by what Nichols has termed an intellectual montage: "A series of images . . . rapidly cut together . . . to evoke the various stages or periods of a process without analyzing . . . the process" (132). The montage ends with Gore's moralizing comment on America: "How in God's name could this happen here?"—meaning *in America*.

To drive his point further, Gore states, "One question we as a people need to decide is how we react when we hear warnings from the leading scientists in the world." The phase "we as a people" conjures up the patriotism of "our forefathers," the complicity of hearing warnings but not taking action, and the importance of science and heeding it's warnings. It is also a not-so-subtle criticism of the Bush administration, which was faulted for not reacting expediently to signs of the disaster or its aftermath. This is followed by an intellectual montage of Florida going to Bush in 2000, amid polling and media confusion, leading one to wonder: Could the devastation of Katrina have been prevented? Gore's concession speech follows: "I accept the finality of this outcome." His humble, confessional voice says, "It brought into clear focus the mission I had been pursuing all these years. . . . I started giving the slideshow again." But had it actually been a "slideshow" previously? Perhaps naming it as such simply lends credence to the vivid graphics used throughout the film, even though Gore's laptop remains closed (presumably connected to the twin plasma monitors and big-screen monitors). The film closes on a similarly sophisticated transition. Gore's final commentary suggests that future generations will ask "What were our parents thinking? Why didn't they wake up when they had the chance?" and leads directly into the closing song, "I Need to Wake Up."

DRAWING ON PROOFS TO DRAW CONCLUSIONS

An Inconvenient Truth could be considered journalism, film, and artwork, all of which are rhetorical. But most simply the film is a call to action aimed at both the individual and the collective. John Louis Lucaites and Robert Hariman write, "American public culture operates in an apparently irresolvable tension between individual sovereignty and collective agency. These tensions are especially pronounced during moments of crisis and disaster . . . where any political response has . . . to meet needs defined in the aggregate, while still maintaining the ideological commitment to the primacy of the individual" (40). Killingsworth and Palmer add, "Environmental rhetoric has thus depended upon a discourse's ability to . . . attract individuals among the general public . . . without seriously challenging the basic institutions of American life" (25). To make a call to action that is both individualistic and collective, the film relies upon public tropes, such as patriotism, nationalism, and Christianity, but emphasizes personal conscious. "Ultimately," Gore says, "this is not really a political issue as much as a moral issue; if we allow that to happen it is deeply unethical." Therefore he places the burden of responsibility squarely on the shoulders of individuals, removing the roadblock of apathy that arises when individuals rely on agencies to resolve problems.

The film pinpoints "three misconceptions": first, that scientists disagree over global warming; second, that we have to choose between the economy and the environment; and third, that we can't do anything about it. By highlighting these misconceptions, Gore is trying to create agency. He describes the difference between the way in which global warming is (in his words, "unanimously," in Killingsworth and Palmer's words, "passively") agreed-upon in peer-reviewed scientific journals and how it is portrayed as a *possibility* in the media. "We already know everything we need to know to effectively address this problem." In other words, don't wait for scientists or politicians to solve it; "we have everything we need save political will."

Yet the film doesn't dismiss the public altogether; rather, Gore appropriates public effort to create a bandwagon for reluctant joiners. Although the US will not ratify the Kyoto Protocol, a list of cities that are pledging to address (in unnamed and likely politicized ways) global warming is shown on the screen behind Gore. To both the individual and the collective he asks, "Are we as Americans capable of doing great things even though they are difficult?" By way of an answer, he employs what Killingsworth and Palmer call "the metanarrative of human liberation," which tells "the story of progress toward an ever broader human liberty" (129). Indeed, Gore runs through the standard list: the American Revolution, abolitionism, the suffragist movement, World War II intervention against fascism, desegregation, and (efforts to) democratize communist governments, despite the racist, hegemonic, capitalistic, and anti-environmental underpinnings of some of these efforts and their problematic consequences. Gore appeals to his audience as patriots, centrists, humanists, and, most of all, revisionists—revisionists in their own future history.

Cara Finnegan writes, "close attention to the specific, institutionally defined constraints of the contexts in which images appear enables a more nuanced analysis of the rhetorical availability of particular modes for framing images" (64). To understand the institutional constraints associated with a film, one might turn one's attention to those who created it: the producers and director. The director's commentary provides a glimpse into the ideology behind the film and the constraints under which it was made, but this is rhetorical as well, and serves as a metarhetoric to the film's primary rhetoric. Put another way, the rhetoric of science is parlayed within Gore's rhetoric, which is scripted into the rhetoric of the film, which is rhetorically positioned by the filmmaker's commentary. These layers of "nested rhetorics" cannot be easily disentangled as they form one blended message being delivered by the film's solitary narrator.

To attend to all of these layers is to attend to the one aspect of the film that is truth: the film is a social construction in which Gore is not (necessarily) the conductor, but (certainly) the performer. The "Behind the Scenes" segment on the DVD is hearteningly "transparent" (inasmuch as a rhetoric can be) about the filmic quality of the documentary. We see the set designers discussing where Gore will stand; we see Gore rehearsing; and we hear the director tell the audience, "This is part of a movie, we are doing it several times." This begs the question: Is he speaking to an audience or to extras? Regardless, he is speaking to a homogenous group of well-dressed, attentive, white "constituents" in their twenties and thirties. When Gore finishes, the producers rejoice, saying: "a standing ovation from the control room, that's pretty good."

We learn other things about the film: Gore's laptop is to be featured prominently; his poor-quality source images have been replaced; his daughter assisted with the scripting; and the stage gives him a three-dimensional appearance. In fact, the producers approached Gore about the film, not vice versa. Once he'd agreed, the director was concerned about adapting a slideshow into a movie: "How do you make a lecture interesting?" The answer: through graphics, charisma, and Gore's "personal journey."

In deciding what to include, the producers also decided what *not* to include. They acknowledge cutting "about 30–45 minutes" from his original speech so the audience wouldn't suffer from "information fatigue." Although we don't know what was cut, we do know what is missing. The film omits interviews with scientists, fellow activists, and politicians. Herein lays one of the film's central truth-building techniques: to rely on science but remain distanced from the scientists who contributed to it. This distancing, according to Killingsworth and Palmer, is important: it keeps the emphasis on "the results and conclusions of the research," not the people or institutions who measured, interpreted, and published that research (144). The people, off "doing" science, "have no interest in influencing actions that lie outside of that research program" (Killingsworth and Palmer, 106). Instead the film uses decontextualized numbers, dates, and rates to represent science, which, paired with vivid visuals, creates truth. This is not to say that the numbers are inaccurate, falsified, or manipulated; it is simply to acknowledge that the purpose of their use is not to explicate details but to create a call to action—in a rhetorical sense, to create agency.

The film also omits discussions about positive efforts being made on a local level or scientific strides toward solutions. The film omits the (sometimes unflattering) environmental negotiations, such as the Northwest timber controversy, that occurred during Gore's vice presidency. The film omits any mention of President Clinton, Gore's wife, or the square footage of Gore's own ecological footprint.

Although the film does address vehicle emissions, it falls short of decisively attacking the oil industry, auto industry, logging industry, home developers, chemical developers, consumerism, partisanship, and military operations. It doesn't look primarily at specific, localized causes or specific, localized results. Robert Cox might consider this a nod to the "aporias of dispersed power" (174). The film seems to distance itself from specifics (individual scientists, localized problems, community solutions) in its effort to create one broad, sweeping truth. It puts the impetus on the individual to take action and press legislators to take action. Perhaps this is because, in the rhetorically impossible hopes of the director, "We don't want this film to be part of a political agenda."

It may be impossible to determine if *An Inconvenient Truth* establishes the scientific, political, and social truth that it seeks to create. Certainly the film has succeeded in helping Gore to reinvent himself and build upon his burgeoning ethos as a humanist and new environmentalist (as well as a businessman and *former* politician). The Noah motif may work well for audiences that traditionally reject notions of climate change; yet the film also allows Gore to redefine himself as a solitary figure when, in fact, scientists around the globe are struggling to address the same issues.

We'll never know if the film succeeded in creating truth (likely for some it did) or agency (likely for others it didn't). Perhaps more importantly, could such truth create agency? Or, more astutely, how would we measure its ability to create agency—through behavioral and policy changes, or through ticket sales and DVD rentals? As Douglas Kellner writes, we can "empower individuals to become more autonomous agents, able to emancipate themselves from contemporary forms of domination and able to become more active citizens, eager and competent to engage in processes of social transformation" (63). In Kellner's sense, awareness *is* agency. Maybe this is all that *An Inconvenient Truth* can hope to do: raise that fuzzy, problematic notion of "awareness." On the other hand, perhaps the film simply fostered our own desire for epistephilia—a pleasure in knowing—even if that which we've come to know is, in Gore's estimation, inconvenient.

WORKS CITED

Bruzzi, Stella. *New Documentary: A Critical Introduction*. New York: Routledge, 2000.

Cox, Robert J. "The (Re)Making of the Environmental President." *Green Talk in the White House: The Rhetorical Presidency Encounters Ecology*. Texas A&M UP: 2004.

Finnegan, Cara A. "Documentary as Art in U.S. Camera." *Rhetoric Society Quarterly* 31.2 (2001): 37–68.

Foss, Karen A. "Celluloid Rhetoric: The Use of Documentary Film to Teach Rhetorical Theory." *Communication Education* 32.1 (1983): 51–61.

An Inconvenient Truth. Dir. Davis Guggenheim. Perf. Al Gore. Paramount Classics, 2006.

Kellner, Douglas. "Reading Images Critically: Toward a Postmodern Pedagogy." *Postmodernism, Feminism, and Cultural Politics: Redrawing Educational Boundaries*. Ed. Henry Giroux. New York: State U of New York P, 1991. 60–82.

Killingsworth, M. Jimmie. "Rhetorical Appeals: A Revision." *Rhetoric Review* 24.3 (2005): 249–63.

Killingsworth, M. Jimmie and Jacqueline S. Palmer. *Ecospeak: Rhetoric and Environmental Politics in America*. Carbondale: Southern Illinois UP, 1992.
Lucaites, John Louis, and Robert Hariman. "Visual Rhetoric, Photojournalism, and Democratic Public Culture." *Rhetoric Review* 20, no. 1–2 (2001): 37–42.
Nichols, Bill. *Representing Reality: Issues and Concepts in Documentary*. Bloomington: Indiana UP, 1995.
Plantinga, Carl R. *Rhetoric and Representation in Nonfiction Film*. New York: Cambridge UP, 1997.
Peterson, Tarla Rai, ed. *Green Talk in the White House: The Rhetorical Presidency Encounters Ecology*. Texas A&M UP: 2004.
Selig, Michael. "The Rhetoric of Documentary." *Post Script: Essays in Film and the Humanities* 9, no. 1–2 (1989): 99–122.
Winston, Brian. *Claiming the Real: The Documentary Film Revisited*. London: British Film Institute Publishing, 1995.

9 Adventure Narratives and the Ethos of Survival

Doug Christensen

One might assume that extreme adventurers would use the stories they tell to make stronger cases for sustainable environmental practices. Unfortunately, so many adventure narratives (often called survival narratives) fail to communicate any noteworthy environmental ethic. Instead we typically get an age-old struggle of conquest, narcissism, and alienation from the land because of unconscious objectification. Adventure narratives, especially when framed as "survival narratives" illustrate how casually people with privilege exaggerate the importance of their own conquests in the overwhelming scheme of people actually living on the margins of survival. The combination of adventure together with the publication of a given narrative precipitates these dilemmas because the focus on self-inflicted struggle for survival is, for the adventurer, so megalomaniacal that writing it down only compounds and reifies the egocentric ontology. That is, by writing about my adventure experience—my brush with death—I further objectify the alien object (nature) because my text is now an additional physical object, as well as a metaphysical layer of distance between me and said object, instead of a catalyst that binds me to the land. I don't suggest that a written narrative can never compliment the actual experience or that extreme adventure stories always fail to reveal acts of great courage, bravery, altruism, or even heroism, but too often self-centered motives complicate such possibilities and even if they don't, the status symbols associated with hero frames, like courage, bravery, and altruism, create distance between the reader and the author-hero.

I am one of many who experiences extreme adventure vicariously—through carefully constructed narratives that tend to textually transfuse at least some of their authors' adrenaline. Although I am neither a climber nor a mountaineer, I am a recreational consumer of outdoor adventure and I connect my enthusiasm for amateur exploits to a romanticized but nevertheless actual appreciation for the earth. At what point and to what degree is the average outdoor enthusiast obligated to an environmental ethic? Is the growing genre of extreme adventure narratives (survival narratives) just another example of American-style arrogance and incorrigible denial about our desire to conquer and colonize otherwise hostile landscapes? I will argue that although adventure narratives shine a unique light on extreme adventure, these stories ironically exacerbate a materialistically driven alienation of the self. My claim hinges on the motive of individual climbers, especially as revealed by their own writing and it presupposes, perhaps idealistically, a ready connection between the adventurer and the natural world. Unfortunately, in the attempt to connect with the land, the water, the rock, the spirit of the wild, the adventurer often perpetuates a solipsistic disregard for responsibilities and opportunities to champion sustainability. At the very least, he or she demonstrates a symbolic denial of sustainable principles, and at most a literal negation of eco-conscious choices.

Some noteworthy adventurers set a high standard for kinship with the land. For example, Henry Thoreau, who saw little more than alienation in the lives of those around him, begins his essay (originally a lecture) "Walking," with this proclamation:

> I wish to speak a word for Nature, for absolute freedom and wildness, as contrasted with a freedom and culture merely civil,—to regard man as an inhabitant, or a part and parcel of Nature, rather than a member of society. I wish to make an extreme statement, if so I may make an emphatic one, for there are enough champions of civilization: the minister and the school-committee, and every one of you will take care of that. (149)

Thoreau is probably not considered an extreme adventurer, but his passion for the earth comes through clearly in his texts. Toward the end of "Walking" he returns boldly to his thesis by lamenting: "We hug the earth,—how rarely we mount! Methinks we might elevate ourselves a little more. We might climb a tree, at least." He then illustrates, as the first tree hugger, this desire to mount—to become one with the earth, by describing an excursion that he made to the top of a white pine where the tree marks him thoroughly with sap—a sign that he has merged with the tree: "Though I got well pitched, I was well paid for it," and then he defines his payment as a view of new mountaintops and new expanses of sky never before seen (175). He also collects a rare blossom from the top of the white pine—a blossom that grows way out on the end of the branches. He takes this prize around to several villagers to see if they recognize it, but of course few have ever been to the top of a white pine. His fascination with the blossom reiterates his common reminder to the reader to drink more deeply, to look more closely—to merge with one's surroundings. There is no doubt that Thoreau's vision is eccentric, nor is there any shortage of criticism for his sanctimonious eco-orthodoxy. Nevertheless, in the context of the rise of environmentalism and conservationism, we cannot take for granted his rendition of a phenomenological circulation between the human and what David Abram calls the "more than human world." Not only does Thoreau become one of the early spokespersons for the environmental cause, he gives Nature a voice of its own when he wishes "to speak a word for nature."

But Thoreau's "Walking" is not only an "extreme statement" about whether one's affinity for nature should precede one's membership in society. It is also a call for people to exercise their lungs, to explore the natural world in order to brush up against the terms of their own survival. In what follows, he highlights the risks of a life indoors:

> When sometimes I am reminded that the mechanics and shopkeepers stay in their shops not only all the forenoon, but all the afternoon too, sitting with crossed legs, so many of them,—as if the legs were made to sit upon, and not to stand or walk upon,—I think that they deserve some credit for not having all committed suicide long ago.
>
> I, who cannot stay in my chamber for a single day without acquiring some rust, and when sometimes I have stolen forth for a walk at the eleventh hour of four o'clock in the afternoon, too late to redeem the day, when the shades of night were already beginning to be mingled with the daylight, have felt as if I had committed some sin to be atoned for,—I confess that I am astonished at the power of endurance, to say nothing of the moral insensibility, of my neighbors who confine themselves to shops and offices the whole day for weeks and months, ay, and years almost together (151).

How does a reader avoid Thoreau's call—a call to be outside but also to be at one with nature? Still, there is something self-righteous in the premise of his writing—something taken for granted when he dings his "neighbors who confine themselves to shops and offices the whole day." Thoreau's privileged career as a single, white, male writer allows him to turn walking into his work, the meager earnings that result from his writing notwithstanding. Moreover, supporting only himself likely required little more than he was able to grow, kill, or catch (clearly we know him to be resourceful: if Thoreau's self described resourcefulness in *Walden*, for example, is not satisfactory evidence, see Emerson's description of Thoreau in *Atlantic Monthly*, volume 10, 1862).

In his introduction to *Walden*, Michael Meyer compares the privileged Thoreau to the anything-but-privileged Frederick Douglass. Meyer compares Thoreau's critique of the slave-driven life of the average city dweller and Thoreau's own heroic journey away from such constraints to the heroic journey of people like Douglass who escape literal slavery. Meyer notes that "readers come away from slave narratives shocked by the descriptions of injustice and human waste, and they come away from *Walden* startled by the realization that they have forged their own limitations, chaining themselves to impoverished values. The ex-slave exposes the welts on his back, and Thoreau reveals the subtler interior scars (where the meanings are, as Emily Dickinson would say) that previously had been covered over by a social fabric" (Thoreau 27). Meyer recognizes the absurdity in this comparison, but one wonders if his recognition goes far enough: "To note these similarities is not to collapse the radical differences that are so painfully obvious when one compares what Douglass had to endure with what Thoreau chose to do without" (28).

Although seemingly unrelated to my thesis, Meyer highlights a subtle, but palpable difference between adventure narratives that result from the escape of dire circumstances, as in the case of Frederick Douglass, or even those in a modern survival story like Pier Paul Read's 1974 book *Alive*, where several members of a rugby team survive a plane crash in the Andes and eventually make their way to safety against terrible odds, versus Thoreau's volitional sauntering, or any of a variety of other narratives about contemporary extreme adventurers who test themselves against inhospitable conditions by choice. Meyer's inadvertent distinction between self-imposed survival and survival of circumstances beyond one's control underscores a crucial difference in terms of privilege. In the latter case, the backdrop of Romanticism can give way to hubris difficult for contemporary adventurers to shake. As already suggested, many of today's adventure narratives presuppose a definition of survival that is limited because of motive. On the other hand, Thoreau's motives seem defensible on the grounds of his clear commitment to what Jeffrey McCarthy calls "contact" and "connection." Thoreau also proves devoted to what has been called naturalism, but what we now call environmentalism and sustainability—motives implied in the fullest sense of what McCarthy means by "connection," but about which we cannot be so sure with the modern adventurer.

In the context of my argument, McCarthy's recent book *Contact* helps in several significant ways. First, McCarthy's is one of very few arguments connecting the action of climbing to the purpose for climbing. He goes so far as to suggest that the ideal contemporary climber does so out of concern for and love of the environment. The first two sentences of his preface are: "*Contact* is a book about climbing. *Contact* is a book about the environment" (McCarthy xi). Second, he brings climbing and the environment together using adventure narratives. Many in the field of professional composition have argued that writing is a way of making knowledge. McCarthy recognizes the effects of bringing adventure together with writing—although often to differing ends. And third, he organizes the narratives around three motives for climbing: conquest, caretaking and connection. "Conquest" obviously grounds the motives in totally personal, solipsistic reasons for climbing. Under this model, exploitative practices are probable. By caretaking, McCarthy means that the environment is understood and designated as a place of use, not development. By partitioning the wilderness into spaces that cannot be developed, caretakers believe these spaces will maintain their natural, wild appeal, while also serving recreational purposes. But they are still objectified in a way that implies that use laws may bend in favor of exploitative practices, like logging. The third, more idealistic frame inscribes a communion with the land. Connection, McCarthy writes, is the "lived expression of a longtime philosophical goal of environmentalists—surmounting the subject/object divide . . . the hierarchy of mind above body, thought above world, leads Western people to treat nature as an object for profit and convenience, instead of a part of ourselves" (169). McCarthy's introduction suggests that contemporary consciousness-raising efforts toward a "connection" ethos are making a difference. Quoting Aldo Leopold and Jack Turner, McCarthy notes that an ontological shift in our self-perception in relation to the earth is the only substantive way to avoid objectification. Although these three models are not mutually exclusive, and one cannot always know why people go into the woods, I suggest that adventure narratives give us our best clues.

Despite his persistent iconoclasm toward almost any institutional structure, Edward Abbey's widely read *Desert Solitaire* renders motives for environmental appreciation that comply with McCarthy's ideal, and, like Thoreau, differ from the norm. In his adventure narrative "Down the River," Abbey is bent on communion and oneness. In the first place, he compares himself to John Wesley Powell because Powell was among the first white travelers down the Colorado and Abbey among the last: "What follows is the record of a last voyage through a place we knew, even then, was doomed" (Abbey 188–89). The undercurrent of adventure comes through in early lines as in the following example:

> We've forgotten a few things, among them life jackets, and I can't help thinking that maybe we should make the trip some other time. One of the things that worries me, besides the missing life jackets and the obvious fragility of our Made-in-Japan vessels, is the fact that Ralph has only one good leg.[1] He can walk, but not hike; he can swim but not far. . . . Ralph paddles on one side, I on the other, giving us some control over our direction. (190–91)

Later Abbey will add: "Actually our ignorance and carelessness are more deliberate than accidental" (195). There is obvious purpose in the uncertainty about the direction and the outcome of their journey. But then we see his motive more clearly:

> We are indeed enjoying a very intimate relation with the river: only a layer of fabric between our bodies and the water. I let my arm dangle over the side and trail my hand in the flow . . . I am fulfilling at last a dream of childhood and one as powerful as the erotic dreams of adolescence—*floating down the river*. Mark Twain, Major Powell, every man that has ever put forth on flowing water knows what I mean. (191–92)

Connection to the elements move seamlessly through Abbey's narrative. They are "thinking river thoughts," they drink the river water, and Abbey plays songs on his harmonica that take him back to the river of his childhood religion where he recalls singing songs of baptismal immersion. They grow accustom to sand: "sand in our food and drink, in our teeth and eyes and whiskers, in our bedrolls and underwear. Sand becomes a part of our existence, which, like breathing, we take for granted (204)." And Abbey's oneness with the river, his immersion, what he calls intersubjectivity, culminates toward the end of their journey down the river. He explains:

> Configurations are beginning to fade, distinctions shading off into blended amalgams of man and man, men and water, water and rock . . . We are merging, molecules getting mixed. Talk about intersubjectivity—we are both taking on the coloration of river and canyon, our skin as mahogany as the water on the shady side, our clothing coasted with silt, our bare feet caked with mud and tough as lizard skin, our whiskers bleached as the sand—even our eyeballs, what little you can see of them between the lids, have taken on a coral-pink, the color of the dunes. And we smell, I suppose, like catfish. We've forgotten to keep a close track of time, we have no clock or calendar, and no longer know for certain exactly how many days and nights we've been on the river (231–32).

If Abbey can ever to be said to be at one with anything, it must be in terms of a oneness with those wild surroundings he describes and defines so elegantly.

Whether taken literally or figuratively, the human-earth oneness narrative is often framed for Western readers by the Genesis account of Adam and Eve: people made by their God from the mud (the word "human" aligned with "humus," meaning soil). In this survival narrative, after Adam (whose name is derived from the Hebrew *adamah*, meaning "ground") and Eve are cast out of the garden, they are thrown into the phenomenological world and exposed to the elements. The burden they bear in the raw world, to "eat their bread by the sweat of their brow," is interpreted by humans in at least two ways, the distinction of which informs much of the contemporary ecological theory. Caring for the earth is either a curse or a duty. All three of McCarthy's frames can be interpolated into the Edenic narrative. In his 1977 essay, "The Body and the Earth," Wendell Berry raises questions about the human relationship to the earth: "The question of human limits, of the proper definition and place of human beings within the order of Creation, finally rests upon our attitude toward our biological existence, the life of the body in this world. What value and respect do we give to our bodies? What uses do we have for them? What relation do we see, if any, between body and mind, or body and soul? What connections or responsibilities do we maintain between our bodies and the earth?" (*The Unsettling of America* 97).

Berry's career-long critique closely follows on this preceding series of questions. As a devout Christian, he explores the possible interpretations and misinterpretations of the Genesis account. In an essay titled "God and Country" he addresses possible misinterpretations, specifically of Genesis 1:28, where God told Adam and Eve to be fruitful, multiply and replenish the earth, and subdue it. Berry writes: "The ecological teaching of the Bible is inescapable: God made the world because He wanted it made. He thinks the world is good, and He loves it. It is His world; He has never relinquished title to it. And He has never revoked the conditions, bearing on His gift to us of the use of it, that obliges us to take excellent care of it. If God loves the world, then how might any person of faith be excused for not loving it or justified in destroying it?" (*What Are People For?* 98). Berry explains the notion of dominion using the word "usufruct," a term he equates most closely to stewardship.

Others agree with Berry's emphasis on an earth-affirming interpretation of the biblical imperatives. In his important book *Our Common Dwelling*, Lance Newman articulates the activist role of the ecocritic:

> First priority has been to mount a negative critique of anthropocentric ways of thinking about nature, such as the idea that people were meant to maintain dominion over nature, or that nature is a passive receptacle of the fertilizing human mind, or that limitless growth is the essence of social destiny. Most ecocritics take to heart Lynn White's observation that: "What people do about ecology depends on what they think about themselves in relation to things around them. Human ecology is deeply conditioned by beliefs about our nature and destiny—that is, by religion." For White, the "victory of Christianity over paganism was the greatest psychic revolution in the history of our culture" and produced an "exploitative attitude" based on "an implicit faith in perpetual progress." In another version of this argument, Glen Love points to the legacy of "humanism," arguing that modern society is deformed by the idea that human well-being is the highest good. Humanism has produced an ecocidal obsession with merely "internal" conflicts over resources, at a time when human domination—never mind the subdivisions of human—of the biosphere is the overriding problem. (Newman 6)

Newman's description of our pervasive denial lays the groundwork for the kind of hubris as easily associated with extreme adventurers as with Thoreau's disconnected city dwellers. David Abram pushes even more forcefully on those boundaries that divide the human and the more than human:

> It is likely that the "inner world" of our Western psychological experience, like the supernatural heaven of Christian belief, originates in the loss of our ancestral reciprocity with the animate earth. . . . Caught up in a mass of abstractions, our attention hypnotized by a host of human-made technologies that only reflect us back to ourselves, it is all too easy for us to forget our carnal inherence in a more-than-human

matrix of sensations and sensibilities. . . . To shut ourselves off from these other voices . . . is to rob our own senses of their integrity and to rob our minds of their coherence. We are human only in contact, and conviviality, with what is not human. (10, 22)

But as I suggest at the beginning, adventure carries its own alienation and existential hostility. Whereas I agree with Abram about the need for deep connection, I am not certain that its ideal precondition arises with adventure, especially adventure in the extreme.

By contrast to my theoretical framework of oneness, the September 2008 issue of *Outside* magazine features a narrative about a climbing fiasco that unfolded in early August 2008, on the world's second highest mountain, K2. According to Michael Kodas, eleven climbers died and ten of the deaths were the result of what Kodas calls "human error." The exception, Rolph Bae, perished after he was suddenly buried by an avalanche of ice. Kodas explains the odds of success on K2 early in his article:

> Everest has been climbed roughly 3,000 times, with hundreds of new names added to the list every year. K2 has seen only 299 ascents—and in many years, nobody summits. According to logs compiled by ExplorersWeb, 10.3 percent of K2 summiters have died on the descent. That's more than five times Everest's fatality rate for summiters, 1.82 percent. Among elite climbers, K2 is known as "the mountaineer's mountain." It's also called "the savage mountain" (1).

Outside magazine is unique when it comes to adventure narratives. A twenty-five page piece written for *Outside's* September 1996 issue about a similar trip to the top of Everest obviously stopped short, prompting Jon Krakauer's nearly 300-page book detailing a misadventure. Unlike the recent K2 article author, Krakauer actually participated in the Everest climb—a witness to the misfortune, although it will not be a surprise when we see a book-length version of the recent events on K2, written by one of the survivors. Accompanying Jon Krakauer's original *Outside* article on the Everest disaster of 1996 is an oddly telling picture—one that reveals a glimpse of the estimated twenty tons of waste (oxygen tanks, etc.) littering the higher camps. Although clean-up efforts have been executed, the task will require a Herculean effort over many years. Obviously one's aspirations for sustainable practices get quickly compromised when oxygen runs low and immediate survival hangs in the balance. But this illustration, although perhaps extreme, raises other questions about sustainability back home. Are people committed to outdoor adventure obligated to a particular environmental ethic?

The example of Swedish native Göran Kropp, who famously rode his bike from Sweden to Nepal and then summited Everest without additional oxygen, posits one exception to the rule. He later climbed to Camp Four with his girlfriend to remove twenty-five oxygen containers. Kropp, whose last name coincidentally means "body" in Swedish, works as proof for my hypothesis because he embodies the ideals of an earth-loving adventurer; he cultivates his devotion to his conquests alongside a persuasive ecological ethos. In his autobiography, *Ultimate High*, he writes of his decision to ride his bicycle from sea level in Stockholm, to Nepal and then continue on foot to the highest place on earth:

> The main idea in my dreams about climbing Everest was to do everything in the most natural way possible—and to use only my own power. I considered how to get to the mountain. Gasoline-powered engines were out of the question. But riding a horse . . . ? Or how about walking . . . ? I decided to bike to Everest. I also planned to make my climb without using bottled oxygen or porters to carry my supplies, and during the climb, I would eat only the food and use only the equipment that I had brought with me on the bicycle from Sweden. (37)

Kropp's tenacity and vision for sustainability is admirable but he is the exception.

No one offers a clearer critique of the extreme mountaineer's motives than Maria Coffey. In her book, *Where the Mountain Casts its Shadow*, Coffey takes exception to the typical interpretation of survival in survival narratives. She argues that those left in the wakes of dead climbers (and even living ones away from home for months at a time) are the real heroes and victims in the stories. Coffey interviews hundreds of climbers and relatives of climbers researching the social and psychic fallout from the climbing lifestyle and especially from the accidents. The variables Coffey most carefully explores include the resentments between partners over conventional home life versus the life on the road—time spent apart—especially when there are children in the mix, and of course there's the risk. Lynn Hill, described as an "American rock athlete," and "the first person to 'free climb' The Nose (in Yosemite), using a rope and equipment only to protect herself from falling, and scaling it in twenty-three hours straight," described her fear of high-altitude mountaineering:

> I loved the challenge . . . but I don't choose to go to those places anymore. For me, there's so much more excitement and beauty in the feel and the aesthetics of warm rock. It's alive. The high mountains are dead places. Nothing lives up there. I understand the adventure and pristine beauty of going to them, but it's not worth the risk and discomfort—or the hurt that it brings to the people who are close to you if you die. And the chances of dying are so much higher in places like that (Coffey 12–13).

That kind of hurt is palpable in story after story.

Coffey carefully analyzes both the motives of the climbers and the silences, resentments, and the wreckage in the aftermath of bad news from Nepal and other high-altitude regions. Of her own loss she writes:

> While Pete and Joe lay still on the mountain, life had gone on for Hilary and me. Our trek to 21,000 feet on Everest had been a hard physical endeavor, but it was easy compared with what awaited us at home—facing the routine of daily life again and making some sense of it all. My first year was one of confusion: I drank heavily, smoked too much pot, drove recklessly. I lurched from day to day, trying to block out the pain, but at the same time I was desperately attempting to regain feelings of aliveness. Then, to others, it appeared that I started to get better. I moved to an old cottage in the countryside and threw myself into renovations. I began training for a marathon and applying for new teaching jobs. But I knew I was still running from despair, fleeing the terrifying emptiness in my life, frantically trying to fill the gap that Joe had left behind, to fill my lost future (113).

According to Coffey's research, climbers have no choice; they have to climb. They do it for the challenge, to walk the existential edge between life and death. The need is described as an incessant nagging from within. Chris Bonington said, "'At the end of the day, climbing is probably irresponsible. But we're better parents because we're doing things that fulfill us.' It's a common argument: climbing is my calling; if you take that away, my spirit will die, I won't be a complete person, and my children will suffer" (Coffey 163).

After so much similar testimonial and explanation by countless climbers, very little is ever made of financial cost. This textual silence[2] may suggest that people will sacrifice whatever it takes to pursue their passion. It may also suggest that people who survive high adventure and write about it live lives of privilege. Even those who abdicate financial responsibilities at home to pursue their adventures somehow manage to catch planes, outfit themselves, and eat during the months of training. Obviously some experts are paid for their exploits, but money doesn't inform the conversation about the complications between partners left at home to tow the line. This omission in Coffey's work, consistent with so much writing about adventure, frames high adventure, if only inadvertently, as exclusive and as privileged. The choice to place oneself into dangerous exotic landscapes, to narrowly survive and then make a career out of telling that story undermines the more mundane survival of millions of people who live on the margins without a voice or opportunity for upward mobility. In other words, most impoverished people, deprived of adequate food, shelter, health, and education, also lack the wherewithal to change their situation. I am not trying to suggest a dichotomy between a person's right to climb or participate in high adventure as opposed to a life dedicated to more altruistic pursuits—an argument perhaps better made by someone like philosopher Peter Singer. But I am arguing that adventurers buy into a system of materialism and cultural alienation instead of a culture of communion and reverence for the earth. Some recognize their own egocentricity—some eagerly admit that theirs is a completely selfish lifestyle. Joe Simpson, author of *Touching the Void*, tells Coffey, "It's super selfish . . . it has to be. You can't do it otherwise" (69). But it's the layer of cultural insensitivity beneath the selfishness; it's the hero frame around such self-centeredness that enables a blindness toward those dealing with actual life-and-death survival in the real world.

At the very least, one might hope that in "survival" narratives the ecocentricity could balance the egocentricity. Despite McCarthy's argument for environmentally sensitive climbing narratives, few of Coffey's illustrations of motive even hint at an environmental ethos. But because adventure narratives already appeal to an environmentally sympathetic audience, couldn't these stories do more to advance literacy about ecologically sensitive issues? Unfortunately, too many adventure stories show how profound self-importance overshadows otherwise sublime connections with and defense of the wild. In Aron Ralston's retelling of his confrontation with death in Blue John Canyon, his passion for adventure and exploration shine.[3] His narrative proves him to be a very resourceful survivor and story teller, and his descriptions of adventures that led up to his fateful solo trip are filled with pathos about the landscapes, with motives couched in a clear appreciation for the outdoor world. But his rather exhaustive retelling could take more advantage of his public moment to raise questions about dire ethical concerns relative to personal responsibility for preservation and sustainability practices. Ralston's story overwhelms readers with details about the choke stone that cost him his arm at the complete eclipse of potential views of the landscape that lured Ralston there in the first place. Ralston was clearheaded enough throughout his ordeal to snap photos and record himself on video and it probably wasn't completely beyond him—even in his emaciated, desperate state—to imagine the story he could tell should he survive. In similar fashion, the droves of climbers summiting Everest seem to have much more to do with spectacle and conquest than with connection to the wild.

Concern along these lines leads Jack Turner to question our motives generally. In his book *Abstract Wild: A Rant* he notes,

> A recent conceit is that certain wild places and animals and forests are "sacred." We have forgotten that sacred is a social word and that "sacred for me" is as irrelevant as "legal for me." We often ignore aspects of our culture that are sacred because we do not distinguish between formal and popular religion. Our national parks are sacred, Disneyland is sacred, the location of President Kennedy's assassination is sacred. These pilgrimage sites are sacred because of the function of entertainment and tourism in our culture. In a commercial culture, the

sacred will have a commercial base. For many people, nothing is more sacred than the Super Bowl (22).

Our Western inclinations toward a philosophical diet of commodification and romance block our view of our own privileged perceptions. In the face of survival, or enveloped in the paragraphs of survival stories, we turn our backs to the complexities of nature and to those not coping so well in other hostile landscapes (like Sub-Saharan Africa and the inner city of Washington D.C.). This hubristic turn toward the self and away from others and from the land (as other) occludes a clear vision of a future where sustainable practices might precipitate a more sublime survival narrative.

Krakauer's recounting of Christopher McCandless's forays into adventure in *Into the Wild* matches Ralston's experience in many respects. Both young men share a youthful zeal for exploration and adventure; both deserted what they considered a mundane, conventional lifestyle for consistent wilderness experience; both approached their adventures without sufficient respect for the land. Much has been made about the naïveté of McCandless's preparation to survive in the Alaskan wilderness, and some of the skepticism is raised by Krakauer himself. But one question that looms silently over both narratives (in fact over all survival narratives) is the question of sustainability. The definition of ecological sustainability suggests an organic circle or circulation of personal responsibility. The reason these stories smack of such hubris is that they so often highlight the inability of an individual to survive, and his practices out in the wild are, therefore, by definition, unsustainable. Krakauer defends McCandless:

> It is hardly unusual for a young man to be drawn to a pursuit considered reckless by his elders; engaging in risky behavior is a rite of passage in our culture no less that in most others. Danger has always held a certain allure. . . . McCandless, in his fashion, merely took risk-taking to its logical extreme. He had a need to test himself in ways, as he was fond of saying, "that mattered." He possessed grand—some would say grandiose—spiritual ambitions. According to the moral absolutism that characterizes McCandless's beliefs, a challenge in which a successful outcome is assured isn't a challenge at all. (*Into the Wild* 182)

Krakauer compares McCandless to Muir and Thoreau and concludes:

> Unlike Muir and Thoreau, McCandless went into the wilderness not primarily to ponder nature or the world at large but, rather, to explore the inner country of his soul. He soon discovered however, what Muir and Thoreau already knew: An extended stay in the wilderness inevitably directs one's attention outward as much as inward and it is impossible to live off the land without developing both a subtle understanding of, and a strong emotional bold with, that land and all it holds. (183)

Krakauer's frame around McCandless's experience rings true. But in the next paragraph he acknowledges what occupied most of McCandless's thought after the charm of the wilderness wore off—food. "The entries in McCandless's journal contain few abstractions about wilderness, or, for that matter, few ruminations of any kind. There is scant mention of the surrounding scenery." In fact the "entries are almost entirely about what he ate. He wrote about hardly anything except food" (183). The question of sustainability here is subtle. In fact, what does it mean to live sustainably? We don't have to invoke Maslow's hierarchy of needs to understand that sustaining one's own personal health comes first; we get that much from the Genesis account. Sustainability requires a symbiotic circulation of understanding and action between the self and the earth. According to the *Oxford English Dictionary*, "sustainability" derives from the word "sustenance," which means to subsist, to nourish, to provide, and to endure. Sustainability connects inextricably with survival. But the term applies broadly to the marketplace, to landscapes, to relationships between people, and to every aspect of survival. Ultimately, Krakauer's *Into the Wild* is a cautionary tale about the requirements of sustainability. Along with Ralston's *Between a Rock and Hard Place*, *Into the Wild* reiterates the absolute demands of an organic, symbiotic relationship to the earth environment.

In 1968 Richard Proenneke pulled up roots in mainstream culture and moved to Twin Lakes in the remote Alaskan Wilderness. He built a log cabin with hand tools, out of trees that he felled the previous summer and he more or less remained in the wilderness from age fifty-one until he was eighty-two years, at which time he decided he could no longer withstand the subzero winter temperatures and he moved to California to spend his final three years with his brother. He recorded his sojourn using a tripod and a camera, and by writing copious journal entries. Proenneke's sustainable lifestyle in the wilderness draws a sharp contrast with Krakauer's narrative, not to mention high-altitude mountain climbing narratives. While Proenneke had occasional contact with the outside world, receiving orders for what he called "life's luxuries," like coffee, spices, sugar, and beans from his close friend Babe, who flew in supplies every two or three months, Proenneke spent most of his thirty years alone with the elements and animals. He created a completely self-sustaining lifestyle in an inhospitable environment. But he also generated an objective humility and respect for his surroundings. His answer to the travails of human society, like Thoreau and Muir, and unlike several misanthropes mentioned by Krakauer in *Into the Wild* (people incapable of sustaining a balanced lifestyle under rigorous conditions[4]), underscores the kind of motive necessary for sustainable practices in the wild. But his narrative also forms a template for more sustainable practices among human populations.

In 1973 Proenneke's journal was shaped into a book called *One Man's Wilderness*. The book comprised his journal entries from his first years at Twin Lakes. But Proenneke complained later that the editor of his book,

Sam Keith, took more creative license with the journal than Proenneke would have liked. "I think Sam probably . . . wanted to be an author so I said you just go ahead, I don't care. [Keith] was the editor, but where does author come into it, but the way he wrote it, it's pretty much . . . he tried to make it sound like it was mine, my thinking . . . He tried to put words in my mouth" (Proenneke vii). Proenneke's second editor, John Branson, compiled Proenneke's journals in Alaska from 1974 to 1980. But Branson doesn't alter the language, instead he organizes the writing into *More Reading's from One Man's Wilderness*. Proenneke's straightforward journal entries calculate the details of his daily habits that never seem repetitive because each day brings a new dance. One day he is protecting his caribou cache from a wolverine and the next he is chasing off a porcupine who keeps returning during the middle of the night to gnaw on his cabin logs. Every day in the Alaskan wilderness is high adventure for Proenneke. His days are filled with hard work and lots of hiking and sightseeing. Like McCandless's journal entries, Proenneke's pages are filled with references to food, but none of his references suggest desperation. He eats well. Moreover, despite his solitary plight, his journal pages are filled with continual flow of visitors. One senses both his separation from society but also his humble recognition that he is part of a family and part of society. McCandless's journey into the wilderness of Alaska reveals a man who severs his supply line to a future. His isolation is absolute and it proves itself as the catalyst to his starvation. On June 30, 1975, Proenneke receives a letter from a young man very similar to McCandless. Jerry Knobton of Rindge, New Hampshire, writes, "[I am] a boy of 21 who wants to live along with nature in the wilds of Alaska and the colder the better." My advice to him," writes Proenneke, "Work until you are 50 and then if you can afford it, do it. He wrote that people thinks him crazy to do such a fool thing. I told him I would have to agree with them" (Proenneke 112). McCandless probably never heard of Proenneke, and the same must be true for Krakauer. If either of them had heard of him, it might have changed McCandless's story because Proenneke demonstrates precisely the kind of preparation required for living in the Alaskan wilderness—for survival. His work reminds the reader of early settlers whose daily affairs were the affairs of survival. When he wasn't tending to his daily needs, he was climbing the surrounding mountains filming and photographing animals. Everywhere his text demonstrates his phenomenological identification with the land in terms of oneness defined earlier: On July 4, 1977, he writes,

> I cleaned my fish and hung them under the roof eave to stiffen. Rain shower over the lower lake and at times it sprinkled pretty good here. . . . I sat under a spruce during the sprinkles and checked on the blueberry crop and the moose situation when it wasn't. Spike has the best crop of fireweed greens in these parts and I loaded up on my way back. Why try to grow something civilized when fireweed, the best

greens ever, does so well? A couple plants of huge dandelions came with Voight's strawberry plants. The strawberries have all but died but the dandelions are high and healthy. . . . My grayling ready for supper. Bite size pieces, no skin, no bones, seasoned well. Fried nice and brown. Beans and a big salad to complete the meal. . . . The showers stopped for the day and now at 8:15 partly cloudy, a light breeze down the lake and 50°. This was a no non-sense 4th of July. The loudest noise I heard was the dishes rattling in the dish pan. (198)

Proenneke's literal experience is not realistic and perhaps not even desirable for many in mainstream culture. But he persuasively shows a way to inhabit a landscape and become part of it. His pragmatic daily experience restores hope in sustainable practices, funded by personal industry and organic responsibility. Proenneke's devotion to a Leopoldian land ethic brings us full circle, back to Thoreau's call:

Speak a word for Nature, for absolute freedom and wildness, as contrasted with a freedom and culture merely civil,—to regard man as an inhabitant, or a part and parcel of Nature, rather than a member of society. I wish to make an extreme statement, if so I may make an emphatic one, for there are enough champions of civilization. (Thoreau 149)

Thoreau's aspiration for connection combined with the aspirations of others mentioned here, raises the possibility that future adventure narratives might explore survival and sustainability in their largest sense—that future hero frames might celebrate symbiotic reverence for the natural world as much as they celebrate individual triumph.

NOTES

1. This concern about Ralph Newcomb's physical condition constitutes another apt comparison to the one-armed Powell.
2. Thomas Huckin coined the term "textual silence" to underscore purposeful omissions in texts that can do as much work as carefully crafted overt terms and phrases.
3. Ralston's story made international news after he survived five days trapped in the desert by a choke stone that pinned his arm to the canyon wall. After he severed his own arm with a pocket knife he hiked eight miles out to his car hydrated only by his own urine.
4. See *Into the Wild*, Chapter 8.

WORKS CITED

Abbey, Edward. *Desert Solitaire*. New York: Ballantine, 1968.
Abram, David. *The Spell of the Sensuous*. New York: Vintage Books, 1996.

Berry, Wendell. *The Unsettling of America*. San Francisco: Sierra Club Books, 1977.

———. *What are People For*. New York: North Point, 1990.

Coffey, Maria. *Where the Mountain Casts its Shadow: The Dark Side of Extreme Adventure*. New York: St. Martin's. 2003.

Emerson, Ralph Waldo. "Thoreau." *The Atlantic Monthly*. Aug. 1862: 239–249.

Huckin, Thomas. "Textual Silence and the Discourse of Homelessness." *Discourse & Society* 13:3, 2002.

Kodas, Michael. "A Few False Moves." *Outside*, September, 2008 [online version], Sept. 26, 008 http://outside.away.com/outside/destinations/200809/k2-disaster-eleven-climbers-die-1.html.

Krakauer, Jon. *Into the Wild*. New York: Anchor, 1996.

———. *Into Thin Air*. New York: Anchor, 1998.

———. "The Story on Everest." *Outside*, September, 1996.

Kropp, Göran. *Ultimate High: My Everest Odyssey*. New York: Discovery Books, 1999.

McCarthy, Jeffrey. *Contact: Mountain Climbing and Environmental Thinking*. Reno: U of Nevada P, 2008.

Newman, Lance. *Our Common Dwelling*. New York: Palgrave MacMillan, 2005.

Proenneke, Richard L. *More Readings from One Man's Wilderness: The Journals of Richard L. Proenneke*. Ed. John Branson. United States Department of the Interior, National Park Service, 2005.

Read, Pier Paul. *Alive*. New York: Harper Collins, 1974.

Thoreau, Henry David. *Walden*. Ed. Michael Meyer. New York: Viking, 1986.

———. *The Essays of Henry D. Thoreau*. Ed. Lewis Hyde. New York: North Point, 2002.

Ralston, Aron. *Between a Rock and a Hard Place*. New York: Atria Books, 2004.

Simpson, Joe. *Touching the Void*. New York: Harper Collins, 1988.

Turner, Jack. *Abstract Wild*. Tucson: U of Arizona P, 1996

10 Fixing Locke
Civil Liberties on a Finite Planet

Eric Zencey

THEORY

For millennia, the assumption that nature has an infinite capacity to offer up its bounty and an infinite capacity to absorb our waste was an unquestionable truth, a condition of life so obvious it didn't need to be articulated; as such it was easily encoded into the theoretical foundations of modern democracy as that foundation emerged in the seventeenth and eighteenth centuries. In no place is this clearer, or more relevant to the experience of the US, than in the work of John Locke, specifically in his influential *Second Treatise of Government, An Essay Concerning the True Original, Extent, and End of Civil-Government*. If we're interested in cataloging ways that rhetorics of unsustainability shape our political experience today, we'd do well to examine the *Second Treatise* with a critical, ecologically wary eye. That examination makes clear: democratic theory needs some rethinking if it is to accommodate itself to a finite planet.

Locke penned the *Second Treatise* to solidify support for the parliamentarian, anti-monarchical political movement that came to power in England in the Glorious Revolution of 1688. His arguments were so successful that the framers of the US Constitution who met in Philadelphia a century later could take his premises as givens; the truths that Jefferson called self-evident in the Declaration of Independence had their disputative origin in the *Second Treatise*. There Locke assembled, codified, and brilliantly extended various strands of disparate and emergent thinking, melding them into a paradigm-case argument for natural rights and the idea that the ultimate source of sovereignty is the just consent of the governed.

In his descriptive subtitle to the *First Treatise*, Locke claimed his purpose as his achievement: "The False Principles and Foundation of Sir Robert Filmer, and His Followers, are Detected and Overthrown." While king and Parliament were at war, Filmer had published *Patriarcha*, an extended defense of the divine right of kings, who, he argued, hold their authority in direct lineal descent from Adam and Noah. In the *First Treatise,* Locke offered a nearly sentence-by-sentence refutation of Filmer's case. Having thus cleared the ground, he could turn in the *Second Treatise* to his positive project: to establish a non-divine foundation for legitimate sovereignty, one that would support a theory of limited rather than absolutist government because it grounded sovereignty in the just consent of the governed, citizens whose rights precede the formation of civil society.

Locke's argument begins with a definition of a human being as having property in himself,[1] and in the crucial chapter "On Property" moves by incremental steps through a "state of nature" argument:

> Though the Earth, and all inferior Creatures be common to all Men, yet every Man has a *Property* in his own *Person*. Thus no body has any Right to but himself. The *Labour* of his Body, and the *Work* of his Hands, we may say are properly his. Whatsoever then he removes out of the State that Nature hath provided, and left it in, he hath mixed his *Labour* with, and joyned to it something that is his own, and thereby makes it his *Property*. (section 27)

Earth and its bounty were given to all men in common; but that doesn't mean that before appropriating from this commons for his sustenance, a man must gain the assent of all who share this God-given title: "If such a consent as that was necessary, Man had starved, notwithstanding the Plenty God had given him." No, a man is entitled "by Law of Reason" to appropriate what he needs for his sustenance, as long as two provisos, the sufficiency and spoilage rules, are met: his appropriation must leave "enough and as good . . . in common for others" and the produce that is appropriated must not spoil before it is used. If a dozen bushels of apples picked from the common bounty of nature rot before Locke's pre-social man can eat them, he's committed an injustice against his fellows, and has the moral status of a thief; what he has taken "is more than his share, and belongs to others" (section 31).

From this pre-social right to appropriate food from the commons Locke thinks it is but a short step to the acquisition of property in land: "I think it is plain that *Property* in that too is acquired as the former" (section 32). Following his two provisos and the logic of his labor theory of value, Locke holds that a man is entitled to stake out a tract of land and cultivate it, excluding others, as long as he continues to allow nothing to spoil and as long as others, too, have the opportunity to enclose land from the commons. And whereas some may complain that in the populated parts of the world there isn't "enough and as good" land left by historical acts of enclosure, Locke has a ready answer: there is land aplenty in the "in-land, vacant places of *America*." (section 36)

From here it is relatively easy for Locke to derive, through a theory of tacit social contract, a legitimate sovereignty that is, unlike Filmer's, limited in scope. The right of an individual to property in himself (and therefore his right to hold secure from others his appropriations from the commons) is inherent and inalienable, and is held by each individual equally by virtue of birth, common humanity, and status as a human being on a God-given planet. In the pursuit of the preservation of that right, individuals can be conceived as having banded together through a social contract to create the civil authority of government. To put the matter negatively: Locke's natural rights theory begins from the premise that human rights and liberties are not the creation of civil society, but preexist it and are merely acknowledged and secured by civil authority.

The change was crucial to the development of a civil society in which the authority of government is limited by rights held by citizens. If, as both Filmer and Hobbes had argued, individual rights and civil liberties are created by the sovereign authority, then the dissolution of that authority would necessarily lead to the extirpation of individual rights and civil liberties.[2] More disturbingly, if rights do not precede the development of sovereignty, then there can be no limit on the sovereign's power that is rooted in civil liberties or individual rights. Indeed, any criticism of the sovereign's treatment of his subjects that refers to the rights of subjects is nonsensical. But in Locke's world, civil liberties limit and trump sovereign authority. In a passage closely echoed by Jefferson in the Declaration of Independence, Locke asserts that "if a long train of Abuses, Prevarications, and Artifices, all tending the same way, make the design [of tyranny] visible to the People . . . 'tis not to be wonder'd, that they should then rouze themselves, and endeavour to put the rule into such hands, which may secure for them the ends for which Government was first erected" (section 225). With Locke government becomes an instrumental, not an absolute good; and when it ceases to serve the ends for which it is an instrument—including primarily the preservation of individual right to property—then, in Jefferson's Lockean phrasing, "it is the Right of the people to alter or abolish it."

An ecologically minded reading of Locke's *Second Treatise* makes clear that to the extent that our concepts of civil liberties and human freedoms are Lockean in origin, they are crucially dependent on a nature that is infinitely bountiful, infinitely capable of absorbing our works and acts. Over and over—half a dozen times in the short chapter on property—Locke adduces the existence of the continental mass of America as justification for his argument; there is always "enough and as good" because America exists as an untrammelled continent awaiting exploitation. "In the beginning," Locke writes, "all the world was America"—all the world was vacant space, held in common, awaiting individual appropriation and exploitation by the entrepreneurial man who, by claiming land and cultivating it, becomes the true originator of civil society. As long as America, with its "inland, vacant places," is a freely exploitable commons, no man can prejudice the interests of another by taking possession of any part of the global commons, because in America there is always "enough, and as good" for others. (In making this argument, Locke not only ignored transportation costs—a commons that is five thousand miles and a difficult sea journey away is scarcely "as good as" a commons close to home—but got his facts wrong: as William

Cronon has shown us, America was not a vacant wasteland. Its ecosystems were being managed by their human participants for maximum production of the services and products that those residents found useful.)

The frequent mention of available land in America is notable for another reason: Locke's argument supposedly doesn't need it. Both the sufficiency and the spoilage rule are, he argues, made irrelevant by the invention of money.

The spoilage rule is obviously circumvented by money. Media of exchange, whether precious metal, rare seashells, or stone wheels, are generally chosen because they are immune to biological decay.

How the invention of money circumvents the "enough and as good" limit on individual appropriation from the commons is less clear-cut, and Locke's argument would be worth examining in detail—if in fact he had offered one. He scarcely bothers to discuss the matter in the *Second Treatise*. (Indeed, some of what he says indicates that the invention of money creates, rather than cures, the problem.[3]) Perhaps an anxiety that his thinking here is muddled accounts for Locke's persistent appeal to the vacant, inland spaces of America; if that continent were in fact as infinite as it seemed to its English settlers, Locke's theory would be freed from the sufficiency rule without any reference to money at all.

Ultimately what Locke presumes about money and spoilage anticipates Adam Smith: within a monetarized, market economy, private greed-based appropriation will increase the amount of goods and services enjoyed within the commonwealth. Because it leads to economic growth, appropriation from the commons does not decrease but actually increases the amount of "enough and as good" available for others. This argument, fundamental to classical free-market economic theory, is also used by those (like Locke) who justified the expropriation of indigenes from the "vacant, inland places" of America and other continents: the locals could not possibly have title to the land because they weren't using it efficiently. To Locke and those like him, land left to go through its natural cycles (which is how the indigenously managed landscapes of America appeared to European eyes) was land that was being *wasted*. The self-interested, accumulative appropriator who would displace indigenes from such land is not a villain but a friend of mankind: "He, that incloses Land and has a greater plenty of the conveniencys of life from ten acres, than he could have from an hundred left to Nature, may truly be said, to give ninety acres to Mankind" (section 37). (In the very next sentence Locke says that this underrates the benefits from "improved" land; the ratio is more like a hundred to one.) "Enough and as good" *land* may not be left behind by the appropriation, but additional value is created through the increased production that the appropriation allows, and this economic growth promises to offer "enough and as good" *wealth* for others.

Thus the foundation of Western civil liberties. There are several problems here. First, the math implies an impossibly infinite series: enclose an acre, give nine acres to mankind; enclose another acre, give another nine acres to the benefit of mankind; and so on. For this process to overcome Locke's sufficiency rule, it has to go on forever. It could do that if the newly enclosed acre could be taken from among the nine acres that a previous enclosure gave to the account of mankind. But even a moderate use of the "natural Reason" that Locke takes as his methodological standard shows that that can't be the case. The nine acres supposedly given to mankind aren't real: they don't hold apples or almonds or water or any other resources, and they can't capture solar energy and turn it, through photosynthesis, into biomass that forms ecosystems, from which humans can extract edible "conveniencys." Those nine acres are *virtual* acres, "as if" acres. Because the per-acre production of human foodstuffs usually increases when hunting and gathering is replaced by agriculture,[4] it's *as if* the amount of productive land available to human civilization increases. Such virtual acreage can grow impressively in the short and medium runs, but real acreage cannot. Locke's sufficiency limit is apparently overcome only because Locke has confused virtual with real acreage. Real humans need real sustenance grown on real acres.

Second, the nine parts of benefit that Locke's commons-encloser creates are not returned to the commons for sharing. Other humans will get to partake of that fruitful harvest only after they've paid for it. When Locke says that in most things ninety-nine one-hundredths of the value is "wholly to be put on the account of labour" (section 40), he holds out the possibility that one one-hundredth part of the value of all wealth is traceable to its origin in a commons. But that's not a very large or firm foundation on which to build the sort of program of social redistribution of wealth that would be necessary for the sufficiency criterion to be met—and in any event Locke doesn't even mention the possibility of such sharing out of the nine-tenths benefit. A Lockean entrepreneurial encloser is not likely to accept a Lockean rationale (especially a Lockean rationale left wholly unstated by Locke) for giving up a significant portion of the fruit of his labors in order to ensure that "enough, and as good" is available to fellow citizens.

Third, Locke's math is clear but isn't sustainable through time. You can't have tenfold increases in agricultural productivity forever. Dramatic increases do come early in the game, when agriculture displaces hunting and gathering, but that transition is a one-shot deal in any region's history. ("Green Revolution" productivity gains don't save Locke's theory, either, although they may have seemed to, thanks to the flush of wealth and agricultural bounty brought about by the industrial revolution's mining of past solar income.)[5] In taking the slope of the seventeenth century's growth-in-agricultural-productivity curve for the permanent slope of that curve, Locke mistook a temporally parochial condition for the permanent state of humanity. Whereas some technological optimists still insist that agricultural productivity can grow forever, it seems wiser to side with Malthusian skeptics, historical observation, thermodynamic reality, and traditional marginal productivity analysis to accept that in agricultural production as everywhere else diminishing returns at the margin must eventually set in, as certainly as sunset must bring to an end the most pleasant of summer afternoons.

Fourth: Locke's mostly implicit argument that money can make moot the sufficiency limitation on land appropriation suffers from a fundamental misconception about money. We can't chastise him too severely for this because the misconception remains common today. Money is a store of value, yes, and it is treated also as wealth; but as Frederick Soddy argued in a series of works published in the 1920s and '30s, money is not wealth (Soddy 1926, 1933, 1935). It is *virtual* wealth: it represents a quantity of real wealth that the community voluntarily denies itself in order to have the benefits of holding a medium of exchange instead. Real wealth invariably has a physical component: it embodies a bit of low entropy that has use value to humans. Real wealth is a useful product, good, or commodity that, being physical, will someday rot and pass away, thanks to the law of entropy—the law, in Herman Daly's apt description, of "random, ravage, rust, and rot" ("Growth Economics" 86). "The ruling passion of the age," Soddy said, "is to turn wealth," which is subject to entropic decay, "into debt," which is not. Humans who have a money income sufficient to accumulate real physical commodities seek to exchange some of that income for a value more completely immune to the depredations of time (*Wealth* 70). They want not just money as a store of value, but something even more abstract, even further removed from devaluation by inflation, theft, or other loss: they seek to own debt, understood as a claim on the future productivity of the economic system.

Problems arise, Soddy said, because no mechanism exists to ensure that real wealth will bear a reasonable relationship to the claims on it. Wealth, being physical, can increase only incrementally, at some historically discoverable rate that is an economy's true rate of productivity increase. (Thermodynamic law tells us that there are only two ways this can happen: real wealth can grow when an economy increases the rate at which it sucks up and processes low entropy from its environment, which increases its ecological footprint; or it can grow by achieving internal efficiencies in its use of an unchanging rate of low entropy uptake, an effort that must sooner or later run into diminishing marginal returns.) Debt, being a complete abstraction, is subject to no such physical constraint, and can increase at any rate we choose to let it: 8, 10, 15, 30 percent per year. It can compound annually and double and redouble in size in fairly short order.

The consequences of this are more easily seen if we demonetarize the transaction contained in debt. Suppose I lend you a gallon of milk this year in exchange for your promise to pay me a gallon and a pint next year: the debt you owe, which I now own as an asset, is for me a claim on next year's production of milk. In effect we are both betting that the agricultural economy will grow: where farmers produced a gallon of milk this year they'll produce a gallon and a pint next year. Generalize the result to all debt, and you see that arrangements like ours require that economy as a whole must grow—in our particular case, by one-eighth per annum overall.

What if it doesn't? What if total debt, the sum of all claims on real wealth, grows faster than total real wealth? In that case, some people holding claims on real wealth must at some point have their claims denied. Soddy's novel insight was to show that when growth in debt outstrips growth in real wealth, the economic system will need some mechanism of debt repudiation—inflation, bankruptcy, loan defaults, bond failures—in order to reestablish the necessary one-to-one ratio between real wealth and the claims on it. I've argued elsewhere that this dynamic is an unacknowledged root of such periodic crises as the subprime mortgage mess (Zencey "Pyramid Scheme"). As Daly pointed out, neoclassical theory treats unrestrained growth in debt as normal, and yet it treats as pathological the mechanisms of debt repudiation that such growth makes necessary (Daly, "Economic Thought" 476). And, as Daly also pointed out, Soddy's analysis of the relationship between money, debt, and physical wealth shows us one strong driver that pushes an economy to grow in disregard of ecological limits: the practice of charging compound interest on debt. Soddy was all for eliminating the practice.[6]

And, finally, an ecologically mindful reading of Locke finds a fifth problem with his argument about property and civil society: that notion of *waste* land. The idea that land left to its natural cycles is being wasted has a long history, and is well-represented in specifically American thinking, where it lies at the root of the conservation movement (Hays 42, 127). There has also been a countertradition in American thought, visible in the works of Muir and Thoreau and a host of other preservationists whose Romantic celebration of wilderness was born in direct opposition to conservation's deeply rooted denigration of wilderness as wasteland (Teale; Fox; Nash). The practical and philosophical tension between these two has been a driving force in American environmental policy for close to a century, ever since Theodore Roosevelt acknowledged the split by giving national forests to the Department of Agriculture and national parks to the Department of the Interior (Utley and Mackintosh). But this old dichotomy, so generative of political wrangling and confusing cross talk over the last century, may be ripe for transcendence. For one thing, both sides have tended to equate "nature" with "untrammeled wilderness," an equation that ignores the considerable value of non-wilderness nature. And the equation has its own problematic metaphysics: as Bill McKibben has suggested, in an era in which pollution (particularly CO_2 pollution) is global in its effect, there is no true wilderness—no ecosystem truly beyond the influence and effect of human presence—left on the planet (McKibben 8). Even supposing we redefine "wilderness" to accommodate the idea that the wild is now no longer wholly other, the division of landscape into two mutually exclusive categories is a bit Procrustean. On the one hand we have wilderness (seen by Romantics as sacred space, needing protection from those who would profane it) and on the other we have profane space—everything else, which, being non-wild, has generally been seen by both groups as appropriately subject to nearly limitless exploitation by humans. This division is dysfunctionally Manichean. Historically it has allowed for many undesirable outcomes, including the removal of "nature" from socially proximate space to ghetto-parks—thus diminishing nature's presence as a practical reality in our consciousness and further discouraging the general public's awareness of healthy ecosystems as a necessary foundation of civilization. No: whereas the romantic celebration of "wildness . . . [as] the preservation of the world" (to quote Thoreau) challenged the idea that wilderness is wasteland, the vision of nature Romantics like Muir and Thoreau proved insufficient to prevent or negate the damage done by the economically rooted vision of conservation. The dichotomy is old and tired and it's time to move beyond it.

One way to transcend the dichotomy is to find a non-Romantic ground on which to challenge the idea that nature left to itself is wasteland. Such a ground is offered by the concept of natural capital.

Natural capital can be defined as healthy ecosystems understood in their capacity as providers of direct nonmarket goods and services to humans. While making a first approximation of the value to human economic life of the goods and services provided by natural capital, Costanza et al. classified ecosystem goods and services into seventeen distinct categories, including regulation of planetary gases; regulation of micro- and macro-climates; regulation of storms, floods, and droughts; regulation, purification, and transport of water; waste absorption capacity; erosion control; soil fertility creation and maintenance; nutrient cycling; pollination services; biological control of natural populations; habitat for species that provide goods and services useful to humans; genetic resources; and recreational, aesthetic, educational, and spiritual values.

When provided by natural systems, these goods and services are not valued by any market but are instead, like Locke's aboriginal planet, a gift to humanity in common.

Of course Locke didn't appreciate the role that natural capital plays in sustaining human culture; the concept is a product of our era, not his. But perhaps we can find a place in Locke for it. What happens within Lockean theory if we take the notion of natural capital seriously?

Let's suppose a man appropriates to himself a forested tract, which he then sets about to denude completely in order to secure for himself the monetary income of lumbering. As he cuts his trees, we can see that our Lockean appropriator of land is making a second, additional appropriation from the commons. A forest provides numerous valuable services that escape its borders, services that are lost when the forest is cut. Particularly noticeable will be the loss of water retention and regulation services; humans living downstream may find it necessary to build levees or construct catch basins and dams in order to moderate stream flows that previously were naturally regulated. But subtler losses—oxygen generating capacity, regional climate moderation, nutrient recycling, soil creation—are no less real. In general, humans living near and even at some distance from the cleared land will suffer a decline in their standard of well-being unless they spend money to replace these lost natural services—with services, usually vastly inferior,[7] that can be derived from humanly built capital.

On a thickly forested, thinly populated planet, the cutting of small tracts of forest leaves "enough, and as good" forest services to be shared in common by others; but, as we are coming to learn, that particular result is not scalable to a world like ours, in which many of the planet's forest ecosystems have been cut, making the forest ecosystem services increasingly scarce. Any further decrement (such as would result from even a single act of lumbering) is in effect an appropriation from a much-diminished commons—an act of appropriation that does not leave "enough, and as good" for others. By Locke's logic, appropriation under these conditions is a taking of property that belongs to others; it is theft.

We can think similarly about global warming. The planet's capacity to absorb greenhouse gases (GHG) with no effect is finite; we can think of that capacity as a service provided by natural capital to all humans in common. In Locke's day, when humans were few and far between and their carbon-based fuel was primarily hand-harvested wood, carbon exhaust fell below the limit of the planet's capacity to absorb it, so an individual's appropriation of that service easily left "enough, and as good" absorption capacity for others. But today every bit of GHG I cause to be emitted adds to the burden that we humans collectively place on this planetary capacity, and collectively we demand more of this service than the planet has to offer. No one's appropriation of any part of the planet's GHG absorption capacity leaves "enough, and as good" for others. Again, by Locke's sufficiency rule, any emission of greenhouse gases is at bottom an act of theft.[8]

It is difficult to see how the invention of money could possibly forestall a Lockean censure of individual GHG exhaust. Does the invention and use of money increase the capacity of the planet to absorb GHGs? No. The expenditure of money could support the discovery and deployment of technologies of carbon capture and sequestration, but this sort of investment is by no means a foregone conclusion within a society of Lockean appropriators, and for us to have a hope of such investment making the sufficiency rule moot, the development of that compensatory human capital must be automatic—at least as automatic as the productivity gains achieved when cultivation of private plots displaces hunting and gathering on a commons (which were themselves, we saw, insufficiently sustainable to overcome the sufficiency limit on appropriation of land from the commons).

At what point does a GHG emitter become a thief? The answer depends less on the existence of a monetarized economy than it does on the quantity of GHG that is being released by all other human and nonhuman activity on the planet, and the capacity of planetary systems (natural or humanly built) to absorb it. Which is to say, in the absence of worldwide deployment of effective carbon sequestration technologies, the moral character of an act of GHG emission depends on the ratio of human culture and its carbon-emitting works to natural capital—to land that Locke described as "waste."

For the Lockean argument justifying property to hold in a modern, ecologically straitened world, the cumulative environmental footprint of human culture must fall below a certain limit, so that there are "enough and as good" ecosystem goods and services left by any individual act of appropriation of them. This Lockean limit is lower than the one necessary for ecological sustainability—probably a good deal lower. The ecologically sustainable limit requires only that an individual act of appropriation leave the flow of natural goods and services into the economy above some civilization-sustaining minimum, whereas the Lockean limit requires that the remaining flow be so far above that minimum that others, too, will be able to appropriate from the source of the flow without endangering the civilization that depends on it. In a Hobbesian or Filmerian world, the sovereign might legitimately run the human economy by command right up to the edge of what society can sustainably take from and sustainably exhaust back into its environment, forbidding other additional encroachments on the collective commons, and leaving little or no room for the experience of human freedom among the general public—a state that could be characterized as "Factory Planet" (Zencey "Taking the Measure," 41). But if we are to have any appeal to Lockean principles, the human economy must operate far enough back from that limit to ensure that when individuals make private appropriations of natural capital they leave "enough, and as good" in the commons for appropriation by others (42–43).

In 1690, with the image of an expansive North American continent firmly in mind, Locke declined to imagine a world in which there wouldn't be "enough and as good" for others. Because nature then seemed infinite, and its role in the production of economic wealth seemed in any event inconsequential, it was easy for Locke to assume that economic growth could proceed forever. (This view is still remarkably current today, especially within academic departments of economics.[9]) The feature of an infinite world that is crucially important to Lockean democratic theory is this: an infinite world can, by definition, infinitely absorb human economic activity without diminishment or harm to the ecosystems that support human life. That is to say, an infinite ecosystem is, by definition, *resilient*. And so, in Locke's derivation of the right to property we find an acknowledgment that the foundation of democratic civil liberty is the resilience of the ecosystems that support human life and economy. A consequence: when that resilience is threatened—as it certainly is today—so too are the civil liberties, the democratic freedoms, that depend upon it.

PRACTICE

As Wendell Berry has suggested, the true condition of our experience of freedom is not some chimerical release from work, duty, or social or familial bonds, but our ability to make and maintain a distinction between behavior that is essentially public and behavior that is essentially private (Berry 97). Although neither the Constitution nor the Bill of Rights specifically mentions a right to privacy, the Supreme Court has consistently interpreted several of the first ten amendments in a way that provides American citizens with such a de facto, if not a de jure, right. The Fifth Amendment makes a strong and appropriately Lockean contribution; it guarantees citizens the right to be secure in their property: "Nor shall private property be taken for public use, without just compensation." In the era in which the Fifth Amendment was written, the paradigmatic taking was the requisitioning of horses, silage, wagons, and provisions in wartime; colonists objected to having the costs of quartered troops imposed on them by military fiat. The subject has become more complicated in the intervening years. As property and concepts of property evolved, so too did the "bundle of rights" that the law conveyed to property owners. Title could no longer convey the right to do whatever one pleased with, on, or to the property, just so long as one avoided causing immediate physical damage to the interests of others off-property (Goldstein); in the first decades of the twentieth century, the practice of urban zoning was instituted and spread rapidly (Whitnall).[10] Regional and in some places rural zoning eventually followed.

Until 1922, the Supreme Court generally held that exercise of the state's police power, when used to stop noxious uses or to prevent harm to the community, did not effect a taking, and its decisions gave no evident weight to future expected income from property. Thus, the owners of a brewery rendered useless by a Kansas dry law were not due compensation for their loss (*Mugler v. Kansas,* 1887); the operator of an existing stable forced to close by newly passed residential zoning rules in Little Rock, Arkansas, was judged not to have suffered a compensable loss (*Reinman v. Little Rock,* 1915); and when the city of Los Angeles expanded its corporate boundaries, enclosing a brickyard, the brickyard could be shut down as a public nuisance with the owner receiving no compensation (*Hadacheck v. Sebastian,* 1915). In 1922, however, in *Pennsylvania Coal Co. v. Mahon,* the Court established the concept of a regulatory taking—a taking of expected benefits—allowing that "if regulation goes too far it will be recognized as a taking."

How far was too far? The Court did not say then, and in the years since has specifically avoided giving any "set formula," preferring to "engage[e] in . . . essentially ad hoc, factual inquiries" (*Goldblatt v. Hempstead,* 1962; *Penn Central Transportation Co. v. New York City,* 1978). In case law no clear line is discoverable between regulatory effects that are noncompensable and regulatory effects that go so far as to amount to a taking. The Court itself has noticed that "[e]ven the wisest of lawyers would have to acknowledge great uncertainty about the scope of this Court's takings jurisprudence" (Justice Stevens, dissenting in *Nollan v. California Coastal Commission,* 1987). But this trend is clear: in a crowded world that lacks ecological resilience, some acts that would otherwise pass as private become decidedly public in their character and consequence. Thus, a man who plants ornamental cedar trees can see them condemned as public nuisances, and cut without compensation, if they carry a form of tree disease fatal to nearby apple orchards (*Miller v. Schoene*, 1928). A property owner who wants to fill in a wetland to build a house finds that he can't—and that he should have known that when he bought the property (*Claridge v. New Hampshire Wetlands Board*, 1984). Whether a man can build houses on land he owns becomes a matter of public interest if the land happens to be environmentally sensitive barrier island, newly protected by state coastal zoning laws (*Lucas v. South Carolina Coastal Council*, 1992). And whether the owner of an auto parts store can expand her building is not simply a private decision if the addition would encroach on green space that town plan identifies as both a bikeway and an environmentally useful drainage swale (*Dolan v. City of Tigard*, 1994).

In the latter four cases, the constitutionality of the regulatory act was never at issue; the question was whether regulation constituted a taking. In *Lucas* and *Dolan*, the Court signaled its acceptance of an expanded definition of private property rights by ordering Fifth Amendment compensation for both plaintiffs. Each was found to have "reasonable, investment backed expectations" of accomplishing some change on their property, an expectation that was frustrated by the law.[11]

In *Lucas* the Court held that the plaintiff, a developer, should receive compensation for the loss of value of two building parcels he owned because those parcels became unbuildable after the passage of coastal zoning regulations forbidding construction of dwellings within twenty feet of the forty-year-average high-tide line. This decision and the reasoning that lay behind it have been roundly criticized, never more scathingly than by dissenting Justice Blackmun, who took technical and philosophical issue with what the court decided.[12]

To Blackmun's principled objections can be added three others: the decision was wrong because unecological, wrong because ahistorical, and wrong because impractical.

In *Lucas* the court presumed that what was taken was taken by a regulating governmental body from the individual. The court did not conceive that in proposing to build on a fragile and mutable ecosystem Lucas would in effect be taking from an ecological commons, denying ecosystem services to the community, and imposing both the risk of further ecosystem degradation and the near certainty of storm-related damage and emergency expense on his fellow citizens.[13] Nor did the court presume that in expanding her auto-parts store into land identified in the town plan as green space, drainage swale, and future bikeway, Dolan would have been appropriating from a collective commons, committing a taking of public benefits that should be prohibited (or, if allowed, be duly compensated at some fair market value). Instead, the Court held that both Lucas and Dolan had a property interest in future economic development of their land.

Since its first use of the phrase "reasonable, investment-backed expectations" in *Kaiser Aetna* in 1979, the Court has had great difficulty in defining the concept (Radford and Breemer "Great Expectations"). One counterintuitive result of the Court's language: the presence or absence of ecological understanding among the American public is the criterion by which the law ought to decide whether a property regulation encoding ecological considerations constitutes a taking that necessitates compensation, or whether it is merely a restriction that does not require payment.

The logic: case law, drawing on common law, clearly holds that landowners do not have a right to create public nuisances. If they mistakenly think that they have that right, their ignorance does not make them eligible for compensation when the noxious use is prohibited. But they do have a right to be compensated for the state's frustration of "reasonable, investment-backed expectations." What counts as reasonable? Before *Lucas*, the court chipped away at a definition, revealing a facet or two here and there, but remained wary of specifying an exact meaning. In *Lucas*'s majority opinion, Scalia offered this large new facet: landowners' expectations are clearly unreasonable only if they violate "background principles of law"—presumably such principles as those embedded in nuisance law, which traces to English common law. Scalia specifically excluded from "background principles of law" principles embodied in legislation, especially legislation of such recent vintage as South Carolina's coastal zoning laws.

Note the resulting circularity in Scalia's decision: in effect it tells Lucas that his expectation of building in violation of the coastal zoning law was not unreasonable, because courts do overturn laws or provide compensation for takings under them; and then, because Lucas's expectation was not unreasonable, it awarded him compensation.

If the court continues to value logic and consistency, that circularity cannot stand. Ultimately the court's definition of "reasonable" must have reference to perceptions of what is and isn't reasonable that are broadly shared in (one hopes) the more enlightened and thoughtful segments of the public. The law can't expect a developer like Lucas to be far ahead of the national or community curve in his understanding of ecology; but then neither should the state be required to use public money to reward individuals for being ecologically ignorant. Among the questions that determine whether Lucas deserves compensation are not "what did he know and when did he know it?" but "what should he have known, and when should he have known it?" What he should have known is the existing state of regulation affecting the property at the point he came to hold title, the purposes of that regulation, and the generally shared understanding, among those knowledgeable about these matters, of the ecological role of properties like the one he was purchasing. These, together, offer "constructive notice" of the likely course of public regulation of such property. If he has had constructive notice that the land is not developable, or that the clear implication of regulation is that the land is likely to be judged undevelopable when permits are sought, the fact that he bought it anyway should not make him eligible for compensation when development on it is denied. If his ownership predated the rise in ecological awareness that led to coastal zoning, he has a claim to be "grandfathered" into compensation. Thus does the public's general level of ecological understanding become a crucial determinant of whether compensation ought to be paid or not.[14]

The Court's opinion in *Lucas* treats property law ahistorically—as though it applied to, and generated cases from, a never-never land untouched by changes in the culture, the environment, or the culture's understanding of its environment. For example, at one point Scalia compares 1971's *Bartlett v. Zoning Comm'n of Old Lyme* (which gave compensation to an owner barred from filling in a tidal marshland) to 1984's *Claridge* v. *New Hampshire Wetlands Board* (which denied compensation to a landowner barred from filling in a wetland). The two cases seem similar enough for their differing results to constitute a problem. Scalia purported to find a difference between them, noting that in *Bartlett* the relevant regulation announced its intent to confer the benefits of proximate unspoiled marshland to residents of Old Lyme, whereas in *Claridge* the relevant regulation sought to eliminate a noxious use that destroyed marshland. The distinction, he said, was between benefit conferral and nuisance prevention, a difference too essentially relative—too much "in the eye of the beholder"—to be a useful legal principle. He then swept away nuisance law by promulgating a new, absolutist rule: when regulation denies all economic development value to a property, even if the regulation prohibits noxious uses that constitute a public nuisance, the regulation constitutes a taking.

But Scalia somehow missed another and larger relevant difference between the two cited cases: *Claridge* and *Bartlett* fell thirteen years apart, and those were culturally transformative years. They saw the OPEC oil embargo, the first gas crisis, lines at service stations and the rippling effect of fuel price increases, publication of the Club of Rome's startling report (*The Limits to Growth*), the celebration of the first Earth Day, and passage of a remarkable amount of major environmental legislation.[15] To miss the ecological ferment of the era, you'd pretty much have to have been resident on the moon; to deny its relevance to property law, you'd have to be working from a legal theory that holds that property rights are in their essence absolute and ahistorical, not a bundle of conventions that society grants to some of its members for the public benefit that derives from the grant. Absolute rights can't evolve or change; a bundle of rights granted for larger social purposes may be modified, stick by stick, as changing circumstances (including changes in our understanding) require. Clearly between 1971 and 1984 both our ecological understanding and the bundle of rights we were willing to convey to property owners were undergoing change, and the difference between *Claridge* and *Bartlett* reflects that evolution. By 1984, it was a truth approaching the clarity of self-evidence that the filling in of wetlands for economic gain was a noxious use constituting a public nuisance.

The result in *Lucas* is, finally, unpragmatic. Lucas was paid the (current) fair market value of two beachfront parcels of land, or close to a million dollars for what amounted to a few dozen feet of shorefront. If the public interest in maintaining a civilization-sustaining flow of goods and services from natural capital is to be served, then barrier island ecosystems must be preserved; but if the public purse has to compensate oceanfront landowners at this rate in order to maintain barrier islands, then sound ecological policy in this area will be too expensive to implement. We will be condemned, through poverty, to further impoverish ourselves through loss of natural capital services and through huge storm-related emergency expenses. In that case, we will let a fundamentalist interpretation of one civil liberty—an absolutist and ahistorical interpretation of property law—deny us the ecological precondition for all civil liberty.[16]

There have been other major takings cases since *Lucas* and *Dolan*, and among them one in particular could prove especially useful to those seeking to move our society toward an ecologically sustainable relationship with nature. In 2005, the Supreme Court decided in *Kelo v. City of New London* that New London, Connecticut's, plan to use its power of eminent domain to take a number of residential properties from long-time owners and to lease the land ($1 for ninety-nine years) to another private party for development was not unconstitutional. The issue was whether the city's donation of the property to a private developer for economic redevelopment (waterfront restaurants, expensive housing) constituted a legitimate public use. Justice Stevens, writing for the majority, held that it was, and noted that the Court gave legislatures "broad latitude" to determine what uses would count as public.

Kelo offers an interesting echo of the Lockean logic by which Europeans expropriated indigenes from their holdings: land used at something other than its most economically remunerative use denies potential benefits to humanity; because income is foregone, the land is being wasted. The decision in *Kelo* thereby embodies a fundamental premise of conservative thinking about property law, a premise that is profoundly unecological: there is no such thing as a public interest separate from the simple cumulation of private greeds expressed in unregulated markets. *Kelo* privileged the private greeds of a developer and his potential customers over the economically inactive desires of residents who simply wanted to continue to enjoy their houses, property they've owned and had reasonable, investment-backed expectations about for years. This is unecological because it takes market valuations as the highest standard for property value—but ecological values (including the values of sustainable use and sustainable flow of services from natural capital) do not find full expression in an unstructured market. Left to itself, the Smithian free hand will never give a society the optimal amount of the nonmarket goods and services that flow from natural capital.

Nevertheless, there may be a silver ecological lining to the cloud of *Kelo*. Certainly using land to maintain healthy ecosystems and to make progress toward establishing a sustainable relationship between nature and culture is a public purpose, and *Kelo* would allow the governmental taking of an ecologically valuable tract of land from one private party and its donation to another, if in the regulatory body's judgment the first party clearly threatened (through, say, proposed development) to harm the public interest by not maintaining the tract as a diverse, healthy ecosystem capable of sustaining a flow of ecosystem goods and services into civil society. Even further: *Kelo* would also justify the expropriation of just about any current landholder if their land could, in the reasonable judgment of some governmental body, be adapted from its current use to a worthier public use as a diverse ecosystem.

Most likely such a shoe-on-the-other-ideological-foot use of *Kelo* wasn't anticipated by the conservative Court that issued the decision. This failure of imagination is consistent with that other feature of Fifth Amendment case law, its failure to evince even the more rudimentary aspects of an ecological understanding. In his majority opinion in *Lucas,* Justice Scalia cites in a footnote the South Carolina legislature's findings in support of its coastal zone act, a set of findings that embody much ecological knowledge; but the findings are cited by the court only in order to be dismissed as irrelevant to the matter at hand. In pursuit of the argument that Lucas deserves compensation despite the ecological unreasonableness of his investment-backed expectations, Scalia cites approvingly, as justification for the court's decision, the biblically cadenced rhetorical question, "for what is property but the profits thereof?"—a sentiment startling for the perfection with which it embodies anti-ecological thought.

CONCLUSION

If we as a civilization choose to maintain a large human population, a population that ever wants to increase the wealth it wrests from nature, we face a choice: either we will see the continued debilitation of ecosystems whose health provides our civilization with real, increasingly valuable, increasingly crucial goods and services, or we'll see our property law change, limiting the realm of individual prerogative over land, and encoding a more fully ecological understanding. If we treat private prerogative over property as an inviolable, absolute right, we not only misread property law's evolutionary, socially constructed history, but we're likely to see our civilization go the way of the ancient ones on Easter Island where the loss of the island's forest cover to competitive tribal statue-building brought about the crash of the entire culture (Diamond, 79–119). If the chieftan who instigated the cutting of the last copse on Easter Island had an inkling of the loss he was about to impose on himself and his fellow islanders, he nevertheless proceeded. We can imagine that he felt powerless and precedentless to do otherwise in the face of long-established cultural and political practice.

What he needed, what we need, is a reversal of the conceptual frame, a resetting of the default. Appropriation of natural capital from the societally shared commons should not be treated as an individual chieftan's or an individual landowner's entitlement. We need to start thinking of the bundle of property rights conveyed with title to land as including only (what Goldstein has called) the "green sticks" of sustainable practice. Following Locke, we could very easily (theoretically) and with considerable difficulty (politically) establish this expectation: if appropriation of natural capital from the commons fails to leave "enough and as good" ecosystem services for the enjoyment of other citizens, then that appropriation of natural capital is a taking from the public commonwealth, a taking that amounts to theft. Such a taking ought to be either prohibited or costed and charged to the appropriator. As even the most avid free-market economist must acknowledge if he or she is to be consistent, charging landowners the social costs, in lost natural capital, of their appropriations would allow the market to be a more efficient allocator of values and resources in this arena.

What is the full cost of the loss of natural capital? In retrospect we can see that the value of the forest on Easter Island was the value of the entire civilization, which any resident of the civilization might reasonably have valued as infinite. "Infinity" is an impractical amount to enter into the cost side of cost-benefit calculations; but this difficulty should not then become a reason to assign natural capital a value of zero instead. Had the political economy of Easter Island been structured to allow some significant valuation to be attached to forests, and had that valuation been entered into decision making about forest use, the island's civilization might well have endured.

The lesson seems clear: if we are to have an ecologically sustainable society, our institutions and practices—property law prominent among them—need to accept that the planet is finite. To live on a finite planet and not limit ourselves to a sustainable rate of economic throughput is simple, dysfunctional stupidity. It ensures the loss of the ecosystems on which civilization depends and thus ensures a great deal of human pain and suffering in the not-too-distant future. (It is also a temporary condition: by definition, an unsustainable system will not last.) If we are to live within a sustainable budget of economic throughput—a sustainable ecological footprint on both the intake and the output side of the economy—we face a difficult reality that Western cultures have never faced: a choice about the size of the planetary human population is also, at least in the short run during which technology is fixed, a choice about the standard of living that that population will, on average, enjoy. We have known as much for decades (although we have consistently refused to acknowledge it). To this insight an ecologically mindful reading of Locke adds something new: it warns us that on a finite planet our choice about our standard of living will also be a choice about our standard of liberty.

NOTES

1. The gender-specific language is of course Locke's, and I won't bother broadening it, because in 1690 only males were considered to be part of the polity.
2. Whereas Filmer saw rights and liberties as resulting from the presence of a sovereign whose right to rule derived from his warrant from God, Thomas Hobbes was a social contract theorist. Other social contract theorists—Rousseau and Locke—saw the precontract state of nature as one in which humans enjoy significant rights and liberties. Hobbes came out in much the same place as Filmer—justifying an absolutist sovereign authority in his *Leviathan*—because in his view humans in the state of nature had no meaningful rights; for them, life in the state of nature is "nasty, brutish, solitary, and short," a war of all against all, and there could be no freedoms or liberties there.
3. "This I dare boldly affirm, That the same *Rule of Propriety, (viz.)* that every Man should have [only] as much as he could make use of, would hold still in the World, without straining any body . . . had not the *Invention of Money* . . . introduced (by [tacit] Consent) larger Possessions, and a Right to them" (section 36).
4. The increases are not permanent if they are not sustainable—and they are not sustainable if agriculture mines the soil, as it did in the Fertile Crescent and in a number of other regions that once hosted now bygone civilizations. See Hyams, *Soil and Civilization;* Diamond, *Collapse*.
5. Basic ecological, thermodynamic, economic, and (some say) nutritional principles tell us that rates of Green Revolution productivity gain are not sustainable; those rates must certainly level off, and in all probability turn negative (where they have not done so already). Economic and thermodynamic reasons: agriculture relies on sunlight, and the amount that falls on any parcel of land is beyond our ability to increase. We can augment that input of current solar energy with past solar energy, the antique sunlight of fossil fuels. But our ability to do that (and to use fossil fuels to run tractors, to serve as fertilizer feedstock, to make pesticide) is not sustainable and has in all likelihood reached a peak (Heinberg, 175–79). When one factor of production is fixed, the addition of more units of other factors of production (labor, pesticide, fertilizer) leads to gains that must eventually level off, or even decline thanks to phenomena like soil depletion, soil salinization, and pest adaptation and recrudescence, all of which occur in accord with ecological principle (Hyams, 138–49). There is some evidence that the simplified diet that comes from monocropped food systems is unhealthy; that sustained reliance on it, even if technically feasible, might be humanly, medically unsustainable; so suggests the Indian Council of Agricultural Research in its 1998 report, "Decline in Crop Productivity in Haryana and Punjab: Myth or Reality?" There are additional reasons that the Green Revolution productivity gains will prove to be unsustainable. Some of the gains in productivity came through increasing the acreage under till, and through conversion of tillable acreage from animal foodstuff to human foodstuff. Neither change gives a rate of productivity change that is sustainable (and demand to feed draft and other farm animals, and to convert biomass into biofuel, may lead to reversal of this trend.) Monocropping makes farmland more vulnerable to ecosystem shock—disruption by such things as pests, diseases, and variable weather—with consequent negative effects on productivity.
6. The proposal seems absurd, but consider: in the 1930s Soddy offered a five-point policy program that grew out of his analysis, and though all five points were dismissed by contemporary economists as being ridiculous and the work

of a crank, four of them are now standard practice—part of the conventional wisdom of economics. The five proposals: 1) nations should get off the gold standard, or indeed any fixed monetary standard, and recognize that money works most efficiently as an abstract creation-by-fiat of national governments; 2) exchange rates between national currencies should be allowed to float freely, one against another and all against all; 3) government budgets should be drawn up with an eye to achieving macroeconomic goals like sustained growth and full employment; 4) governments should create bureaus of economic statistics to collect system-wide information useful to this effort; and 5) banks should stop creating money through the practice of lending deposits at compound interest, and should finance themselves by charging for the legitimate services they provide. Only the last of these remains beyond the pale of (currently) acceptable economic discourse (Zencey 1985, chapter 6). The histories of many disciplines illustrate a pattern: change often comes from outsiders, like Soddy, whose lack of familiarity with reigning dogmas frees them to rethink conceptual muddles from a novel perspective. As a chemist led to political economy by his revulsion at the use of mustard gas in World War I, Soddy was familiar with the laws of thermodynamics, and his case of disciplinary relocation offers a classic illustration of Kuhnian paradigm change: Soddy was prepared to reconceptualize various muddles in economics and to offer new perspective on the emperor's supposedly stylish clothing. See Thomas Kuhn, *The Structure of Scientific Revolutions*.

7. When the ozone layer was shown to be under assault, the cavalier attitude of the Reagan administration was that people can wear sunscreen and sunglasses when they go outdoors. This is a classic illustration of replacing a natural-capital service with a built-capital service, and only a fool would think that the replacement comes anywhere near to being the equal of the original.

8. Lockean logic thus says that we humans are all thieves by virtue of the simple act of breathing (CO_2 and water vapor being greenhouse gases). The unforgiving moral ground of ecological absolutism is something I criticized in "Ecology and Guilt."

9. To be fair: most neoclassical economists have abandoned the myth of infinite factor supply from an infinite nature and have rallied behind the equally improbable myth of infinite factor substitutability.

10. "Proto-zoning" had existed for a few decades before that, based primarily on nuisance law; and city planning and de facto zoning is in evidence in Europe and elsewhere long before that. In the US, zoning regulations grew in application following their introduction in New York City in 1916.

11. The phrase "reasonable, investment-backed expectations" from *Kaiser Aetna* represents a modification of the phrase "distinct investment-backed expectations," which entered into case law in *Penn Central Transportation Co. v. City of New York*. The analysis used in that decision, including the phrase itself, traces to Michelman. Radford and Breemer contend that "the court has never provided more than a vague sense of what this term means, or how it should be applied" ("The (Less?) Murky Doctrine"). In the absence of clear guidance from the Supreme Court—and, one may say, in the presence of the casuistry the court does offer—some state courts have carved out independent treatments of this crucial aspect of takings law, and on occasion have specifically rejected reasoning found in Supreme Court precedent. Thus, the New York State Supreme Court held in *Gazza v. New York Department of Environmental Conservation* that a landowner could not have reasonable, investment-backed expectations of development if that development falls afoul of regulations that were in place when title passed to the owner seeking the development; the existence of regulations serves as constructive

notice that the permits necessary for the development may be denied. This common-sense construction of "reasonable" is not supported by relevant US Supreme Court decisions (including *Lucas,* discussed in the text).
12. Blackmun found the decision to be grounded on dubious facts that were never reviewed; that it reached far beyond the case at hand to articulate categorical principles supposedly applicable to other kinds of takings; that it misread the development of law and case law in the area; that it claimed as precedent decisions that are distinctly hostile to its line of argument; that it arrived at a particular decision that was unsupportable by the principles it articulated; and that it did little, therefore, to clarify the ongoing muddle about when and why the state must compensate for a regulatory taking. See the additional dissent by Stevens and the "statement"—neither a concurring nor dissenting opinion—by Justice Souter. And see also Glicksman, "Making a Nuisance of Takings Law."
13. During storm surges, beachfront homes that fall to wind and water don't simply dematerialize; their constituent lumber and other elements become battering rams that exponentially increase storm damage further inland. Ecological considerations aside, the prevention of construction on barrier islands protects the rights of one class of property owner against encroachment by another.
14. Another wrinkle: the fair market value that Lucas sued for is different depending on the level of ecological knowledge among the citizens present in the market. A market of ecologically astute citizens will assign a different valuation than one that contains as few as two ecologically oblivious bidders competing. Thus do markets systematically encourage unrealistic optimism in the valuations they assign. Widespread ecological ignorance is thus costly to the public purse, as it will make the phasing in of sustainability regulations more expensive under takings law. To the many virtues of ecological education (Zencey "Transcending the Culture Wars") can be added another: it will save the public money.
15. On January 1, 1970, President Nixon signed the National Environmental Protection Act, creating the Council on Environmental Quality. Later that year, an administrative reorganization created the Environmental Protection Agency. The Clean Air Act amendments of 1970 and the Federal Water Pollution Control Act amendments of 1972 were passed, and were the object of much discussion and debate for being "technology forcing"—the standards that they put in place were unattainable with existing technology. The 1970 Clean Air Act resulted in the development and adoption of catalytic converters, greatly reducing automobile pollution and also requiring a nationwide switch to unleaded gas. These changes were, in sum, hard to miss.
16. Additionally unpragmatic is the incentive that *Lucas* gives to the purchase of property encumbered by recent zoning for the sole purpose of seeking public restitution for the denial of development.

WORKS CITED

Berry, Wendell. "Feminism, the Body, and the Machine." *The Art of the Commonplace: The Agrarian Essays of Wendell Berry.* Ed. Norman Wirzba. Washington, D.C.: Counterpoint P, 2002. 93–108.
Costanza, Robert, et al. "The Value of the World's Ecosystem Services and Natural Capital." *Nature* 387 (1997): 253–60.
Cronon, William. *Changes in the Land: Indians, Colonists, and the Ecology of New England.* New York: Hill and Wang, 1983.

Daly, Herman. "The Economic Thought of Frederick Soddy." *History of Political Economy* 12.4 (1980): 469–88.

———. "Growth Economics and the Fallacy of Misplaced Concreteness," *American Behavioral Scientist* 24.1 (1980): 79–105.

Diamond, Jared. *Collapse: How Civilizations Choose to Fail or Succeed.* New York: Viking, 2005.

Filmer, Robert. *Patriarcha and Other Writings by Sir Robert Filmer.* ed. Johann P. Sommerville. New York: Cambridge UP, 1991.

Fox, Stephen. *The American Conservation Movement: John Muir and his Legacy.* Madison: U of Wisconsin P, 1985.

Glicksman, Robert L. "Making a Nuisance of Takings Law." *Journal of Law and Policy 3* (2000): 149–94.

Goldstein, Robert J. "Greenwood in the Bundle of Sticks: Fitting Environmental Ethics and Ecology into Real Property Law." *Boston College Environmental Affairs Law Review* 25:2 (1998): 347–431.

Hays, Samuel P. *Conservation and the Gospel of Efficiency.* Pittsburgh: U of Pittsburgh P, 1999.

Heinberg, Richard. *The Party's Over: Oil, War, and the Fate of Industrial Societies.* Gabriola Island, British Columbia: New Society Publishers, 2003.

Hobbes, Thomas. *Leviathan: With Selected Varients from the Latin Edition of 1668.* ed. Edwin Curley. Indianapolis: Hackett, 1994.

Hyams, Edward. *Soil and Civilization.* London: Thames and Hudson, 1952. Repr. New York: Harper Colophon, 1976.

Indian Council of Agricultural Research (ICAR). "Decline in Crop Productivity in Haryana and Punjab: Myth or Reality?" New Delhi, 1998.

Kuhn, Thomas. *The Structure of Scientific Revolutions.* 3rd ed. Chicago: U of Chicago P, 1996.

Locke, John. *Two Treatises of Government.* Ed. Peter Laslett. Cambridge: Cambridge University Press, 1963; repr. New York: New American Library, 1965.

McKibben, Bill. *The End of Nature.* New York: Random House, 1989.

Michelman, Frank I. "Property, Utility and Fairness: Comment on the Ethical Foundation of 'Just Compensation' Law," *Harvard Law Review* 80 (1967): 1165.

Nash, Roderick. *Wilderness and the American Mind.* 3rd ed. New Haven: Yale UP, 1982.

Radford, R. S., and J. David Breemer, "Great Expectations: Will *Palazzolo v. Rhode Island* Clarify the Murky Doctrine of Investment-Backed Expectations in Regulatory Takings Law?", *New York University Environmental Law Journal* 9:3, 449–531.

———. "The (Less?) Murky Doctrine of Investment-Backed Expectations After Palazzolo, and the Lower Courts' Disturbing Insistence on Wallowing in the Pre-Palazzolo Muck," *Southwestern University Law Review*, 2005.

Smith, Adam. *The Wealth of Nations.* Buffalo, NY: Prometheus, 1991.

Soddy, Frederick. *Money Versus Man.* E. P. Dutton, 1933.

———. *The Role of Money.* New York: Harcourt Brace, 1935.

———. *Wealth, Virtual Wealth, and Debt.* London: George Allen & Unwin, 1926.

Supreme Court of the State of New York. *Gazza v. New York Department of Environmental Conservation* 679 N.E.2d 1035 (N.Y. 1997).

Teale, Edwin Way, ed. *The Wilderness World of John Muir.* Boston: Houghton Mifflin, 1954.

United States Supreme Court, Washington, D.C. *Bartlett v. Zoning Comm'n of Old Lyme* 161 Conn. 24, 30, 282 A. 2d 907, 910 (1971).

———. *Claridge* v. *New Hampshire Wetlands Board* 125 N.H. 745, 752, 485 A.2d 287, 292 (1984).
———. *Dolan v. City of Tigard*, 512 U.S. 374 (1994).
———. *Goldblatt v. Hempstead*, 369 U.S. 590 (1962).
———. *Kaiser Aetna v. United States*, 444 U.S. 164 (1979).
———. *Lucas v. South Carolina Coastal Council*, 505 U.S. 1003 (1992).
———. *Miller v. Schoene*, 276 U.S. 272 (1928).
———. *Nollan v. California Coastal Commission*, 483 U.S. 825, 866 (1987), Stephens, J., dissenting.
———. *Penn Central Transportation Co. v. City of New York*, 438 U.S. 104 (1978).
———. *Pennsylvania Coal Co. v. Mahon*, 260 U.S. 393 (1922).
Utley, Robert M., and Barry Mackintosh, *The Department of Everything Else: Highlights of Interior History*. U.S. Government: U.S. Department of the Interior Online Books, 1989, Dec. 29, 2008 http://www.nps.gov/history/history/online_books/utley-mackintosh/interior7.htm.
Whitnall, Gordon. "History of Zoning," *Annals of the American Academy of Political and Social Science* 155 (1931): 1–14.
Zencey, Eric. "Ecology and Guilt," in *Virgin Forest: Meditations on History, Ecology, and Culture*. Athens, GA: U of Georgia P, 1997.
———. "Is Industrial Civilization a Pyramid Scheme?" *History News Network*, March 24, 2008, Dec. 29, 2008 http://hnn.us/articles/47330.html.
———. "The New Physiocrats," in *Entropy as Root Metaphor*, Diss., Claremont Graduate School, 1985.
———. "Taking the Measure of the Incalculable: Democratic Freedom as a Function of Ecological Reslience." In *Proceedings of the Third International Conference on Environmental Accounting and Sustainable Development Indicators*, Prague: Jan Purkyne U, 2007: 31–46.
———. "Transcending the Culture Wars: Environmental History as Meta-Metanarrative," *Liberal Education* 94:2 (2008): 42.

11 Toward Sustainable Literacies
From Representational to Recreational Rhetorics

David M. Grant

> O chestnut-tree, great rooted blossomer,
> Are you the leaf, the blossom, or the bole?
> O body swayed to music, O brightening dance,
> How can we know the dancer from the dance?
> —William Butler Yeats, "Among School Children"

> I should believe only in a God who understood how to dance.
> —Friedrich Nietzsche, *Thus Spoke Zarathustra*

In offering "some preliminary definitions" of ecocomposition, Sid Dobrin and Christian Weisser note that many scholars increasingly see identity as "shaped by more than social conventions and . . . influenced by our relationships with particular locations and environments" ("Breaking" 567). As a result, they see an opportunity for "how the two massive cultural projects of composition studies and ecology might inform each other" (567). Like one of their predecessors, Derek Owens, they talk about addressing "the current environmental crisis" (574) not only by promoting pedagogies that understand environment or "place" as a critical category, but also by "identifying the ecological relationships between humans and surrounding environments as dependent and symbiotic" (574). Seen this way, ecocomposition is decidedly a move to address issues of sustainability within English studies. Because of an assumed symbiosis between human activity and environment, both are necessary for the continuation of the other.

However, Owens and Dobrin and Weisser run into trouble when they attempt to spell out just how that relationship works. Broadly speaking, nature is kept separate from discourse and theorized mainly as a tool for representing external reality. Byron Hawk notes a similar concern in that Dobrin and Weisser "seem to be held back from pushing the concept of ecology to its limits by continuing to rely on forms of social-epistemic rhetoric and social construction" (223). Rather than detailing an ecology of writing, they instead focus on how "discourse *communities* become ecological systems in which *writers* interact with and react to one another and their environments" (*Natural* 74, emphasis added). This focus on writers rather than writing emphasizes atomistic social relationships and assumes writing's role as a representational medium. The emphasis and assumption here, I argue, undercuts our efforts toward sustainability because there is no point in which our discourse literally matters to its environment. At every turn "nature" or "environment" is taken as that which is outside and divorced from discourse rather than each term being part of the other. As such, language is severed from the world, forever reaching toward an external reality it can never reach.

I contend that this helps explain why many environmental education efforts have simply not led to effective or desired actions. Despite decades of persistently repeated alarms about global warming, the polar ice caps and mountain glaciers continue to melt, the rate of species extinction continues to increase, storms continue to be more violent and frequent, and humans continue to transform land, air, and water at the expense of ecological health. Environmental educators and those who teach with some attention to environmental problems often respond by formulating new strategies of representing these horrors or rush to utilize the latest technologies in order to remain "competitive" in a game of representing these disasters to more and more people. Yet, for every group like Sierra Club, Greenpeace, or CREDO Action who spend millions on lobbying, media advertising, self-promotion, and fund-raising, well-funded interests from Daniel Inhofe to John Stossel, and Exxon Corporation to Western Fuels continue to up the ante. As with the sudden popularity of CFLs, our current capitalist system might accommodate ecocentrism, but it will never capitulate to it. Rather, environmentalists are led into the trap of ever-expanding, direct, continual competition with unsustainably consumptive forces. This is hardly a sustainable practice.

Recent work in composition and rhetorical theory, however, points us in a productively different direction. Recent theorists have begun to look at different ways of conceiving writing that are less new strategies of representation and more what Gregory Ulmer calls "the thought of a different kind of writing (without representation) and a different mode of value" (66). These theories are already attentive to conceiving rhetoric and literacy as an ecological endeavor, although they are only beginning to address the dynamic roles between place and language. I look here at the history of ecological thinking in composition and rhetoric to provide a basis for understanding how this new thinking about writing (without representation) might help us. Dobrin and Weisser were certainly correct when they argued that the "link . . . to connect ecological thinking with composition is simply to revisit composition studies in an ecological light" ("Breaking" 576, *Natural* 73). However, I take this to mean that language helps us *recreate* our environment, not merely represent it. An understanding of language founded on representation reduces everything to discourse and subjects nature to our own power. It is, therefore, not an ecological theory. A truly ecological perspective is similar to Yeats's insights about chestnut trees and dancing: no one point of any system, cultural or ecological, can determine meaning. Rather, the system moves and its relationships are primary. Who, indeed, can tell the dancer from the dance?

LEARNING THE STEPS: ROMANCING THE MIRROR

One of Dobrin and Weisser's main contentions is that "we cannot know nature, except through language" (*Natural* 48). Language allows us to "triangulate" or come to an intersubjective understanding of the world. However, this triangulation is "the moment at which humans construct, map, and elicit power over nature" (48). Although they acknowledge the extra-discursive reality of nature, that reality remains forever outside anything with which ecocomposition might concern itself. Instead "nature" and "environment" are just as discursive as culture. In their formulation, external reality is separate from language. They do acknowledge that "the place where a culture, where a discourse evolves, has tremendous effect on the evolution of that discourse," but they are careful to point out how it is "problematic to suggest that environment precedes culture, discourse, or ideology" (69). Rather, language's power to represent always distorts "nature," "wilderness," or "environment," even though "ideologies and discourses always grow from environments" (69). However, this growth is not really explained except that communities organize themselves in places. And, despite their call to question "a narrowly anthropocentric system of belief" (54) about language, they nonetheless arrive at an impasse where language can only get nature wrong and where human activity can only do violence to natural activities.

Derek Owens relies on a similar bifurcation with his metaphor of "chameleon vision" in *Composition and Sustainability: Teaching for a Threatened Generation*. For Owens, the metaphor works like a mascot or symbol for his own perspective. One eye sees with a kind of "hopeful pragmatism" about the state of our environment while the other sees a more bleak picture, and "the more it regards current trends, arrives at unsettling conclusions that literally cause me to lie awake some nights and fear for my son's future" (9). Thus, a discursive construct—a metaphor—allows Owens to act with respect to the environment, even if that action is simply and quite understandably lying awake at night. Whereas Owens here acknowledges the contingencies of perception involved in the relationship between natural and discursive systems, his metaphor breaks down as the eyes are simultaneously sensory and cognitive organs. They do more than just see, they evaluate. In adopting the chameleon as a mascot for the book, Owens asks, "Does the animal see in split screen? Or are the separate images somehow fused?" (8). Sadly, he doesn't answer these questions, but simply juxtaposes the two in subsections of the chapter. Perhaps this implies the split-screen approach. But what, then, provides a point of reference for understanding the images? What is the faculty by which the two images are made meaningful in relation to one another so the subject can act more and not less sustainably?

Owens ultimately relies on another animal metaphor, the spider, as a way out of this conundrum. He calls for a reconstructivist "arachnid consciousness" that "reaches forward and backward simultaneously, aware that to look behind is also to look ahead" as well as "choreograph immediate future conditions" and recognize that humans "don't exist in place but *are* place" (156). This is a powerful metaphor and the beginning of a powerful ethic. But like the chameleon, the metaphor is ultimately problematic. How is the way an arachnid "extend[s] itself into and thereby altering, maintaining, its limited, local universe" fundamentally different from what humans are able to do with their tools, ideas, or words? Owens lists several models for creating this reconstructivist ethic, such as the work of C. A. Bowers, Ted Trainer, and David Orr. However, these "blueprints, heuristics, or design proposals for imagining sustainable environments" need only someone like ourselves to "apply and revise them for our own local, curricular needs" (159). This resolution hinges on two points. First, it requires the extension and application of representations created by the imagination. Second, it assumes a rather unproblematic rhetorical means of that extension and application. But how are we to determine the degree of sustainability in these representations? Beyond following the models, beyond "cross-disciplinary, cross-temporal thinking," how do we engage in the process of reconstruction Owens calls for? What makes the difference between ethanol and solar fuels? Both require advanced technological systems as well as industrial processing and refining of raw earth materials. Moreover, what is it Owens wants us to reconstruct and how does that lead us away from engaging in unsustainable practices without shutting out other people and practices?

At the risk of oversimplifying what I consider one of the most undervalued works in composition studies, Owens's plan rests on hoping that something—anything—might someday work. But this process appears to be rather positive in character, or at least emphasizes the positive and downplays any function of the negative. As such, it remains undertheorized. Moreover, as a course of action, it seems somewhat haphazard, filled with pitfalls, and resting on a great deal of hope. As appealing as it may be, arguing for hope in education alone again oversimplifies the issue and begs for a more complex accounting of discourse's relationship with nature. In his book *Last Child in the Woods: Saving Our Children from Nature-deficit Disorder*, Richard Louv interviews Robert Stebbins, professor emeritus at the University of California, Berkeley. Stebbins showed Louv pictures of desert ecologies ripped apart by ATVs. And Louv describes the "grooves and slashes, tracks that will remain for centuries. Desert crust ripped up by rubber treads, great clouds of dirt rising high into the atmosphere; a gunshot desert tortoise, with a single tire track cracking its back" (138). As a result, according to Stebbins, such desert areas suffered a 90 percent loss of invertebrate life. "If they only knew," Louv quotes Stebbins as saying in response to such atrocities.

The sad truth is that they—and we—already know. American children are inundated with earth-friendly messages from kindergarten onward. The 2005 National Environmental Education and Training Foundation report, "Environmental Literacy in America" estimates that "30 million K–12 students and more than 1.2 million teachers participate in environmental instruction" (Coyle 1). It does not count the thousands of colleges and universities, post–high school programs, media, zoos, aquariums, museums, and other institutions where environmental education occurs. But according to their own surveys conducted between 1997 and 2001, the result of this effort is that "the public fails to understand the basic principles underlying many of the major environmental subjects discussed in the media" and, moreover, "there was no appreciable difference in knowledge levels between people who finished high school prior to 1970 and those who graduated after 1990 when EE [environmental education] was more commonplace in schools" (3). Despite an increase in curricular, pedagogical, and rhetorical effort, then, environmental literacy has remained stagnant. Owens's hopeful pragmatism, it would seem, is already being tried, but our efforts are not succeeding. Given that corporate interests spend so much effort in making themselves appear "green" in the eyes of consumers, it seems that there is enough broad-based social understanding and even collective will to take care of the environment lest we harm future generations. So why don't we do it?

DOING THE TWO-STEP: ECOLOGY AND COMPOSITION IN THEORY AND PRACTICE

My contention here is that neither Dobrin and Weisser nor Owens are wrong; they are just oversimplified. Part of the reason for this, I think, is found in Tim Taylor's *A Historical Understanding of Ecocomposition: The Greening of University Rhetoric*. In it, Taylor sees two approaches within ecocomposition: environment as subject (EAS) and environment as metaphor (EAM). For Taylor, EAS designates those approaches that take up a systematic understanding of discourse referencing nature or the environment. EAM approaches, on the other hand, take ecology as a starting metaphor for thinking about language or discourse. Written shortly after Owens's *Composition and Sustainability* and concurrent with Dobrin and Weisser's *Natural Discourse*, Taylor shows how ecocomposition had already encompassed two radically different combinations of ecology and discourse. I use Taylor's categories here to trouble those combinations and thereby resituate composition's ecological discourses, pointing out how more recent perspectives might better equip us to approach issues of sustainability.

EAS approaches can be seen in much of the scholarship on environmental rhetoric, and to some degree, ecocriticism. That said, ecocriticism remains distinct as a study of aesthetic reception, and much of what I say here may or may not apply to that area of inquiry. Nonetheless, EAS scholarship often works, in Palmer and Killingsworth's words, to "delineate patterns of rhetoric typically used in written discourse on environmental politics" (1). Their project connects the political and technical, in that "technological and bureaucratic solutions to environmental problems will be ineffective—or impossible—unless accompanied or preceded by free and broad access to special knowledges and relevant information as well as by deep psychological and social adjustments" (2). Thus, they recognize that political policy, persuasive activity, and ethical deliberation in contemporary Western societies all depend upon technical discourse. As such, *Ecospeak* takes as its object of study those discursive artifacts surrounding the construction of a techno-political environmental issue. The purpose of environmental rhetoric, then, is to analyze the ways that technical documents, political speeches, metaphor, and the like represent nature, orient speakers to the natural world, and allow or foreclose certain types of activity. In many respects, EAS approaches follow cultural studies in their notion that nature is a social construction and ought to be seen as a critical category along the lines of race, class, and gender.

This connection between language and the environment emphasizes a dialectic of representation. We see this demonstrated in Carl Herndl and Stuart Brown's *Green Culture: Environmental Rhetoric in Contemporary America*. This anthology analyzes several rhetorics about the environment "as part of a contested cultural exchange, a contest not only about the nature of the world, but also about the identity and place of those involved in the debate" (215). Herndl and Brown also argue that their collection aims toward "suggest[ing] how rhetoric as a discipline can help resolve environmental disputes" and, taking a postmodern world as a world of things missing, they add that "rhetorical analyses of how we talk about the environment provide a means to recover some of what is missing" (19). In other words, they focus on rhetoric's power to mediate between representations and things represented. The collection's diverse rhetorical analyses demonstrate the complex ways social groups relate to the environment and point out that there is no unified way to see how human beings use discourse to interact with the environment. Rather, there are many different ways to investigate such a complex phenomenon or set of phenomena.

What remain in their analysis, however, are schema of representation. They offer rhetoric in its capacity to presence and figure, to fill in what is not there or what is not seen because there is no access to anything beyond signification, not even the very nature they claim to defend. Nature might exist, but as humans we can never make it fully present. To this end, they provide an adaptation of the rhetorical triangle that lays out possible ways humans can talk about the environment or the ways we "read" the book of nature and its signs. As they admit, "these discourses are not pure" (12) and their anthology suggests "that writing for a large public audience is most successful when it combines the rhetorical resources of more than one kind of discourse" (19). However, only "sentimental" ecocentric discourse is left able to speak for nature's interests, and in many ways it is opposed to the other two points, the ethnocentric and anthropocentric. Like Kant with his faculties of the mind, Herndl and Brown appear to offer a tribunal of rhetoric where sustainability would come from pathos motivating logos to understand a situation so ethos can act. But their triangle pits both singular and collective human identities against nature. The discourses of ethos and logos must collude as the regulatory nature of ethnocentric discourse tries to enact what is "discovered" about nature by the objective and objectifying logocentric discourses of the natural sciences. More simply put, regulatory discourses all too often take their cue from positivistic discourses of science where nature is objectified and the "greater good" is served by further conversion of nature into commodifiable products.

Within approaches that treat environmental discourse as subject for rhetorical analysis, however, neither theory nor method for that analysis need be "ecological" in any regard. Such approaches simply take the environment as a common topic—literally a *topos*, or common-place—for discourse and debate about cultural attitudes, societal norms, or ideological investments. This works, however, only by way of separation between sign and signified, between "environment" and "discourse," between "human" and "nature." Indeed, as Herndl and Brown so clearly exemplify, for these theories to work, nature must remain outside and disconnected from discourse except via political, regulatory, or metaphorical action. Contra Owens, then, we are always separate from the spaces we occupy, always placing our own limited human forms on things external to us. This approach takes environment as subject and thereby subjects it to our own ideas.

In contrast to EAS, Taylor sees in environment-as-metaphor (EAM) approaches the attempt to explain language in the terms of ecology. Many of these can be described as "post-process," such as Marilyn Cooper's "The Ecology of Writing" and Richard Coe's "Defining Rhetoric—and Us: A Meditation on Burke's Definitions," both of which Dobrin and Weisser cite as defining moments for ecocomposition theory. Ecological metaphors in composition, rhetoric, and writing studies imply a particular set of ways to theorize, investigate, and describe what happens when a social subject engages in the act of writing. In order to forward these theories and investigations, scholars have had to do more than simply point out how human discourse represents nature. Rather, they have needed to advance an account of written discourse informed by post-structuralism's insights on identity, agency, and invention. In this sense, EAM approaches often posit an ecology of information and endless post-structural play. However, as Bill McKibben has wondered, "an awful lot of people have come to see this 'information ecology' as a sort of substitute for the other, older, natural ecology" (quoted in Heise 163). In other words, whereas EAM approaches often escape the postitivist and cultural-theory stances of EAS approaches, they often do so by sacrificing the natural environment altogether.

First writing about ecology during the mid-1970s in "Eco-logic for the Composition Classroom," Richard Coe critiques modes of rhetorical analysis and their problematic theories of "phenomena in which the whole is roughly equivalent to the sum of its parts" (232). Drawing on anthropology and psychology, Coe problematizes the act of perception, noting that "many patterns can be perceived in any batch of sensory input. In order to see one of them, the observer must (consciously or unconsciously) make a set of choices about what to emphasize, what to de-emphasize, and what to ignore" (235). Such choices, he argues, are effects of socialization. Teaching writing, therefore, is about teaching multiple ways of seeing, through attention to context. It is this context, Coe argues, that requires an adequate response, because "within the past few decades the world has changed so much that our perceptions, logic, and rhetoric are no longer as well adapted as they once were" (237).

A decade later, in her response to the cognitive figure of the solitary author, Cooper proposed "an ecological model of writing, whose fundamental tenet is that writing is an activity through which a person is continually engaged with a variety of socially constituted systems" (367). For Cooper, this meant not only a more dynamic image of "author," it also meant a dynamic image of the systems with and within which that author is engaged. However, Cooper is clear to point out that by using the term "ecology," she does not signify "context." To do so would "abstract writing from the social context in much the way that the cognitive process model does" (367) because the contextual categories must necessarily be thought of as "formal or transcendent" (368). We are all, even the most "objective" of scientists, engaged with certain systems of knowledge and power, acting within them as much as acting upon them.

If Coe and Cooper took the first steps toward an ecological theory of writing, Louise Phelps took those steps further and in greater detail. Phelps's work is explicitly ecological, centering on how to develop critical consciousness in both students and teachers in a "modern society [where] the life-world is really many worlds" (121), each impinging on one another, sometimes refining, sometimes conflicting. She sees these worlds as a social ecology structured by and structuring various ideological formations around a finite and irrevocable traumatic human experience in discourse. She critiques what she sees as "a belief in the naturalness of writing" (108) within composition pedagogy. The problem with such naturalness, Phelps explains, is "the human attachment to the natural, which embodies a nostalgia for the immediate that is constantly undercut by the critical, reflective impulse" (110). Such natural attitudes toward literacy suppose a romanticized, Eden-like space, such as the home or classroom, as origin. Such approaches are dangerous in their "implicit arrogance of trying to create the perfect, controlled environment that excludes or ignores the negatives and complexities" of literacy learning (119). Phelps turns to Gadamer's interpretation of phronesis as a mechanism to handle such negatives and complexities. She reasons that because "science, in the form of general laws, cannot tell us precisely how to make practical-moral decisions in everyday life," a concept like phronesis, or "the case by case analysis application of ethical concepts to concrete practical situations," can be used "as a model for hermeneutical understanding" (205).

This is not merely a theory for composition or even the humanities, but for the expanse of human knowledge-making. As Michael Bernard-Donals recognizes, Phelps's intention here is to place the discipline of composition "squarely at the juncture of the human and the natural sciences in a postmodern paradigm" (131). This epistemic process of knowledge-making, then, is what Phelps refers to as an "ecology." It is the knowledge-making itself that is circumscribed and generated by the interactions of modern society. Such an ecology has only tangential grounding in the real, mostly through what she quotes Gadamer as believing when he writes "a scientific approach disciplined by *phronesis*" (in Phelps 205). For Phelps, it is postmodern epistemology that is ecological in its processes and arrangement.

Margaret Syverson conducted an empirical study that uses the work of chaos and complexity theorists to posit an ecology of writing. Like writing, complex systems are a "network of independent agents—people, atoms, neurons, or molecules, for instance—[that] act and interact in parallel with each other, simultaneously reacting to and co-constructing their own environment" (3). Furthermore, complex systems are both adaptive and dynamic, properties distinguishing them from "simple" systems such as a pendulum or "complicated" systems such as an engine (4). In other words, the forces that factor into the ecology of writing are not deterministic except in hindsight. All that can be determined in advance are probabilities, because one can never know how one aspect of the complex system might adapt to another. This is similar to Phelps, although where Phelps holds out for some discipline of sign and signified through phronesis, Syverson breaks any such connection between sign and signified.

Most importantly, like Phelps and Cooper, there is no explicit attention to how writing, discourse, or language works in Syverson's ecological system comprised of both discursive and nondiscursive elements. Cooper's theory explicitly limits itself to "socially constituted systems" in an effort to avoid abstraction and complete contingency of knowledge. Phelps uses terms like "ecologies," "naturalness," and "environment," but her aim is so large that these remain abstractions. Syverson turns to the virtual instead of nature or "the natural" in order to investigate the complexity of social systems and "demolish the folk model of readers as standing outside the system of text production" (127). As a result, even Syverson's ecology metaphor leaves us searching for nature and finding only more texts. When EAM approaches have used ecology, then, it has always been a matter of sociocultural, technological, and human political systems.

Given this brief history, we might say that EAM approaches take as their object of study the ecology of discourse, whereas EAS approaches take as their object the discourse of ecology. Both approaches hold complicated views on how human beings use language to produce certain material effects. However, talking about the language of environment is different than talking about an ecological theory of language. In EAS approaches, "nature" can be known only as a social construction because the natural environment remains external to human understanding. The best case for sustainability within this approach is a privileging of ecocentric perspectives within scientific discourse coupled with sufficient political will through regulation. Whereas EAM approaches offer the idea that with each utterance we participate in the ongoing maintenance of our environments, their scope has thus far been limited to a particularly human or social ecology, eliding the "nature" of texts and technology. As Dobrin and Weisser attest, these metaphors have been influential to ecocomposition, although I question their compatibility.

In both cases, the central movement is one of discursive effects upon an external environment. Both EAS and EAM approaches deal in hermeneutics, representation, and their persuasive and communicative effects. But if we follow Owens in taking sustainability to be an ethic whose motivation stems from the fact that we are *of* our environment, not separate from it, then we need theories of rhetoric and literacy that proceed along these lines. Nature has long been associated with poetry, heightened consciousness, and transcendence, but the explanations for this still rely on bridging a fundamental disconnect or a projection of our own inner psyche onto that which we can never completely comprehend. Of what use, then, is this arrangement? There is no hope for sustainability if we are fundamentally removed from that which we try to sustain. Looked at this way, the question for ecocomposition and environmental rhetoric becomes how to understand discourses about the environment not as determinative actions by subjects on the object of the environment, nor as simple reflections of the environment on our own subjectivity, but as interrelated systems or circuits of activity.

TOWARD SUSTAINABLE LITERACIES: A VERY STRANGE AND DIFFERENT DANCE

Taken by themselves, neither EAS nor EAM approaches can really lay claim to offering new ways of configuring our relationship with nature, environment, or place, because neither has convincingly explained how discourse and place operate with respect to each other. Rather, because the totality of place can never be fully signified, its reality has been relegated to that which lies beyond all discourse; it is the "other" par excellence, capable of neither representing nor of being fully represented. But this is not the only possible arrangement. Kristi Fleckenstein, for example, looks to emplaced material bodies as a potential nexus that links the discursive with the physical. She argues that composition has sacrificed material bodies "to some illusion of transcendent truth or culturally constituted textuality" ("Writing" 281). In reclaiming material bodies without abandoning contemporary insights such as social constructionism, Fleckenstein posits the somatic mind, "a permeable materiality in which mind and body resolve into a single entity which is (re)formed by the constantly shifting boundaries of discursive *and* corporeal intertextualities" (286). In other words, Fleckenstein looks at how discourse and nature operate as a circuit of activity that flows across different areas of experience. Her arrangement is one that recognizes as inseparable those systems of discourse and material bodies.

Drawing on feminist insights and Gregory Bateson's use of "ecology," Fleckenstein argues elsewhere that the *is* logic of image and sensory experience is interlocked with the *as if* logic of language to form a range of possible meanings. As she explains, "We cannot point to any one part of the system and say here lies meaning because it is a property emerging from the entire configuration, traceable to no single causal force but only to the resonance of its transient pathways" (*Embodied*, 33–34). Like social construction, there is no "unmediated access to the flow of the stimuli that constitutes existence" (34). What we have access to are the differences among stimuli. Thus, "Any idea comes to be, becomes a something, by means of the valuation of differences because an idea is an array of relationships that exists through those differences" (35–36). Fleckenstein thus reiterates and strengthens Cooper's distinction between "ecology" and "context" here, arguing that differences cannot be abstracted from the situation but are immanent within them. Although it is tempting to see this as an argument for difference and diversity, this is not Dobrin and Weisser's value of difference as a sign of ecological health. Rather, it is a more constrained, regulated, and embodied notion of difference that arises only through emplaced bodies. Rather than simply placing language within an ecological metaphor or pointing out the gaps between discourse and ecology, Fleckenstein theorizes a way to understand an ecology of meaning that centers on the writer writing in response to being emplaced as distinct from the writer already written and put into a situation.

Thus, it appears that Fleckenstein accounts for a *literal* ecology of discourse rather than discourse's *metaphorical* ecology. She takes the *logic*, or the very fact that systems operate productively, as her starting point, rather than center her investigations of how to make logical *sense* of those systems. This does not eliminate incommensurabilities between the discursive and the actual, but employs them as the basis upon which meaning gets made. On one hand we have the logical order of language as a social system, whereas on the other we have the paralogical order of an embodied life. These logics come together *in* an environment, at the point of the writer writing. Although writers might manage to temporarily override one or both of those logics, effectiveness with discourse will be diminished should that discourse fail to recognize either logic.

This is not too far from Stephen Yarbrough's "discourse studies" that begins with Donald Davidson's challenge to "'the very idea' of language" (Yarbrough 6). Although both Yarbrough and Dobrin and Weisser cite Davidson's work, Yarbrough focuses on his theories of discourse where Dobrin and Weisser focus on triangulation. For Yarbrough, re-visioning discourse "erases . . . the distinction between linguistic ability and our 'ability to get around in the world generally'" (10). Moreover, Yarbrough explains, this does not proceed by discovery of objective truths, nor by "recovering" truth, and "unlike postmodern rhetoric, it does not invent truths through merely contingent associations" (10). Rather, the kind of discourse studies he advocates "can help students to take note of the effects of power . . . and . . . aim[s] less at representation and more at experimentation, less at argumentation and more at problematization, less at 'taking a position' and more at 'entering a conversation,' less at applying principles and more at engaging in social actions" (11). Yarbrough thus sees a way through the "mastery" of triangulation. Its distortions are not eradicated but dealt with as part of human limitations. With this we see again that the environment of discourse is what matters, not the ability of discourse to represent that environment.

In claiming that neither EAS nor EAM approaches alone can help, I do not dismiss either. Rather, I take both as important and necessary while offering some clues as to how we might "invent a practical style of engagement that doesn't just repeat the structure of negation and refusal" (Muckelbauer 12). The crucial question for me is how the relationship between environment and discourse is construed. Up to now, the history of ecocomposition has emphasized language's capacity to represent an environment or things in the environment. As such, it has kept nature external and thereby limited our ability to literally matter. This sets up a binary between world and word, and even ecocomposition's attempts to offer a synthesis of the two have only reinforced their opposition. But if these syntheses attempt to determine a shared reality, what if we understood that reality as dynamically interwoven from complex systems such as bodily logics, be they individual or social? As Owens points out, writing about any environment cannot be separated from it. So discourse must do more than simply represent place but be somehow bound to it. Yarbrough and Fleckenstein are two possibilities to sustainably rethink ecocomposition.

To follow this thinking of sustainability through ecocomposition is to shift our focus from place as *topos* to *chora*. Following Thomas Rickert's tracing of the term, we take place or environment as "the 'in which' (*en ho*) and 'out of which' (*ex hou*) rhetorical and cognitive activity occur" (269).

Etymologically, Rickert notes that for the ancient Greeks, *chora* implied a territory around the city and from which the city was woven. But for Plato, *chora* "takes on far greater cosmological import as the Receptacle, the matrix or mother of all becoming" (255). In *Timaeus*, it becomes important in Plato's "addressing the question of the available means of creation, and how we give life to and make a place for (static) ideas" (257). For Plato, *chora* acts as a kind of midwife. Itself being neither ideal form nor determinable as a thing, it is of a "'third kind' approachable as in a dream through a bastard discourse" (258). It is not a mold that forms things, thereby leaving its imprint and the memory of its forming, but something that goes beyond boundaries "not to abandon them, but to establish them as what will have been the beginning points" (260).

Seeing environments or places as *chora* is admittedly disruptive of representation and rhetoric since Aristotle. However, that is what makes understanding the interplay between discourse and place so important. As Gary Snyder writes, "The greatest respect we can pay to nature is not to trap it, but to acknowledge that it eludes us and that our own nature is also fluid, open, and conditional" (v). Rather than proceed on the assumptions of representation and hermeneutics—assumptions which always privilege human consciousness as well as the discursive power associated with it—we can look instead to the emplaced ecologies of discourse, what discourse does in particular ecologies, and the interactions that occur within the *as if* and the *is* logics. Similar to Randall Roorda's discussion of "the antinomies of participation in literacy and wilderness," we recognize the importance of not settling structured oppositions between action and passivity or between outside and inside. Just as there is no point from which we cannot *not* affect the earth, we find no outside to participating in nature or, by extension, literacy. Paraphrasing Ivan Illich and Etienne Vern, we have worked too long on a problem-solution axis that implies a kind of global managerial mindset antithetical to sustainability.

Rather than adjudicate the use of nature through social and physical commonplaces, then, we might instead look at ecocomposition in two ways. First, ecocomposition is a way to understand the full complexity of the relationship between our uses of language and those environments in which language gets used. This complexity moves in multiple ways so that what is said, the speaker, writer, are present as part of the environment. Second, it is a way to make room for agency. Writing and discourse is no longer representative of anything, but *recreative*. It is literally a process of recreation, continuing some patterns and modes of the world's emergence but also potentially altering it. In short, recreation makes our discourse matter and have a real effect on the world. We continually invent our way out of the problems of the past. We will create new problems, but as both Yeats and Nietzsche point out, this is part of a holistic movement, not the arrangement of partial objects. We cannot look at just one part of our tree or just one activity isolated from the whole body. A truly sustainable ecocomposition and environmental rhetoric honors the recreative potential of emplaced discourse. It looks at environments as places to play and to cultivate wonder. It is not a kind of literacy *about* the environment, it is literacy *in* and *with* the environment.

WORKS CITED

Bernard-Donals, Michael. *The Practice of Theory: Rhetoric, Knowledge, and Pedagogy in the Academy.* Cambridge: Cambridge UP, 1998.

Coe, Richard M. "Eco-logic for the Composition Classroom." *College Composition and Communication* 26.3 (Oct. 1975): 232–37.

Cooper, Marilyn. "The Ecology of Writing." *College English*, 48.4 (Apr. 1986): 364–75.

Coyle, Kevin. *Environmental Literacy in America: What Ten Years of NEETF/ Roper Research and Related Studies Say About Environmental Literacy in the U.S.* Washington, D.C.: National Environmental Education and Training Foundation, 2005.

Dobrin, Sid, and Christian Weisser. "Breaking Ground in Ecocomposition: Exploring Relationships Between Discourse and the Environment." *College English* 64.5 (May 2002): 566–89.

———. *Natural Discourse: Toward Ecocomposition.* Albany, NY: SUNY P, 2002.

Fleckenstein, Kristie. *Embodied Literacies: Imageword and a Poetics of Teaching.* Urbana, IL: NCTE, 2004.

———. "Writing Bodies: Somatic Mind in Composition Studies." *College English* 61.3 (Jan. 1999): 281–306.

Hawk, Byron. *A Counter-History of Composition: Toward Methodologies of Complexity.* Pittsburgh, PA: U of Pittsburgh P, 2007.

Heise, Ursula. "Unnatural Ecologies: The Metaphor of the Environment in Media Theory." *Configurations* 10 (2002): 149–68.

Herndl, Carl, and Stuart Brown, eds. *Green Culture: Environmental Rhetoric in Contemporary America.* Madison, WI: U of Wisconsin P, 1996.

Illich, Ivan, and Etienne Verne. *Imprisoned in the Global Classroom.* London: Writers and Readers, 1981.

Killingsworth, M. Jimmie, and Jacqueline Palmer. *Ecospeak: Rhetoric and Environmental Politics in America.* Carbondale, IL: Southern Illinois UP, 1992.

Louv, Richard. *Last Child in the Woods: Saving Our Children from Nature-Deficit Disorder.* Chapel Hill, NC: Algonquin Books of Chapel Hill, 2006.

Muckelbauer, John. *The Future of Invention: Rhetoric, Postmodernism, and the Problem of Change.* Albany, NY: SUNY P, 2008.

Owens, Derek. *Composition and Sustainability: Teaching for a Threatened Generation.* Urbana, IL: NCTE, 2000.

Phelps, Louise. *Composition as a Human Science.* Oxford: Oxford UP, 1988.

Rickert, Thomas. "Toward the *Chora*: Kristeva, Derrida, and Ulmer on Emplaced Invention." *Philosophy and Rhetoric* 40 (2007): 251–73.

Roorda, Randall. "Antinomies of Participation in Literacy and Wilderness." *ISLE* 14.2 (Summer 2007): 71–87.

Snyder, Gary. "Preface." *No Nature: New and Selected Poems.* New York: Pantheon, 1992.

Syverson, Margaret. *The Wealth of Reality: An Ecology of Composition.* Carbondale, IL: Southern Illinois UP, 1999.

Taylor, Timothy. *A Historical Understanding of Ecocomposition: The Greening of University Rhetoric.* Diss., U of Alabama, 2002. Ann Arbor: UMI, 2002.

Ulmer, Gregory. *Heuretics: The Logic of Invention.* Baltimore: Johns Hopkins UP, 1994.

Yarbrough, Stephen R. *After Rhetoric: The Study of Discourse Beyond Language and Culture.* Carbondale, IL: Southern Illinois UP, 1999.

Contributors

Jeff Bergin is a doctoral candidate in rhetoric and composition at Arizona State University. He has taught sustainability-themed undergraduate writing courses, and his research interests include rhetoric and representation in documentary film; digital and environmental literacy; and democratized media. Jeff has produced more than forty documentary films and published entries on documentary criticism in the *Encyclopedia of Documentary Film*.

Doug Christensen is a doctoral candidate in rhetoric and composition at the University of Utah. He holds an MFA in creative nonfiction from the University of Utah. He has taught writing at Salt Lake Community College and Weber State University, and currently teaches at the University of Utah. His research interests include cultural literacy, rhetoric of the environment, rhetoric of religion, credo writing, and the essay. Outside his academic work, he enjoys building heirloom furniture, backpacking, hiking, running, biking, and skiing.

Elizabeth Giddens is associate professor of English at Kennesaw State University in Georgia where she teaches in the Master of Arts in Professional Writing program. She has previously been communications director for the RAND Institute for Civil Justice in Santa Monica, California, and associate director of communication at the Southern Regional Education Board in Atlanta, Georgia. Recent publications include "Context Matters: Recognizing the Effects of Epistemic and Agonistic Contexts in Public Policy Debate" in *Issues in Writing*, and "Qualitative Research on What Leads to Success in Professional Writing," with Margaret Walters and Susan Hunter, in the *International Journal on the Scholarship of Teaching and Learning*.

Peter Goggin is associate professor of English at Arizona State University in Tempe. He is author of *Professing Literacy in Composition Studies* (Hampton Press) and has published in such journals as *Composition Studies* and *Rhetoric Review* as well as in the collection *Trauma and* *the Teaching of Writing*. His current and ongoing research focuses on environmental stewardship and rhetorics and literacies of sustainable development in island communities. He is founder and co-director of the annual Western States Rhetoric and Literacy conference with Maureen Mathison of the University of Utah.

David M. Grant is assistant professor at the University of Northern Iowa where he teaches writing and rhetoric. He has previously taught at the University of Wisconsin–Madison, Winona State University, and Northern Arizona University. His interest in place as an aspect of writing comes from his time spent in the Boundary Waters Canoe Area, Colorado Plateau, Black Hills, and the Driftless Region of the upper Midwest. He is currently revising a book-length manuscript focusing on emplaced journal writing in a course that combined writing and recreation studies

Elenore Long is a visiting professor at Arizona State University. With Linda Flower and Lorraine Higgins she published *Learning to Rival: A Literate Practice for Intercultural Inquiry*. They recently published a fifteen-year retrospective for the *Community Literacy Journal*. She recently completed a book entitled *Community Literacy and the Rhetoric of Local Publics*, published by Parlor Press.

Anne Faith Mareck is associate director of writing programs at the University of Kentucky. Her interest is in the development of biospheric literacy, with research focus on the critical intersections of rhetoric, discourse, literacy, science and technology, and professional communication. Academic publications include "Computer Gaming as Literacy," with Cynthia Selfe and Josh Gardiner, in *Gaming Lives in the Twenty-First Century*; "Student-based Case Studies in Software Communication," with Charles Wallace et al., in *Proceedings of the Conference on Software Engineering Education and Training*; and "A Review of Technical Communication and the World-Wide Web," in *Technical Communication Quarterly*.

Lynda McNeil holds a PhD (1980) in comparative literature from the University of Maryland, College Park. She published her dissertation, *Recreating the Wor(l)d: The Mythic Mode as Symbolic Discourse* (SUNY Press 1992) and has been a full-time instructor in the Program for Writing and Rhetoric at the University of Colorado, Boulder, since 2000, teaching, researching, and publishing on topics encompassing ethnographic writing, folklore, and rock art as iconographic narrative and a form of visual rhetoric. Her current research interests include Ute rock art as an iconographic discursive strategy in response to forced removal from Colorado.

Contributors 219

David Metzger is chair of English and professor of rhetoric at Old Dominion University. He is the author/editor of several works, including *The Lost Cause of Rhetoric: The Relation of Rhetoric and Geometry in Aristotle and Lacan* (SIUP 1995) and *Medievalism and Cultural Studies* (Boydell & Brewer, 2000). His current research interests include Jewish rhetorical thought and rhetoric in the public sphere.

Kimberly Moekle received her PhD in comparative literature from the University of California-Irvine in 2000. She served as an assistant director in the composition program at UC Irvine before joining the Program in Writing and Rhetoric at Stanford University, where she teaches undergraduate writing and is the lead writing faculty member in a pilot program of the Interdisciplinary Graduate Program on the Environment and Resources. Moekle also mentors graduate and undergraduate students in the Hume Writing Center, and is affiliated with the School of Earth Sciences and the Woods Institute for the Environment at Stanford.

Sally E. Said teaches Spanish language and linguistics at the University of the Incarnate Word in San Antonio, Texas, where she cochairs the Department of Foreign Languages. Her research interests include writing pedagogy, Spanish dialectology, Navajo culture and literacy, Sudanese women's literacy and folklore, and the rhetoric of social activism. She has published a collection of Sudanese folktales retold in English and Arabic, and numerous articles, including a coauthored history of the Headwaters Project. With her late colleague Rebecca Cross, she developed an approach to writing pedagogy for use in schools and organizations locally and in the Navajo Nation.

Hannah Scialdone-Kimberley is a doctoral candidate studying rhetorical and textual studies at Old Dominion University in Norfolk, Virginia. Her current research interests include travel narratives of women adventurers (particularly Annie Smith Peck), eco-criticism, and the visual rhetoric of environmental advocacy.

Eric Zencey is Visiting Associate Professor of Historical and Political Studies in the Graduate and International Programs at Empire State College, State University of New York. He teaches environmental history and ecological economics in New York and Europe. He is the author of a novel, *Panama* (Farrar, Straus and Giroux, 1995), a collection of essays, *Virgin Forest* (University of Georgia Press, 1997), and the forthcoming *Freedom on Factory Planet*.

Index

A
Abbey, Edward 168–169
Abbott, Patrick L. 119
Abelson, Donald E. 22
Abram, David 165, 170–171
action alerts 98–100, 105–106, 111
activist rhetoric 15, 32, 106
adversarial rhetorics 10, 99–100, 106, 109, 112
aesthetics 79–80, 83, 88, 172
agency, rhetorical 9–10, 19, 40–41, 43, 111, 127, 134, 150–151, 159–162, 208, 214
Alinsky, Saul 27–28
ambiguity (Burke) 49–50
American Environmental Values Survey 90
American wilderness 82–83
ancestral memory 116, 170
Appalachian farmers 56
archaeological sites 98, 103, 106, 119, 126, 129
Aristotle 145–146
Atwill, Janet 15–18, 20, 32, 33n4

B
Bakhtin, Mikhail M. 109
Ban, Raymond 137
Barringer, Mark D. 58
Barthes, Roland 136
Barton, David 25
Basso, Keith H. 116
Batten, Frank 143
Bazerman, Charles 1, 28, 93n7
Benford, Robert D. 108
Benhabib, Seyla 24
Benoit-Barne, Chantal 111
Bercovitch, Sacvan 81, 93n6
Berlin, James A. 93n8

Bernard-Donals, Michael 210
Berry, Wendell 90, 169–170, 189–190
Billig, Michael 104, 106
biodiversity 8, 55–57, 59–73, 128
Biodiversity Project 57, 66, 68–69, 73
Bitzer, Lloyd 26
Booth, Wayne 17
Bourdieu, Pierre 31
Brace, Peter B. 79
Branch, Kirk 16, 32
Brandt Commission 48
Breemer, David J. 192, 198n11
Brill, David 72
Brown, Doug 3, 8
Brown, John 139, 142
Brown, Stewart C. 6, 91, 207–208
Brundtland Commission 6, 13, 48
Bruner, Michael 81, 91
Brush, Lisa D. 18–19, 22
Bruzzi, Stella 150, 153, 156
Bryson, John 25
Bureau of Land Management (BLM) 93, 98–102, 104–106, 108–111, 113n4
Burke, Kenneth 40–47, 49–51, 52nn2–3, 52n6, 87, 208
Burkett, Elinor 79–80
Buzzards Bay 78, 87–88, 92n1

C
Cantrell, Geoffrey 72
Carley, Kathleen M. 104
Carson, Rachel 134
Chandler, C. K. 119
Chess, Caron 60
chora 214–215
chronos 26, 32
Cicero, Marcus T. 1
Cintron, Ralph 17

222 Index

civil liberties 182–183, 189
Clancy, William 142
Club of Rome 6, 193
Coe, Richard M. 208–209
Coffey, Maria 172–174
collective anxiety 17
Collins, Allen 139, 142
Colomb, Gregory 17
communicative action 32–33n2, 57, 61–62, 73–74, 143
community literacy 4, 8, 13–17, 21–22, 24–26, 32
Community Think Tank 22–24, 26–27, 30
composition studies 20–21, 167, 202–203, 205–210, 212
Comstock, Michelle 34n7
Connelly, Robert 125–128
conservation 59, 89, 111, 186–188
conservationism versus protectionism 78, 82–88, 93n10, 94n17, 186
Consigny, Scott 26
Coogan, David 16–20, 26, 30, 34n8
Coogan, Jim 94n14
Cooper Marilyn 208–210, 212
Coppola, Nancy 33n2
Corbett, Julia B. 57
Costanza, Robert 187
Council on Competitiveness 3
Cox, I. Waynne 122
Cox, Robert J. 72, 161
Coyle, Kevin 73, 206
crisis (environmental) 3, 59, 151, 159, 202
Cronon, William 183
cultural heritage 58–59, 64, 69, 124, 129
cultural myths 137–138
cultural resources 56, 97–98, 105–112, 119
cultural value 91
Cunningham, James 27
Cushman, Ellen 14–15, 26

D

Daly, Herman 185–186
de Bruijn, Theo J. N. M. 33n2
de Certeau, Michel 32
Deans, Thomas 19
Deems, Julia 22
DeLaughter, Jerry 63, 70
deliberative democracy 99, 104, 106, 111

deliberative rhetoric (and discourse) 18, 21, 23, 25, 64, 112
Deloria, Jr. Vine 119–120
DePoe, Stephen P. 6
design literacies 22–23
Dewey, John 13
diachronic perspective/process 81, 117–118, 129
dialogic discourse 57, 99, 109
Diamond, Jared 195, 197n4
discourse community 21, 91, 117, 125–126, 128–129, 202
Dobrin, Sidney I. 2, 6, 18, 21, 26, 33n2, 33–34n5, 202–204, 206, 208, 211–213
drilling 97–110, 123
Duffy, Dennis 87
Duguid, Paul 139, 142
Dunlap, Riley 134, 138
Dunne, Joseph 146
Dunwoody, Sharon 73

E

Easter Island 195–196
ecocomposition 11, 18, 32n2, 202, 204, 206, 208, 211, 213–215
ecocriticism 52n2, 133, 170, 207
ecology: Burkean notion of 40, 45; definition of 202, 206, 208–220, 212; human/social 170, 211; and writing 11, 202, 209–211
ecosystems 1, 64, 67, `33, 135, 137, 183–184, 187–189, 194–196
ecotourism 108
Ehrlich, Paul 133–134
Elliot, Norbert 81–82, 84, 93n6
Emerson, Ralph W. 82–83, 93n8, 166
Emerson, Robert 136
energy: conservation 90, 101; demand and consumption 79–80, 88–89, 97, 100–101, 137, 141; production 78, 86, 100, 102, 106; sources 79–80, 88, 92, 104, 133, 141, 184
Enlightenment 81–82
environmental discourse 8, 24, 26, 32n2, 33n5, 78, 81, 84, 89, 208
environmental education 203, 206
environmental footprint 189
environmental literacy 2, 10, 73, 206
Environmental Protection Agency (EPA) 99

environmental rhetoric 4, 6, 9, 14, 21, 32n2, 40, 78, 81, 88, 91, 151, 159, 207, 211, 215
environmentalist(s): ethos/identity 79, 84–86, 90–91, 99, 124, 132, 153–154, 158, 162, 168, 203; perspective 81, 89; rhetoric 14, 21
ethos 74, 84–86, 94n14, 151–157, 162, 168, 172, 174, 208

F

Faber, Brenton 34n7
Fairclough, Norman 134
Farrior, Marian 66
fear appeals (environmental/rhetorical) 67, 69, 73, 101, 103, 133, 141, 204
Fels, John 136
Ferguson, Sherry D. 67
Fifth Amendment (to the US Constitution) 11, 190–191, 195
Filmer, Robert 180–182, 197n2
Finnegan, Cara A. 150, 160
Fleckenstein, Kristie 212–213
Fleming, David 15
Flower, Linda 13–14, 16–20, 22–24, 26–27, 29–32, 32n1, 34n7
formal voice 153–154
Foss, Karen A. 150
Fox, Stephen 186
framing: strategies 17, 20, 99–111, 160 diagnostic 108–110; prognostic 108–110
Fraser, Nancy 21–22, 24, 29, 33n5
Freire, Paulo 19
Fretz, Rachel 136

G

Gee, James P. 19, 30, 136, 138–139
Geertz, Clifford 13
gender equity 4–5, 34n5, 43–61, 207
Genesis 169–170, 176
Georg, Susse 13, 24
Giddens, Anthony 104
Glacken, Clarence J. 1
Glicksman, Robert J. 199n12
global warming 90, 133–135, 151–160, 188, 203
Goggin Maureen D. 104, 106
Goggin, Peter 32n2
Goldblatt, Eli 16, 18, 24, 27–30
Gonzalez, Jennifer 144

Gove, Doris 65
Grabill, Jeffrey 14–16, 18, 32, 32n1, 33nn2–3, 34nn7–9
Great Depression 71
Green Revolution 184, 197n5
Greene, Ronald W. 16
greenhouse gas emissions 94n17, 132–135, 188, 198n8

H

Habermas, Jürgen 24–25, 30, 32n2, 33–34n5
Habitus (Bourdieu) 31
Halloran, S. Michael 93n7
Halstead, Lacey 118, 128–129
Hamilton, Mary 25
Hansen, James 133
Hariman, Robert 152, 155, 159
Harrigan, Stephen 119
Harris, Joseph 20, 26
Harris, Joyce L. 15
Haskins, Ekaterina V. 20\
Hauser, Gerald A. 98, 100, 111, 113n4
Hawk, Byron 202
Hays, Samuel P. 186
Heath, Shirley B. 19
Heifetz, Ron 34n6
Heinberg, Richard 197n5
Heise, Ursula 209
Heller, Caroline E. 29, 34n7
Herndl, Carl G. 2, 6, 91, 207–208
Hetch Hetchy controversy 82–85, 88, 93n10
Higgins, Lorraine 13–14, 17–20, 22, 34n7
Hobbes, Thomas 182, 197n2
homesteading 55, 58, 65, 69, 71
Horstman, Lisa 65
Horton, Sally 113n5
Houk, Rose 70, 71
Huckin, Thomas 17, 178n2
Hurricane Katrina 151, 157–159
Hyams, Edward 197nn4–5

I

identity, in pentadic analysis 40–12, 45–46, 49
ideographic analysis 19–20, 29
Illich, Ivan 214
Ingham, Zita 60
instrumental rationality 33n5, 57, 112, 113n4
intellectual virtues (Aristotle) 145–146

intervention, rhetorical 15–18, 20
invention, rhetorical 9, 15–17, 20, 23, 29–30, 45, 150, 208
Irwin, Alan 13, 24

J
Jacobson, Susan K. 57, 64–65, 69
Jamieson, Dale 57, 74
Japp, Phyllis M. 6
Johnson, Branden B. 60
Johnson, Robert 145
Jolley, Harley E. 71
Jordens, Christopher F. C. 117, 125

K
kairos 26, 32n1
kairotic moment 26–27, 112
Kamhi, Alan G. 15
Kareiva, Peter 59
Karis, Bill 33n2, 73
Kaufer, David S. 104
Kellner, Douglas 161
Kelly, John 137
Kemp, Steve 56–63, 66–67, 69–70, 72
Kennedy, Jr. Robert F. 85–87, 94nn12–13, 94n15
Kidd, Charles V. 6
Killingsworth, Jimmie M. 2, 6, 8, 10, 18, 21, 24, 26, 33n2, 33n5, 57, 67, 84–85, 89, 91, 100, 103, 112, 113nn1–4, 151, 154, 157–161, 207
knowledge activism 27–30, 34n9
Kodas, Michael 171
Krakauer, Jon 171, 175–177
Kravitz, Derek 92
Kress, Gunther 104
Kropp, Göran 171
Kubal, Timothy 109
Kuhn, Thomas 198n6
Kyoto Protocols 155, 160

L
Lakoff, Robin Tolmach 117, 126
land ethic 178
land management
Langsdorf, Lenore 14
language (environmental concerns) 65, 91, 106, 117, 126–127, 192, 203–214
language isolate 120
Lauer, Janice 20
Lave, Jean 136, 139, 142
León-Portilla, Miguel 129
Lindquist, Evert A. 22
literacy
Little, Miles 117, 125
Littlejohn, Margaret 55, 60
Locke, John 180–190, 194, 196, 197nn1–2, 197n8
logging 56, 58, 68, 71, 140, 161, 167
logos 151–152, 154, 157, 208
Long, Elenore 13–15, 17, 20, 22–23, 25–28, 33n5, 34n7
Louv, Richard 205–206
Lovelock, James 135
Lucaites, John L. 152, 155, 159

M
Mackintosh, Barry 186
Mansbridge, Jane 22
Marback, Richard 144
Marcel, Detienne 32
Mareck, Anne 135
Masauki 121
Maser, Chris 13, 15
Maslow, Abraham 64
material discourses 10, 133–134, 139
material(ist) rhetoric 17, 19–20, 30, 133–134, 139, 143–144, 146
Mathieu, Paula 16–17, 29, 32
Maynard, Charles W. 72
McCarthy, Jeffrey 167–169, 174
McConnell, Grant 83
McCracken, Dick 123–124
McGee, Michael 19, 143–144
McKibben, Bill 186, 209
Meister, Mark 6
Merchant, Carolyn 135
metasigns 136–139
Michelman, Frank I. 198n11
Milbrath, Lester 133
Miller, Carolyn 26, 93nn6–7, 134
Milligan, Bryce 124
Mitchell, Margaret 120–121
Monmonier, Mark 143
Morrison, Toni 5
Moser, Susanne C. 57, 67
Muckelbauer, John 213
Muhlbeier, Barbara 56, 57
Muir, Star A. 6
multicultural literacy 29
multicultural publics 21–22
multi-stakeholder dialogue 39–44, 48, 52n4
Murphy, Patricia 27
mutuality 18–19

N
Naess, Arne 135

Nantucket Sound 78–79, 88, 90, 92, 94n12
narrative(s) of change 5, 22, 39, 112, 120, 151–152, 164
Nash, Roderick 186
National Energy Plan (Federal Energy Initiative) 97
National Environmental Education and Training Foundation 73, 206
national treasure ideal 80, 86, 92, 94n16
National Trust for Historic Preservation 100, 102
Native American: culture 56, 118, 121; early settlements 56, 118–119; tribal organization and influence 100, 102, 121
natural capital 187–189, 194, 196
natural resources 62, 69, 70–71, 82, 84, 100, 143
natural rights 180, 182
nature: as adversary 10, 81–82, 90, 134, 138, 170, 175, 186–187; as object 85, 91, 164, 168, 194, 202–215; as resource 1, 11, 57–59, 85, 88, 127, 180–183, 189, 195, 197n2; as spirit 73, 82–85, 90, 165–166, 177–178
Newman, Lance 170
Nichols, Bill 150–152, 154, 157, 159

O
Oelshlaeger, Max 81, 91
Oldenburg, Ray 9
Olson. Leslie 17
Opie, John 81–82, 84, 93n6
Oravec, Christine J. 82–84
Orr, David 135
Orr, Diane 112
Ortiz, Simon 120
Owens, Derek 2, 5, 6, 8, 133, 202, 204–206, 208, 211, 213

P
Pachauri, Rajendra 135
Palmer, Jacqueline S. 2, 6, 8, 10, 18, 21, 24, 26, 33n2, 33n5, 57, 67, 84–85, 89, 91, 100, 103, 112, 113nn1–4, 151, 154, 157–161, 207
pathos 101, 103, 152, 156, 174, 208
patriotism 83, 101, 159
Peck, Wayne 27
pedagogy 21, 209

Pérez, Gary 116, 121, 128
Pérez-Peña, Richard 93n4
performance rhetoric 20, 22–23, 26, 34n8, 152–153, 157
Pergams, Oliver R. W. 59
Peterson, Tarla R. 2, 6, 8, 45, 48, 153
Phelan, James D. 84
Phelps, Louise 209–210
phronesis 17, 145–146, 210
Pierce, Daniel 71
Pirages, Dennis 133–134
place-making 10, 116–118, 126, 128
Plantinga, Carl R. 150, 152–155
Plato 140–141, 145–146
Plevin, Arlene 57, 61, 67
polarization (in environmental debate) 84–84, 110
Pollock, Karen E. 15
praxis 3, 17–18, 118, 120, 127, 146
preservation 59, 78–79, 81–90, 94n17, 99–105, 111–112, 119, 125, 174, 186–187
Proenneke, Richard L. 176–178
progressivist/ism 8–9, 82, 137
property, right to 11, 134, 138, 181–182, 188–196, 199n13
protectionism (see conservationism)
public policy 73, 100, 133
Puritan culture 81–82

R
Radford, R. S. 192, 198n11
radical centrist ideal 103
Ralston, Aron 174–176, 178n3
Ramism 81
rationalist/ism 21, 33n5, 81–82, 85, 87, 153
Read, Pier P. 167
Reardon, K. E. 61
recreation 59, 61, 71, 74, 84, 103–104, 110, 164, 167, 187, 214
restoration ecology 125–129
reticulate public sphere 10, 98–99, 103, 106
rhetorical proofs (see also: *ethos*; *logos*; *pathos*) 10, 151–152, 158
Rickert, Thomas 213–214
Righter, Robert W. 93n10
Roberts-Miller, Patricia 21
Romantic(ism) 78, 82–83, 85, 88, 90, 113n1, 137, 164, 176, 186–187, 210
Roorda, Randall 214
Ruekert, William 40
Ryan, Eilish 123

S

Said, Edward 126
Sauer, Beverly 14–15, 33n2
Sayers, Emma-Jane 117, 125
school reform 19–20
scoping letters 98–101, 103, 105–106, 108–109, 112
Scott, James C. 32
Seigel, Marika 52n2
Selig, Michael 152
Senecah, Susan L. 6
Shafer, William 143
Shaw, Linda 136
Sheedy, Jack 94n14
Shelley, Mary 146
Simmons, W. Michele 14–16, 18, 32, 33nn2–3
Simpson, Joe 174
Simpson, John W. 93n10
situated learning 135, 139, 142–144
Slattery, Margaret P. 122–123
Smith, Adam 183
Snow, David A. 107–108
Snyder, Gary 214
Soddy, Frederick 185–186, 197, 198n6
Soja, Edward, W. 9
Spanish colonization 116–122
spoilage rule (Locke) 181, 183
Stark, Mike 111
Stevens, Sharon M. 100, 104, 106–109
stewardship 69–70, 73, 109, 118, 124, 127, 133–135, 170
Stothert, Karen E. 119, 121–122
sufficiency rule (Locke) 181, 183–185, 188
Supreme Court (of the United States) 190–195, 198n11
sustainababble 1–2
sustainability in the humanities 2, 4–6, 11, 118, 125–127, 210
sustainability, definitions of 1–7, 26, 29, 32n2, 41, 45–46, 48, 167, 175–176
sustainable development 1, 6–8, 39, 42, 45–46, 48, 52n4
Swift, Jonathan 147
symbiosis 10, 202
synchronic perspective/process 10, 116, 118, 129
Syverson, Margaret 210

T

Taylor, Timothy 206, 208
Teal, Edwin W. 186

techne 15–20, 27–29, 31–32, 140–141, 145–146
terministic formulae (Burke) 45–46
textual silence 173, 178n2
Thoms, Alston V. 120
Thoreau, Henry D. 165–167, 178, 187
tourism 58, 79–80, 100, 103, 108–109, 174
transcendentalists 82, 103, 113n1
Travis, W. 100
Trimbur, John 20
Tukker, Arnold 33n2
Turner, Jack 168, 174

U

Ukaga, Okechukwu 13, 15
Ulmer, Gregory 203
United Nations (UN) 6–7, 9, 13, 39, 43, 48–51
urban community action 13–14, 32
Utley, Robert M. 186

V

Van Liere, Kent 134, 138
Vatz, Richard E. 26
Vaught, Carl G. 117–118
Veenendall, Thomas L. 6
Vernant, Jean-Pierre 32
Verne, Etienne 214
video games (as learning tool) 133, 138–139
visual rhetoric 78, 88, 90–91

W

Waddell, Craig 6
Waldvogel, Merikay 72
Wang, Wilfried 132
Warner, Michael 25
Warnick, Christopher 17
waste: culture of 133, 141, 166, 180, 187; hazardous; 18, 141; on Mount Everest 171–172
wasteland, concept of 183, 186–187
Weisser, Christian R. 2, 6, 18–19, 21, 26, 33n2, 33–34n5, 202–204, 206, 208, 211–213
Wenger, Etienne 136, 139, 142
Wess, Robert 52n3
West, Cornel 20
Whitcomb, Robert 90, 92n1, 93n11, 94n12, 94n14
Whitnall, Gordon 190
Wild, John 140
wilderness, definition of 186–187

Williams, Don 72
Williams, Joseph 17
Williams, Rhys 109
Williams, Rosalind 139
Williams, Wendy 90, 92n1, 93n11, 94n12, 94n14
Williamson, Judith 136
Wilson Edward O. 55, 59
wind energy, rhetoric of 80
Winner, Langdon 139, 141–142
Winston, Brian 150, 152
WOCAN (Women Organizing for Change in Agriculture and National Resource Management 48–51

Wood, Denis 136
Woodruff, Jr. C. M. 119

Y

Yagelski, Robert 3
Yale Center for Environmental Law and Policy 90
Yarbrough, Stephen R. 213
Young, Amanda 14
Young, Iris M. 24

Z

Zaradic, Patricia A. 59
Zencey, Eric 186, 189, 198n6, 199n14
zoning rules/laws 190–193, 198n10